AF361600

DUNS SCOTUS'S DOCTRINE OF CATEGORIES AND MEANING

DUNS SCOTUS'S DOCTRINE OF CATEGORIES AND MEANING

MARTIN HEIDEGGER

TRANSLATED BY
JOYDEEP BAGCHEE AND JEFFREY D. GOWER

INDIANA UNIVERSITY PRESS

This book is a publication of

Indiana University Press
Office of Scholarly Publishing
Herman B Wells Library 350
1320 East 10th Street
Bloomington, Indiana 47405 USA

iupress.org

Manufactured in the United States of America
First printing 2022

Cataloging information is available from the Library of Congress.
ISBN 978-0-253-06264-2 (hardback)
ISBN 978-0-253-06265-9 (ebook)

Heinrich Rickert
in grateful veneration

CONTENTS

TRANSLATORS' PREFACE

HEIDEGGER'S *HABILITATIONSSCHRIFT* OR POSTDOCTORAL THESIS, titled *Die Kategorien- und Bedeutungslehre des Duns Scotus* (*Duns Scotus's Doctrine of Categories and Meaning*), was submitted to the University of Freiburg im Breisgau in the spring of 1915.[1] Completed under Heinrich Rickert, an exponent of the Southwestern or Baden school of neo-Kantianism, the text consists of two parts.[2] Part 1, titled "The Doctrine of Categories," offers a treatment of John Duns Scotus's doctrine of the categories (primarily referencing Duns Scotus's *Opus Oxoniense* and the commentaries on Porphyry's *Isagoge* and Aristotle's *Categories* and *Sophistic Refutations*),[3] whereas part 2, titled "The Doctrine of Meaning," is a meticulous exegesis of the *Grammatica speculativa* (full title, *De modis significandi sive grammatica speculativa*).[4] This work in medieval grammar is now known to

---

1. Robbins's 1978 translation (see below) is titled *Duns Scotus' Theory of the Categories and of Meaning*. We prefer "doctrine" for Heidegger's *Lehre*.

2. For Rickert's evaluation, see Heinrich Rickert, "Gutachten über die Habilitationsschrift des Herrn Dr. Heidegger, dated July 19, 1915," in *Martin Heidegger–Heinrich Rickert: Briefe 1912–1933 und andere Dokumente*, ed. Alfred Denker (Frankfurt a.M.: Vittorio Klostermann, 2002), 95–100.

3. S. J. McGrath, *The Early Heidegger and Medieval Philosophy: Phenomenology for the Godforsaken* (Washington, DC: Catholic University of America Press, 2006), 90. McGrath discusses the *Habilitationsschrift* in chapter 4; the conclusion, which Heidegger composed later and which differs in key respects, is the subject of chapter 5.

4. An English translation may be found in G. L. Bursill-Hall, ed. and trans., *Grammatica Speculativa of Thomas of Erfurt* (London: Longman, 1972). An earlier translation, by Charles Glenn Wallis, *On the Modes of Signifying. A Speculative Grammar. The First Translation into English of "De modis significandi, sive grammatica speculativa"* (Ann Arbor, MI: Edwards Brothers, 1938), is not widely available.

have been authored by the Modist grammarian Thomas of Erfurt.[5] Heidegger's thesis was originally published in 1916 by J. C. B. Mohr with the addition of a conclusion composed specially for the occasion.[6]

Editions and Translations—The present translation is based on the text of volume 1 of Heidegger's *Gesamtausgabe* (complete edition; henceforth GA 1), first published in 1978 (with reprints in 1981, 1987, 2003, and 2018). An earlier edition of the text was published in 1972, also under the title *Frühe Schriften*, though not as part of the *Gesamtausgabe* and with a smaller selection of Heidegger's early writings (for details of the additions made in GA 1, see Friedrich-Wilhelm von Herrmann's editor's afterword, also translated in this edition). The present edition includes the translation of *Die Kategorien- und Bedeutungslehre des Duns Scotus* and the foreword Heidegger composed for the 1972 edition of *Frühe Schriften*. The index of names and the subject index are both based on von Herrmann's indexes in GA 1. This translators' preface and the English–German and German–English glossaries are the only additions.

Heidegger's postdoctoral thesis has been translated into English previously, in whole and in part. A complete translation is available in Harold J. Robbins's PhD dissertation at DePaul University,[7] and three partial translations (of the

---

Bursill-Hall's translation is based on the Latin text of Mariano Fernández-García, ed., *B. Joannis Duns Scoti Doct. Subtilis O.F.M. Grammaticae speculativae nova editio* (Quaracchi: College of St. Bonaventure, 1902), which it reprints on facing pages. Heidegger cites the text according to the Paris edition, *Joannis Duns Scoti Opera omnia* (Paris: L. Vivès, 1891–95). He also consults the earlier Wadding edition, on which the Vivès edition is based: Luke Wadding, ed., *Joannis Duns Scoti opera omnia*, 12 vols. (Lyons, 1639). See p. 10, n. 11 of our translation. For a description of the editions and their relation, see Robert Mathiesen, review of *Grammatica Speculativa by Thomas of Erfurt*, by G. L. Bursill-Hall, David Abercrombie, and R. H. Robins, *Language* 51, no. 3 (1975): 731–36.

5. See Martin Grabmann, "De Thoma Erfordiensi auctore Grammaticae quae Ioanni Duns Scoto adscribitur speculativae," *Archivum Franciscanum Historicum* 15 (1922): 273–77. Despite having known Grabmann personally, Heidegger never corrected the ascription.

6. See the bibliographical reference in Martin Heidegger, *Gesamtausgabe, I. Abteilung: Veröffentlichte Schriften 1914–1970*, vol. 1: *Frühe Schriften*, ed. Friedrich-Wilhelm von Herrmann (Frankfurt a.M.: Vittorio Klostermann, 2018), 436. The reference is translated on p. 169 of this volume and includes details of the first publication of both the postdoctoral thesis and the author's notice.

7. Harold J. Robbins, "Duns Scotus' Theory of the Categories and of Meaning, by Martin Heidegger, Translated from the German and with Introduction by Harold Robbins" (PhD diss., DePaul University, 1978).

conclusion) have been published, in *Man and World, Supplements,* and *Becoming Heidegger.*[8] The last two also translate the *Selbstanzeige* or "author's notice" from the postdoctoral thesis. Despite Robbins's valuable introduction to the text, the translation has several shortcomings, necessitating a retranslation. John van Buren's and Aaron Bunch's translations of the conclusion are both based on Roderick Stewart's, which they variously modify. Finally, we also referred to Hans Seigfried's translation of Heidegger's inaugural address to the Heidelberg Academy of Sciences, which Heidegger quotes in extenso in his foreword.[9] We gratefully acknowledge these previous efforts at translation: we consulted them and, where appropriate, also drew from them.

Glossaries, Indexes, and Apparatus—Although the glossaries provide a guide to our word choices, a few require clarification. Notably, we translate *Bedeutung* and its compounds such as *Bedeutungsmodi, Bedeutungsakt,* et cetera consistently with "meaning" (hence, "modes of meaning," "act of meaning," et cetera).[10] Although this diverges from the standard English translation of Thomas's *Grammatica speculativa* (which renders *modi significandi* as "modes of signifying"), we felt it was more important to maintain consistency with the title and independent usages of *Bedeutung.* Because Heidegger is concerned with establishing the relationship between the *modi essendi* (the modes of being) and the *modi intelligendi* (modes of understanding), which "in turn demands an investigation into the structure of the meanings through which these objects can be meant (*modi significandi*),"[11] "modes of meaning" seemed preferable to varying between "meaning" and "signifying" (or "signification"). "Meaning" also preserves the relationship to intentionality, which is crucial to Heidegger's project of mediating between phenomenology and medieval thought.

---

8. Roderick M. Stewart, "Signification and Radical Subjectivity in Heidegger's *Habilitationsschrift," Man and World* 12, no. 3 (1979): 360–86; Roderick M. Stewart and John van Buren, "The Theory of Categories and Meaning in Duns Scotus," in *Supplements: From the Earliest Essays to* Being and Time *and Beyond,* ed. John van Buren (Albany: SUNY Press, 2002), 61–68; Aaron Bunch, "Supplements to *The Doctrine of Categories and Meaning in Duns Scotus,*" in *Becoming Heidegger: On the Trail of His Early Occasional Writings, 1910–1927,* ed. Theodore Kisiel and Thomas Sheehan (Evanston, IL: Northwestern University Press, 2007), 73–78.

9. Hans Seigfried, trans., "A Recollective 'Vita' 1957," in *Becoming Heidegger: On the Trail of His Early Occasional Writings, 1910–1927,* ed. Theodore Kisiel and Thomas Sheehan (Evanston, IL: Northwestern University Press, 2007), 9–10.

10. Heidegger uses *Bedeutungsmodi* and *Bedeutungsweisen* interchangeably. We translate both as "modes of meaning." By contrast, the nearly identical *Bedeutungsformen* is rendered as "forms of meaning."

11. Maren Kusch, *Language as Calculus vs. Language as Universal Medium: A Study in Husserl, Heidegger, and Gadamer* (Dordrecht: Kluwer Academic, 1989), 145.

Three other challenging terms may be mentioned: *Bewandtnis, Inhalt,* and *Gegenstandsverhalt.*

1. *Bewandtnis,* a seldomly used word, is typically encountered only in expressions such as *mit jmdm., etw. hat es seine besondere, seine eigene Bewandtnis.* It means something like, "there is a specific background with regard to someone or something, matters stand thus" (*Wörterbuch der deutschen Gegenwartssprache,* s.v. "Bewandtnis"). Heidegger's use of *Bewandtnis* is idiosyncratic, and Theodore Kisiel has rightly called it "the most difficult of the early Heidegger's words for the translator."[12] We have chosen "relational context" and are aware that no English word really conveys the sense of the German idiom.

2. Although *Inhalt* is straightforwardly "content," English lacks a corresponding adjective for the German *inhaltlich.* The *Oxford English Dictionary* lists "contentual," but this word is clearly a new coinage resorted to by translators of German (*OED,* s.v. "contentual"). We render *inhaltlich* either with phrases centered on the noun "content" or by "conceptual"/"substantive." The latter should be taken to imply neither the metaphysical concept of substance nor the grammatical substantive, which Heidegger also discusses. This also applies to our translation of *Sachhaltigkeit* as "substantiality."

3. *Gegenstandsverhalt* occurs four times in the text, in the context of a discussion of the meaning function of the verb.[13] Along with *Gegenstand,* it reproduces Thomas's distinction between *modus entis* and *modus esse.* Whereas "the *modus entis* is the mode or form of habit and permanence of things; the *modus esse* is the mode of flux and succession."[14] Bursill-Hall translates *modus entis* and *modus esse* as "mode of an entity" and "mode of being," respectively. Although we could have retained Bursill-Hall's expressions, because Heidegger uses *Gegenstand* and *Gegenstandsverhalt* to gloss this very passage,[15] we felt it was more important to

---

12. Theodore Kisiel, *Heidegger's Way of Thought: Critical and Interpretive Signposts* (New York: Continuum, 2002), 120.

13. *Gegenstandsverhalt* should not be confused with *Sachverhalt,* "the actual relationships and processes, the state of things, conditions" (*WdG,* s.v. "Sachverhalt"), which we consistently translate with "state of affairs." Note, however, that, in one place, just prior to his introduction of the distinction between *Gegenstand* (*modus entis*) and *Gegenstandsverhalt* (*modus esse*), Heidegger also uses *Gegenstands-Sachverhalt,* which we translate as "object's state of affairs" (see also n. 18).

14. Robert G. Godfrey, "The Language Theory of Thomas of Erfurt," *Studies in Philology* 57, no. 1 (1960): 26.

15. In Bursill-Hall's translation, "The mode of an entity is the mode of condition and permanence inherent in the thing from which it has essence. The mode of being is the mode of change and succession inherent in the thing, from which it has becoming." *Grammatica Speculativa of Thomas of Erfurt,* 153.

maintain fidelity to the semantics and morphology of the German term.[16] We have thus chosen to render *Gegenstandsverhalt* as "(an *or* the) object's way of comporting itself."[17] By contrast, Heidegger's hyphenated compound *Gegenstands-Sachverhalt* is simply rendered as "(an *or* the) object's state of affairs."[18]

As noted earlier, the index of names and the subject index are based on their respective counterparts in GA 1. The subject index retains the terms and the arrangement of the GA 1 index while updating its page references. Translating its entries into English and reorganizing the index around these new terms would have fragmented the unity of the page references that fall under a given concept, besides replacing individual German entries with a potentially unwieldy mass of equivalents. However, because the glossaries list all of the German terms in the subject index, it is relatively easy to cross-reference the text with the latter, either by first locating the term of interest in the English–German glossary and then consulting its German equivalent in the index or, for readers with a knowledge of German, by first looking up a term in the index to identify its occurrences and then consulting the German–English glossary to find the English translation(s) we have adopted. These translations can then be found on the pages listed in the index.

Quotations of works in languages other than Latin are from the standard English editions of these works; we note whenever these translations are modified.

---

16. *Verhalt* can have any one of three meanings depending on the sense in which the underlying verb *sich verhalten* is taken, that is, either as "the way in which something holds on to or stops something" (*sich verhalten = festhalten, anhalten*), as "the way in which a person comports or carries him or herself" (*sich verhalten = das sich verhalten, sich betragen; von Personen*), or as "the way in which something relates to another, the relation, or their mutual relationship" (*sich verhalten = das verhalten einer sache zur andern, das verhältnis, die wechselbeziehung*) (*Deutsches Wörterbuch von Jacob Grimm und Wilhelm Grimm*, s.v. "*Verhalt*"). Context suggests that it is the second meaning Heidegger intends.

17. The French translation of this work—Martin Heidegger, *Traite des categories et de la signification chez Duns Scot*, trans. Florent Gaboriau (Paris: Gallimard, 1970)—renders *Gegenstandsverhalt* with "*le rapport objectif,*" that is, "the objective relationship." But this would be *objektiver Sachverhalt* or *gegenständlicher Sachverhalt*, formulations Heidegger never uses. We felt it best to be guided by the meaning of the Latin term.

18. We have chosen to retain the standard English translation of *Sachverhalt* (*OED*, s.v. "state of affairs": "in the philosophy of Ludwig Wittgenstein: a combination of objects"; see also "*Sachverhalt*"), even though it does not adequately capture the original's dynamism. Whereas Wittgenstein typically uses *Sachverhalt* to denote complexes of facts, Heidegger means the actual content that is intended by a judgment. As the correlate of an intentional act, *Sachverhalt* thus potentially encompasses more than a mere object (*Gegenstand*) or fact (*Tatsache*).

Where standard editions were unavailable, the translations are our own. Latin quotations are not translated because Heidegger provides a running commentary on them. Where we cite a translation, the first reference is to it, followed by "Heidegger cites" and Heidegger's original reference. Where an English translation is available, but we do not cite it (either because we could not source it or because we could not identify the passage corresponding to Heidegger's reference), we cite Heidegger's source first, followed by the reference to the translation (the latter is placed on a new line and set off by "Tr.:"). In all cases of the latter type, the translation of the quoted text is ours, though it is not marked as such.

Where we provide Heidegger's original German (usually a concept, more rarely a complete phrase), we always do so in square brackets. The German is provided exactly as in the original, reproducing roman or italic type to preserve Heidegger's emphasis and giving the term or phrase just as it is declined or conjugated in Heidegger's text. We also use square brackets to enclose clarificatory insertions into the translation. Note, however, that Heidegger also uses square brackets to mark his addition of emphasis or his insertions into passages he is quoting (sometimes with the additional remark "d.V." [*der Verfasser*], which we translate as "Heidegger" to avoid ambiguity). Context will always make it clear whether the insertion is ours or Heidegger's, because our insertions occur only within Heidegger's own words. Square brackets are also used for the references to *Husserliana* inserted in GA 1 in the footnotes.

Following the conventions established in GA 1, we use numbers for Heidegger's footnotes (the numbering is identical in GA 1 and the separate edition of *Frühe Schriften*) and lowercase letters for the handwritten marginalia in Heidegger's personal copy of the text. Asterisks mark translators' notes; they are not further marked with "tr.," "translators' note," or the like. When two translators' notes occur on the same page, a double asterisk indicates the second note. The numbers in braces refer to the pagination in GA 1 and the 1972 edition (the reference is always to the end of the page). The first number is from GA 1; the second is from *Frühe Schriften*.

The Latin text in the notes is based on the text of GA 1; we did not compare Heidegger's Latin text with any of the Latin editions of Scotus's or Thomas's work. There are small differences between the Latin text of the 1972 edition and that of GA 1. Heidegger's internal references in the notes have been updated to refer to the relevant sections of the present edition. Finally, we scrupulously reproduce Heidegger's use of roman or italics in our translation, even though this differs from the dictates of style. Although this leads to some inconsistency (in fact, Heidegger's use of italics or quotation marks to indicate terms is decidedly erratic), we felt it important to preserve Heidegger's emphasis. This principle also applies to Heidegger's placement of certain words in quotation marks: even if he doubles italics and quotation marks, we do not omit either in the interest of fidelity to his (potential) meaning.

ACKNOWLEDGMENTS

IT REMAINS FOR US TO thank the people who made this book possible. We do so individually.

Joydeep Bagchee—Words cannot express my love and gratitude to Prof. Dr. Adluri. He not only taught me Heidegger; he also taught me to think as a philosopher. The circumstance that I took up Heidegger's *Habilitationsschrift* of all his works (my own preference was for GA 62) is due to him: he insisted I translate it, noting Reiner Schürmann always said the core of Heidegger's thought was already contained in it. Vishwa also introduced me to Arbogast Schmitt's *Modernity and Plato*, without which I would not have appreciated Duns Scotus's significance for modern philosophy. Prof. Dr. Schmitt recommended me to Vittorio Klostermann, thus securing the translation license. Dee Mortensen at Indiana University Press was instrumental in setting up translation contracts. Her faith in me was unwavering. My thanks to Jeff, my friend, cotranslator, and fellow Heideggerian.

Jeffrey Gower—I gratefully acknowledge the friends and colleagues who contributed to this book in various ways. Walter Brogan's generosity and mentorship over many years proved essential to my involvement with this project. I thank Joydeep Bagchee for the invitation to work on this project and for a convivial collaboration. Thanks to Christopher Noble for setting the collaboration in motion. Wabash College and the John J. Coss Memorial Fund supported travel that made it possible to collaborate in person. A debt of gratitude is due to Dee Mortensen for her patient stewardship of this project and to Ashante Thomas, Gary Dunham, and others at IUP for seeing the project through to its completion. My parents continue to offer love and support. I am deeply grateful to Adriel M. Trott, who encourages and inspires me through her vitality and her thoughtful provocations. None of this would have been possible had I not had the great good fortune to become friends with my German language mentor at Whitman College, James Soden. I dedicate my efforts on this volume to his memory.

FOREWORD TO THE FIRST EDITION OF *FRÜHE SCHRIFTEN* (1972)

WHEN I WROTE THESE EARLY and literally helpless attempts, I knew nothing of the problem that would later beset my thinking.

Nonetheless, they indicate the beginning of a path, although it was closed off to me then: the question of *being* in the guise of the problem of the categories and the question of *language* in the guise of the doctrine of meaning. The relationship of the two questions remained obscure. I could not even intuit the obscurity, because their treatment was unavoidably dependent on the dominant measure for all onto-logic, the doctrine of *judgment*.

Of course, these domains of inquiry point to Aristotle, from whose texts I attempted, clumsily enough, to learn to think even before I wrote these treatises. I had no hope of presenting medieval thought's historical dependence on Aristotle fittingly.

The inaugural lecture I presented in 1957 on admission to the Heidelberg Academy of Sciences discusses some features of the intellectual world that implicitly shaped my early efforts. It reads:†

At every station, the path shown me appears in a different light in retrospect and prospect. It appears with a different nuance and evokes other interpretations. Of course, several features, which are hardly recognizable even for me, lead in the same manner through regions of thought. Their countenance is revealed in the little text *The Pathway* [*Der Feldweg*] written in 1947–1948.

I learned Greek, Latin, and German fruitfully under excellent teachers at the humanistic gymnasiums in Constance and Freiburg im Breisgau between 1903

---

† See the *Sitzungsberichte der Heidelberger Akademie der Wissenschaften: Jahresheft 1957/58* (Heidelberg: Carl Winter, 1959), 20–21.

and 1909. Outside of {55/IX} school, I encountered something in this period that would have a lasting influence.

I read [Adalbert] Stifter's *Colorful Stones* [*Bunte Steine*] for the first time in 1905. In 1907 Dr. Conrad Gröber, a paternal friend from my hometown who later became the archbishop of Freiburg im Breisgau, presented me with a copy of Franz Brentano's dissertation *On the Several Senses of Being in Aristotle* (1862). The many, mostly lengthy quotations from the Greek compensated for the lack of an Aristotle edition. A year later, however, a copy borrowed from the school library could be found in my school desk. The question that was awakened then, although obscurely, hesitantly, and helplessly—the question of the unity of the manifold of Being—*remained* through many reversals, blind alleys, and confusions *the* unrelenting spur for the treatise *Being and Time*, which appeared two decades later.

In 1908 I encountered Hölderlin in a small Reclam volume of his poems that I still possess.

In 1909 I embarked on a four-semester program in theology at the University of Freiburg im Breisgau; this yielded in the following years to the study of philosophy, the humanities, and the natural sciences. Beginning in 1909 I attempted, although without proper guidance, to penetrate into Husserl's *Logical Investigations*. Rickert's seminar exercises introduced me to the writings of Emil Lask, who, mediating between the two of them, likewise attempted to pay heed to the Greek thinkers.

I cannot adequately express what the exciting years from 1910 to 1914 brought, but a short selective list may provide some indication: the second edition of Nietzsche's *Will to Power*, expanded to twice its size; translations of the works of Kierkegaard and Dostoevsky; an awakening interest in Hegel and Schelling; Rilke's compositions and Trakl's poems; and Dilthey's *Collected Writings* [*Gesammelte Schriften*].

The decisive influence (and hence one that cannot be captured in words) for my later academic career came {56/X} from two men, who should be expressly mentioned here in remembrance and gratitude. The first was professor of systematic theology Carl Braig, the last representative of the tradition of the speculative Tübingen School, whose engagement with Hegel and Schelling gave Catholic theology rank and breadth. The second was art historian Wilhelm Vöge. Every hour I spent in lectures with these two teachers continued to work on me through the long semester breaks, which I always spent in uninterrupted work at my parents' house in my hometown Meßkirch.

The successes and failures in the following years on the path I chose exceeds self-interpretation, which could only name what does not belong to one. This includes everything essential.

I reluctantly acceded to Dr. Klostermann's recommendation that we reissue these writings, but I thank him for their realization. I also thank Dr. Feick and University Docent Dr. von Hermann for carefully proofing the reissued texts.

Freiburg im Breisgau, March 1972

M.H. {57/XI}

FOREWORD TO *DUNS SCOTUS'S DOCTRINE OF CATEGORIES AND MEANING*

EXCEPT FOR SOME INESSENTIAL CHANGES and the concluding chapter, which was written later, the present investigation was completed in the spring of 1915. I submitted it as a postdoctoral thesis to the Philosophical Faculty of the University of Freiburg im Breisgau in the summer semester of the same year.

The dedication expresses my gratitude and debt. While freely preserving its own independent "standpoint," it simultaneously testifies to my conviction that the philosophy of value, in its character of a *worldview* that is *attentive to problems,* is destined to advance and deepen the treatment of philosophical problems decisively. Its *intellectual-historical* orientation provides fertile ground for creatively shaping problems arising from intense personal experiences. Emil Lask's philosophical creativity proves this. I address a word of grateful and loyal remembrance to him in his distant soldier's grave.

The support of the Wissenschaftlichen Gesellschaft in Freiburg im Breisgau enabled this work's publication, difficult at present for so many reasons. I thank its board, Councilor Finke, and Professor Husserl sincerely.

Freiburg im Breisgau, September 1916.

Martin Heidegger

INTRODUCTION

The Necessity of Examining Scholasticism from the Perspective of the History of Problems

Motto:

With regard to philosophy's inner essence
there are neither predecessors nor followers.

HEGEL, W. W. I, 169.

HISTORICAL RESEARCH INTO THE CULTURE of the Middle Ages has attained such a pinnacle of achievement today, both in penetrating understanding and objective [sachlichen] evaluation, that it is unsurprising that earlier judgments, which were hasty and based on mere ignorance, are disappearing while scientific and historical interest in this period is constantly increasing.

If we recall how philosophical-theological intellectual life was a driving force and enduring power in medieval man's attitude toward life, whose basic structure consists in the soul's transcendent primordial relationship to God, it is not hard to agree that historical research into this aspect of medieval culture is both indispensable and fundamentally significant. Clemens Bäumker and his school are working exemplarily and untiringly to this end. Martin Grabmann's instructive inaugural address in Vienna demonstrated that large areas of the history of medieval philosophy—a history that is by no means straightforward—remain unexplored.

Major, philosophically rich sententiae and summae of early and high Scholasticism are unedited still. Even the works of major Scholastics such as Albertus Magnus have not been fully published. In order to determine Aristotle's influence on {193} Scholasticism (the "action d'Aristote," as Mandonnet calls it), {135} conclusive investigation into and publication of the Latin translations of Aristotle and research on and publication of the unpublished Scholastic commentaries and lexica on Aristotle are future tasks for science. Much that is obscure must be illuminated. Much that is unpublished and unknown must be evaluated to understand the transition from early Scholasticism to high Scholasticism and to present the phases of development of the Franciscan school from Bonaventura to Scotus. Likewise, Aquinas's far-reaching philosophical influence, which is revealed in the partially unpublished works of his immediate or remote disciples, presents investigators with a wide field.[1]

Editions of texts and comprehensive and reliable materials are indispensable foundations for penetrating further into Scholasticism's intellectual content. Creating this foundation demands confident work using all the tools at the disposal of modern historical research. But by merely collecting, registering, and reproducing their contents, we do not yet meet all the preconditions for evaluating the philosophical thought of the Middle Ages.

Certainly, the rich results of this research force us to reconsider established views about Scholasticism's formulaic nature, its "slavish" relationship to Aristotle, or its "handmaiden role" vis-à-vis theology, thereby securing a more reliable, *historical* verdict about this subfield of medieval philosophy.

Pure philosophical talent and a genuinely productive capacity for historical thinking rarely coexist in one person. It is therefore understandable that a genuinely *philosophical* evaluation of Scholasticism is possible only in exceptional cases, particularly if we consider the difficulty and tediousness of this pioneering work of trawling libraries and manuscript collections with utmost critical accuracy. {194/136} A *division of labor* is needed. A historian of medieval philosophy can hardly work without philosophical training, just as, contrariwise, a systematic theoretical evaluation of Scholasticism is impossible without some degree of historical interest. More historical and literary-historical investigations and primarily theoretical and philosophical investigations would enrich each other mutually.

The history of philosophy is not *just* history. It cannot be this if it is to belong to the field of scientific work in philosophy. The history of philosophy has a different relation to philosophy than the history of mathematics to mathematics, for example. The reason does not lie in the *history* of philosophy but in the history of *philosophy.*

Outsiders to philosophy—and occasionally supposed insiders too—feel obligated to view the history of philosophy as a series of more or less frequently

---

1. Martin Grabmann, *Der Gegenwartswert der geschichtlichen Erforschung der mittelalterlichen Philosophie.* Akad. Antrittsvorlesung (Vienna: Herder, 1913), 7f.

repeating displacements of "errors." Add the fact that philosophers have never agreed on what philosophy is at all, and the complete dubiousness of philosophy as science appears a fact.

But to someone who really understands, a completely different situation reveals itself.

We consider philosophy a cultural value like every other science. At the same time, philosophy is unique in that it asserts its validity and applicability as a *value for life*. Philosophical ideas are more than scientific material we busy ourselves with either out of a personal predilection or because we wish to encourage and form culture. Philosophy exists simultaneously in tension with the vitality of the individual. It draws its content and normative claim from the depth and the fullness of life of that individual. {195/137} This is why the philosopher's personal viewpoint often underlies every philosophical conception. With his unrelentingly caustic style and plastic gift for expression, Nietzsche expressed how the subjectivity of the thinker influences all philosophy by the well-known phrase "*Drive, that philosophizes.*"[2*]

Given the constancy of human nature, it is understandable that philosophical problems repeat themselves in history. But we cannot identify a *development* in the history of philosophy in the sense of a constant advance to new questions taking place on the basis of previously attained solutions. Rather, we mainly find an ever more productive *unpacking* and *creative drawing out* of a circumscribed sphere of problems. This ever-renewed concern with a set of problems that remain more or less the same, this enduring identity of the philosophical spirit, not

---

2. Recently, *von der Pfordten* has undertaken an interesting attempt at presenting the history of philosophy from this aspect and working out the fundamental value judgments of philosophers. See Otto v. d. Pfordten, *Die Grundurteile der Philosophen: eine Ergänzung zur Geschichte der Philosophie, I. Hälfte: Griechenland* (Heidelberg: Carl Winter, 1913).

*Heidegger encloses the expression in quotation marks and sets it in italics. However, such a quotation cannot be found anywhere in Nietzsche's corpus: Heidegger appears to be paraphrasing *Beyond Good and Evil* §6. See Andreas Urs Sommer, *Kommentar zu Nietzsches* Jenseits von Gut und Böse (Berlin: de Gruyter, 2016), 108, particularly, "Heidegger does not reference the passage; such an indicative quotation cannot be found in N., but only the expression with the auxiliary verb in 20, 16f. Heidegger here makes N. a spokesperson for a personalistic understanding of philosophy, according to which every philosophy is determined from out of the subject. Whether the language of 'drive' in JGB6 [*Jenseits von Gut und Böse* §6] is really suited as evidence of such an understanding of philosophy can be set aside; at any rate, the concept of drive here seems rather to imply something transindividual and transpersonal."

only enables but also *demands* a corresponding understanding of the "history" of philosophy.

Even though an age's religious and political aspects and its cultural aspects in the narrower sense are indispensable for understanding a philosophy's *genesis* and historical contingency, these aspects can be disregarded in the interests of a purely philosophical view that is, as such, only concerned with problems *in themselves. Time*—understood here as a *historical* category—*is put out of play, as it were.* The various related solutions to the problem converge centripetally in their orientation toward the problem itself.

Thus, the history of philosophy has an essential relation to philosophy as long as and *only* as long as it is not "pure history," a science of facts, {196/138} but rather has projected itself into the purely philosophical system. The distinguished historian of philosophy A. Trendelenburg writes, "Where history ceases to be the mere past, it spurs spirits on most effectively."[3]

In what follows, we shall examine Scholasticism on the basis of this understanding of the essence and task of the history of philosophy—an understanding that we cannot further articulate here.

Given that development in philosophy has the character of an *unpacking* of specific problems, progress in philosophy mostly consists in a deepening and a renewed posing of questions. Perhaps in no other discipline do questions determine solutions so forcefully as in philosophy. A "historical" examination of philosophy in this sense must accordingly focus on how problems are posed. But it can only do this if it has somehow recognized the problems arising in its field of investigation in their theoretical uniqueness, in themselves and as such, and has understood their connection with other problems. We may not overlook this latter moment, for no problem stands alone. Rather, it is always entwined with other problems, growing out of them and itself engendering new ones.[4]

However we view the results of research in modern philosophy, we cannot dispute that it is both strong and impressive in its depth and in the acuity of its

---

3. Adolf Trendelenburg, *Geschichte der Kategorienlehre* (Berlin: Bethge, 1846), 197.

4. Because Grabmann ignores the statement of the problem and merely contrasts stock thoughts taken out of context in a superficial fashion, the third part of his inaugural address is unsatisfying. Rather than repeat what I have already said, I refer to my discussion of Charles Sentroul's *Kant und Aristoteles* (*Literarische Rundschau für das katholische Deutschland* 40, no. 7, ed. Joseph Sauer [1914]: 330–32), where I clarify the relationship between Aristotelian-Scholastic philosophy and modern philosophy and the necessary criteria for treating this relationship.

Tr.: Heidegger's book review, "Charles Sentroul, *Kant und Aristoteles*," is reprinted in GA 1, 49–53.

questions. The reason for this strength {197/139} lies in its pronounced *method-ological consciousness*, a consciousness of *the manner in which we come to grips with a problem* and the necessity of doing so. This basic trait of modern science is only a *reflex* of modern culture in general, which has established itself as revolutionary through its self-consciousness (this should not be understood in an ethical sense) of its own effects.

The Middle Ages seemingly lack this methodological consciousness, this highly developed *drive to question* and *courage to question*, the constant testing of every step of thought.

The dominance of *the idea of authority* and the high value placed on *tradition* provide clear indication of this. These moments are unique to medieval thought and life in general, and reveal themselves as more than a merely external peculiarity of the period.

But we come closer to the thought pattern characteristic of medieval man when we recall the unique circumstance that I wish to characterize as *absolute dedication to and fervent immersion in the content of traditional knowledge*. Because it steadfastly surrenders itself to this content, the subject is, as it were, riveted in *one* direction and hence deprived of the inner ability and indeed the desire to move freely. The value of facts (objects) dominates more than the value of the "I" (subjects).

The individual thinker's individuality is, as it were, submerged under the wealth of the *material* he must master, a phenomenon that effortlessly fits the image of the Middle Ages as a period that emphasized the universal and the fundamental. But precisely this pronounced domination of the *universal* is supposed to have forced method into the horizon of the science of that period, because method, distancing itself from individual peculiarities, aims at universal lawfulness. One confidently cites the structure of philosophical summae with their uniform arrangement and their constantly recurring formulae and forms of questioning. As if this were not enough, {198/140} we can also point to the greater respect for *dialectic*, beginning particularly in the thirteenth century, and so completely destroy the claim that the Middle Ages lacked methodological consciousness.

Should this indication prove irrelevant, however, this can only mean that in our previous characterization, we had a *different meaning* of the concept of method in mind. Although this characterization seemingly reached a negative conclusion, this is in no way a reproach.

In fact, what we mean by method is not so much the specifically fixed form that the *presentation* and *communication* of thought takes, but rather the spirit guiding research and *the posing of problems*. More precisely, deficient methodological consciousness means medieval man cannot raise himself—with a certain spiritual wrench—above his own work so he can consciously reflect on problems as *problems*, on the possibility and means of mastering them, their relationship with other problems and range of application. At the very least, this is how things stand with the philosophical thought of the Middle Ages.

The Middle Ages lack an essential trait of the modern spirit: freeing the subject from his bondage to his environment, his immersion in his own life. Medieval man is not centered in himself [bei sich selbst] in the *modern* sense of the expression. He is embedded in a metaphysical tension. Transcendence hinders him from a purely anthropological attitude to reality. For him, reality as reality, as real environment, is a bound phenomenon in that it appears, from the very beginning and constantly, *dependent* when measured against transcendent principles. This is why medieval epistemology, for example, despite its undeniably profound insights, lacks the free range and breadth of its modern counterpart. Medieval epistemology remains bound to transcendence—the problem of how to cognize the supersensory. In this context, being bound does not mean lacking freedom or being subordinate, but rather, a partial orientation of intellectual life. {199/141}

For medieval man, the stream of his own life with its manifold entwinings, its reversals and returns, in its variform and ramified conditionality, remains buried to a great extent. It is not recognized as such. However, this does not settle whether, finally, the thought of transcendence should not prevail over everything in a philosophy. But this can occur only once the domain of transcendence has been determined in its boundaries and taken up on all sides into one's own life.

We may wonder whether the absence of a developed methodological consciousness is really a deficiency. Does not constant deliberation and discussion of the path on which to proceed, in place of brisk progress, signify weakness? Is it not a sign of being unproductive? "Constant whetting of the knife is boring, if one does not plan to cut anything."[5]

It would indeed be equally useless and uninteresting if methodological consciousness accomplished nothing more than reflecting on pure possibilities, solving all sorts of so-called preliminary questions to realize the projected solution to a problem but without ever forcefully seizing hold of the topic. Productive methodological reflection can and may get underway only once the work of actual research has been carried out. But what good is a knowledge of method, if it no longer applies to anything once the problem has been solved? Can the word "method" be understood in a different sense, one that relates it entirely to principles?

---

5. Hermann Lotze, *Metaphysic in Three Books, Ontology, Cosmology, and Psychology*, trans. Bernard Bosanquet (Oxford: Clarendon, 1887), 16 (translation modified); Heidegger cites *Metaphysik: Drei Bücher der Ontologie, Kosmologie und Psychologie* (Leipzig: S. Hirzel, 1879), 15.

Admittedly, we can also understand methodological consciousness as knowing or being attuned to the fundamentals that originally enable a certain sphere of problems, that is, as demonstrating the existence of utterly unique principles that ground a specific cognitive context and first grant it its sense. {200/142}

What we mean is not merely knowing these *principles* but rather *a knowledge of the* relation *between them and that for which they are principles.* What is decisive is not merely the That [Daß] and the What [Was] but the *How* [*Wie*] of the relationality of principles [des prinzipiellen Zusammenhangs].

Thus, *method* presents itself as the form of the epistemic sphere's substantive unity.

"Something that is, in reality, not an intentionally followed path of discovery, but merely expresses a mystically known totality of meaning should not be called 'method.'"[6] This seems immediately applicable to our use of the word. And yet it is not too much to say that our concept of method is a broad one. Specifically, it is fundamentally deepened and ultimate. It first makes the other, genetically real, epistemically *practical* concept possible and endows it with sense.

A similar concept of method seems to have been familiar in Scholasticism, at least to the extent that Scholasticism is imbued with the authentic spirit of Aristotle. Reference to the treatment of first principles and to the entire metaphysics as a science of principles speaks for this. We will have to decide this in the course of the following investigation.

In order to productively examine and fundamentally evaluate Scholastic ideas, we must heed what Scholasticism does *not* say. Expressed more concretely, we must not lose sight of the fact that Scholasticism does not lapse into *empirical-genetic explanations* in its analyses of meaning. Rather, it seeks to retain the objective content of meaning and does not simply explain away what it comes across in "opinion." It seeks to remain attuned to the descriptive content.

Given the metaphysical orientation of its thought, another question concerns how far Scholasticism works with metaphysical realities. But despite these metaphysical "involvements" {201/143}—which are comprehensible from the perspective of Scholastic thought's overall orientation and which as such annul the "phenomenological reduction" or, more precisely, render it impossible—elements of phenomenological observation lie hidden in the Scholastic thought pattern, perhaps more strongly here than elsewhere.

In keeping with the *basic principles* we discussed earlier, in what follows, we shall take up a definite problem and place it in the perspective of modern research. We have chosen a problem that modern logic is intensively preoccupied with: the *doctrine of categories.*

---

6. Hans Driesch, *Ordnungslehre: ein System des nicht-metaphysischen Teiles der Philosophie* (Jena: Diederichs, 1912), 34.

Windelband, to whom we owe many valuable suggestions that advanced this problem, writes, "For those familiar with the history of science, there is no question that this task [projecting a system of categories] is the pivot for the movement of logical science since Kant. Almost everyone agrees that Kant failed in his attempt at a solution."[7] Eduard von Hartmann, author of the first modernly constructed doctrine of categories, refers to the "decisive role the interpretation of the doctrine of categories has consistently played for a philosophical worldview." In his view, the history of the doctrine of categories determines the history of philosophy.[8]

Scholastic logic has been regarded until now mostly as hairsplitting syllogistic and an imitation of Aristotelian logic. But if we try for once to understand it out of modern problems in logic, another aspect immediately reveals itself. It acquires a totally new character, such that we can systematically present the basic concepts that encompass and form what can be experienced or thought in its entirety.

We shall not trace the problem of categories {202/144} in the entire history of Scholasticism. Rather, we shall examine and evaluate its treatment by the Franciscan Duns Scotus, whom Dilthey called the "subtlest of all Scholastics."

However, the critical thinking for which Duns Scotus is rightly famed and which is utterly necessary in logical problems is not the sole reason for directing our attention to him. What is decisive is his entire personality as a thinker with its undeniably modern traits. He discovered a greater and finer proximity (haecceitas) to real life in its manifoldness and potential for tension than the Scholastics before him. At the same time, he knew how to turn, with similar facility, from the fullness of life to the abstract world of mathematics. The "forms of life" are as familiar to him (as far as this was at all the case in the Middle Ages) as the "gray on gray" of philosophy.

Consequently, all preconditions for working out the problem of categories are fulfilled in Duns Scotus.

Furthermore, we find among his works a "doctrine of the forms of meanings"—to use Husserl's expression—that stands in an essential relation to the doctrine of categories insofar as it presents the different categorial formations of "meaning in general" and lays the foundation for all further work on logical problems of sense and validity.

When we consciously invoke *modern* problems and solutions and a certain kinship between them and Scholasticism suggests itself, this is far removed from an attempt to deny the originality or indeed the independence of modern logic.

---

7. Wilhelm Windelband, "Vom System der Kategorien," in *Philosophische Abhandlungen: Christoph Sigwart zu seinem siebzigsten Geburtstage 28 März 1900 gewidmet* (Tübingen: J. C. B. Mohr, 1900), 45.

8. Eduard von Hartmann, *Kategorienlehre* (Leipzig: Haacke, 1896), vii.

Apart from the dubious nature and scientific worthlessness of such an attempt, it remains excluded from the outset insofar as the intellectual milieu in which modern logical investigations were born is completely different from that of Scholasticism. {203/145} This by no means prevents Scholastic thought and modern thought from being concerned with the same problems in the same intellectual areas. But we can subject Scholasticism and modern thought—traditions that are initially and in a certain respect really disparate—to a comparative analysis only if we raise the entire investigation, which *seems purely* historical, to the level of a systematic philosophical examination.

In this initial attempt at a fundamentally new treatment of medieval Scholasticism—that is, its interpretation and evaluation in terms of the contents of its philosophical problems as such—it is initially not all that decisive that we circumscribe the doctrinal system of the individual philosopher (in our case, that of Duns Scotus) against contemporary and earlier systems down to each individual statement and compare them against each other, bring out their *common* ideas, and finally, contrast its doctrinal content against Platonic, Aristotelian, and Stoic philosophy. We can take up such a complete presentation and comparison (which, in my view, should not impair the significance of the individual researcher's independence all too much) only with some prospect of *philosophical* success, when we have succeeded beforehand in making available the systematic content of medieval Scholasticism, at least in the spheres of its most important problems.

Given contemporary theoretical philosophy's energetic will to problems and its corresponding strength to come to grips with problems, philosophical-historical understanding is simultaneously enriched and deepened, but completing these tasks also becomes more urgent—as we just noted.

To touch on a specific task, it is impossible to consider writing a *philosophically* valuable *history of Scholastic logic in the Middle Ages* until the final and most difficult problems of Aristotelian logic {204/146} and metaphysics have been posed clearly—as Emil Lask indicated in a book on judgment that is rich in problems.[9]

---

9. Emil Lask, *Die Lehre vom Urteil* (Tübingen: J. C. B. Mohr, 1912), 39ff. Besides applying a *systematic* understanding of Aristotle down to the last details, a history of Scholastic logic must just as urgently consider the historical process by which Aristotelian philosophy penetrated into Scholasticism's philosophical activity. Recently on this topic, see Arthur Schneider, *Die abendländische Spekulation des zwölften Jahrhunderts in ihrem Verhältnis zur aristotelischen und jüdisch-arabischen Philosophie*, Beiträge zur Geschichte der Philosophie und Theologie des Mittelalters, vol. 17, no. 4 (Münster: Aschendorff, 1915).

If we are even remotely to achieve a philosophically satisfying solution to this task, we must include Scholastic psychology. Today, where we have fundamentally overcome the nonphilosophy of *psychologism*, we will hardly consider this demand justified.[10] But the sole issue here is whether Scholastic psychology coincides, without remainder, with the psychology of modern natural science. We deny this. On the contrary, we must become conscious of the fact that Scholastic psychology, because it is not attuned to the dynamically flowing psychically real, is objectively and noematically oriented in the fundamental problems, and thus greatly facilitates our visual orientation toward the phenomena of intentionality.

In my view, a philosophical—or more precisely, phenomenological—analysis of the mystical, moral and theological, and ascetic writings of medieval Scholasticism is particularly urgent for decisive insight into this fundamental characteristic of Scholastic psychology. {205/147} Only thus will we first advance to medieval Scholasticism's vital life, which decisively founded, enlivened, and consolidated a cultural epoch.[11] {206/148}

---

10. See the introduction to my dissertation, *Die Lehre vom Urteil im Psychologismus* (Leipzig: Johann Ambrosius Barth, 1914), and above p. 160ff., where I note Husserl's decisive significance in developing ideas of a "pure logic." Of course, its domain of objects must be further problematized with regard to its form of reality. However, we can only do so with the systematic means of a philosophy oriented, *in principle*, toward *worldview*.

Tr.: In the original 1916 edition, Heidegger references p. 86ff. of his 1914 dissertation. The reference here is to the reprint in GA 1, *Frühe Schriften*.

11. I cite the text according to the Paris edition: Joannis Duns Scoti, *Opera Omnia* (Paris: apud Ludovicum Vivès, 1891–95). Where this new edition seemed less reliable, I compared the Lyon edition of 1639 (Lugduni: sumptibus Laurentii Durand, 1693). The treatise *De modis significandi* is more easily accessible in a separate edition: B. Joannis Duns Scoti Doct. Subtilis O. F. M. *Grammmaticae speculativae* nova editio cura et studio, ed. P. Fr. Mariani Fernàndez Garcia (Quaracchi: College of St. Bonaventure, 1902).

PART I

THE DOCTRINE OF CATEGORIES
Systematic Foundation of an Understanding of the Doctrine of Meaning

A *PHILOSOPHICAL* INTERPRETATION AND PRESENTATION of Duns Scotus's *Grammatica speculativa** as a doctrine of meaning necessarily demands a preliminary investigation into the elements and conditions that enable an understanding of the domain of the stated problem.

Research into the *historical* conditions and the genetic formation of the field of knowledge under discussion within the [broader] development of scientific consciousness is a necessary task in the *history* of science. Its completion, though deferred to later investigations within the framework of a comprehensive presentation of medieval logic, will provide the *purely philosophical* interpretation with the lively and unique form and fullness that always arises from a deeper grasp of history.

But it will *not* lead to an enrichment or a systematic philosophical understanding of the doctrine of meaning.

The doctrine of meaning must first be raised to a concept. This can be achieved only in a manner appropriate to the essence of the conceptual. The content of the specific concept of the doctrine of meaning dictates that it can be understood

---

* See the translators' preface for this text's correct attribution (to Thomas of Erfurt).

only when we recognize the *universal* elements of meaning that ground and constitute it. Preliminarily, albeit indisputably, we must conceive of the doctrine of meaning—"grammar"—as a specific segment of the totality of the knowable, that is, the theoretically determinable. {207/149}

The uniqueness of this particular *science*, as we call the theoretical treatment of the domain of the objective in a nutshell, must be understood by contrasting it with the remaining sciences or, better yet, by assigning it a specific place within a complete grouping, a system of sciences, provided one exists.

The expression "system of sciences" is ambiguous. We can understand it to mean an arrangement of the sciences actually extant at a specific time and oriented toward particular vantage points. But such a grouping of what is currently historically given, what has been achieved up to a specific epoch in intellectual history, can only have limited validity. Like everything else subject to historical becoming, it must change. Practically, such a system of sciences can become enormously significant in its time, and from the perspective of intellectual history, it may be a fruitful way to characterize a cultural epoch. But when considered purely theoretically in terms its content, it must be assessed as of minimal value. Only a system of sciences that does not limit itself to arranging the currently extant sciences, but rather encompasses all sciences in general within it, can be theoretically valuable. How is such a "system" possible?

How is one supposed to know at any given time which new sciences will emerge in the future, when their number will be exhausted, or whether this can be exhausted at all?

The system and theory of science is a matter for philosophy. One might think that the individual sciences should be derivable from philosophy as the "universal" science. But when we recall that philosophy itself and *in particular* is subject to dramatic transformations, we face the same shortcoming as in the first concept of the "system of sciences" we discussed. Clearly it is preferable, because more fruitful, to make do with an order of extant sciences {208/150} rather than seeking to create new ones and busying oneself with utopian possibilities. And yet the demand for a system that goes beyond the purely practical arrangement of extant sciences is not an impossible demand. Only, we must not demand too much.

It *cannot* be a case of inventing new sciences. Beside the fact that this would require long historical development and definite conditions of origination and continued formation, such a new creation is not a purely theoretical enterprise, as the system under consideration must be. Thus, we are left with treating what is historically given. Or is there an opportunity to fulfill the demand for a purely theoretical system of sciences?

Such a system is indeed possible provided we do not expect *more* from it than it can deliver. It should only provide an outline, as it were, of the potential main groups of the sciences and the nature of their relationship, a grid into which we can insert new formations. The concept of a "system of sciences" in this sense has not always been clearly recognized. The most diverse opinions have existed and still exist concerning how to produce such a system. For the most part, purely theoretical considerations and practical orientation toward the existing sciences are entwined. This explains the manifold systems of sciences found in intellectual history.

It remains beyond the scope of this investigation's tasks to unfold the problem of the theory and system of science in its entire breadth and depth. A complete enumeration of the many attempts at a solution with their greater or lesser divergences is equally inappropriate. We shall mention only the main perspectives that have so far guided the varied attempts at a system of sciences. {209/151}

Some divisions of sciences such as Baco von Verulam's, which is oriented toward the psychic faculties, are strongly oriented toward cognitive psychology. We can attempt a division in light of the aim of the individual sciences (theoretical and practical sciences). The demarcation can also occur according to the methods predominantly employed in the individual sciences. This is possible in two ways: first with regard to the procedure employed in *gaining* knowledge (methodology of research: explanatory and descriptive sciences), then with reference to the difference in the structure of *presentation* of the *knowledge gained* in the sciences (methodology of presentation: generalizing and individualizing sciences). Finally, a system of sciences can reflect on the object region peculiar to the individual sciences and their form of reality (ideal and real sciences). Like every other attempt of this sort, the last-mentioned demarcation will not arrive at any securely grounded results unless it pays fundamental attention to and incorporates the logic of the structure of presentation and—less, by contrast—[the logic] of the research methodology. Which of these different possibilities of division are relevant for our task?

The principle for choosing from the different classifications results from what this division should achieve for our task of laying foundations for understanding. We want to know what grammar (as a doctrine of meaning) in Scotus's sense deals with. Its object region should become recognizable in its uniqueness. Thus, we find ourselves led back to something prior, to the *object regions*, and thus the sole way our task can be fulfilled is indicated.

The individual sciences deal with different object regions or with one and the same region from different perspectives, "from another side." {210/152} On observation, we recognize the individual object regions as belonging to specific domains of reality. According to its type [Artung], each of these has its own specific structure and constitution. Thus, we find ourselves confronted with a task that has been commonly summarized under the name *"doctrine of categories."* What is important here is not, for example, presenting in full breadth how Duns Scotus deals with the number and arrangement of the *Aristotelian* categories as handed down to the Middle Ages. Our task of a categorial characterization of the domains of reality and their initial and preliminary separation extends much further, such that the Aristotelian categories appear as a *specific class* [of categories] *of a specific domain* and not as *the* categories *tout court*. Indeed, our entire investigation rests emphatically on showing that, if distinct regions of reality exist, they should be recognized in their uniqueness and fixed and distinguished from one another accordingly.

Such an exclusive foregrounding [Abheben auf] of the categorial character may appear completely one-sided. In fact, it is so, but it may not in any way be portrayed as unjustified. This is the case only when the contemplative attunement alters the phenomena to be investigated, falsifies them in their What [in ihrem Was] and thereby imputes a view to Duns Scotus that, the evidence shows, he nowhere maintained. Certainly, this investigation of a highly specific stratum of the *categorial* should bring out this aspect of Scotist philosophy more clearly and sharply than it may have been clear to Duns Scotus himself. But this changes nothing about the fact that everything to be presented belongs to the thought world of the philosopher, and *this alone is decisive*. Given the situation that Duns Scotus treats the categorial structure of the different domains without full awareness of their meaning and novelty, it should simultaneously be understood that he did not solve these problems in their systematic order and totality. {211/153} Our task therefore is *not* to systematically complete [this solution] and fill in the gaps but rather to *integrate* what is scattered here and there *into a clearly visible whole*.

We therefore treat Duns Scotus's doctrine of categories from a highly *specific perspective*. This can be carried out at least until we have distinguished the different domains and have *the totality of what can be thought* outlined in *such* clarity before us that we can assign the domain of *meanings*, which will be treated later, its place.

It is therefore more than a cherished expression among logicians when they speak of a phenomenon's logical place. What underlies this expression is a specific conviction—not discussed further here—of an immanent structure grounded in the essence of the logical that is responsible for the fact that every phenomenon that belongs to the domain of what can be at all thought demands, in keeping with its very content, a specific place. Every place is founded on a spatial determination that qua order is only possible on the basis of a referential system. Hence *"place" in the logical sense* is based on *order*. Something that has a logical place fits in a specific way into a specific *relational whole*.

Not only does Scholastic thought thereby reveal itself from a new side, but more important, we attain the authentic foundation for understanding the doctrine of categories. Of course, the fact that we introduced the doctrine of categories prior to the doctrine of meaning as a basis for understanding the latter does not settle anything about the *logical* relationship of the two spheres. We can first answer this question once both phenomena have become adequately clear *in themselves*, thus easily enabling a decision about their hierarchy.

As yet, we do not know that there are *several* different domains of reality. {212/154} When we stated this, it was, strictly speaking, only speculation. How do we attain certainty about this question and what kind of certainty can it be? We cannot demonstrate that there is one domain of reality (and even less that there are several) in an a priori, deductive manner. Factualities [Tatsächlichkeiten] can only be *exhibited*. What is the sense of such *exhibiting*? What is exhibited stands before us as itself. Figuratively speaking, it can be immediately grasped and requires no detour via something else; this *one* thing that is to be exhibited holds our glance. From a practical cognitive perspective, we have only one duty here: to look closely, to really grasp everything that can be grasped, to exhaust the pure being of what offers itself to us. There can be no doubts, probabilities, or illusions in relation to the immediate inasmuch as it, *qua* immediate, does not have, as it were, anything between itself and our apprehension of it (simplex apprehensio).

Because we can only gain a knowledge of the domains of reality via exhibition, nothing can be decided in advance about their number and the totality of what has been exhibited. This is why it is fundamentally irrelevant which domain is first characterized in such exhibition. But practically, we first seek to grasp what is initially given to us, what is most familiar to us. What is proximal is likely the empirical reality within which we move every day, what is given in space and time—*physical natural reality*. To be sure, one view holds that what is truly immediate is the *psychically* given. Apart from the fact that initially many do not become conscious of this at all as their own world, or if they do it is only upon longer reflection, this view is initially too heavily encumbered by presuppositions that cannot be elucidated without difficulty—for example, when people say that the psychic is most proximate to the cognitive (logical) subject and indeed *is* this subject itself. This may hold true in a *certain* sense, but from the perspective of method, what is initially and immediately given is the sensory world, the "environment."

And yet in what follows we shall not take it as our point of departure. {213/155} Even though we just said that we cannot decide anything about the domains of reality, about their kind and number, in an a priori deductive manner, we can nonetheless proceed from general reflections. Indeed, there is a certain need for this, if we wish to give some account of our procedure.

ONE

—ᴍ—

THE UNUM

Mathematical, Natural, and Metaphysical Reality

EVERY OBJECT *REGION* [GEGENSTANDSGEBIET] IS *an object* region [*Gegen-standsgebiet*]. Even if we know nothing more about the domains of reality in question, merely in virtue of the fact that we speak of them as problematic in every respect, something confronts us, an object.* Anything and everything is an object. *Primum objectum est ens ut commune omnibus.* This ens is given in every object of cognition insofar as it is an object. Just as every object of sight, whether white, black, or variegated, is *colored*, so every object *in general* is an *ens*, irrespective of the content it represents.

We find an almost modern observation in Duns Scotus: we often have the experience that we have something objective [etwas Gegenständliches] before us, without knowing whether it is a substance or an accident. In other words, the objective entity lacks a more precise categorial determination. When we have such an objective entity intellectually in view, doubt can arise as to the category to which it belongs, whether it exists for itself or in another thing. The character of its reality is still not determined at all, and nonetheless something is given. *Aliquid indifferens concipimus*: we grasp something that exists prior to every definite categorial formation. The ens thus means the totality of sense of the objective

---

* Heidegger uses both *Gegenstand* and *Objekt* (the latter less frequently). We translate both as "object." The morphology of *Gegenstand* is identical to that of Latin *obiectum*, but Heidegger uses it preferentially in contexts where the sense of opposition or confrontation to the subject is intended (*gegen* = against). In contrast, he uses *Objekt* when he wishes to emphasize the objective, that is, independent nature of the appearance or phenomenon vis-à-vis consciousness. The occurrence of *Objekt* is signaled in square brackets.

17

sphere *as such*, {214/156} the moment that endures in everything objective. It is the category of categories.[1] The ens remains preserved (salvatur) in every *object*, irrespective of how it is differentiated in the fullness of its content.

This ens belongs to the *maxime scibilia*. We can understand this in two ways. A maxime scibile is something that is known primordially. This term must be understood less in a temporal, genetic sense than in a *logical* sense. The "maxime" here contains a logical and theoretical idea of *value* and characterizes the primordial element of the objective, namely, *objectivity*. The ens, understood as maxime scibile in the sense just described, means nothing other than the *condition of the possibility of cognition of objects in general*.

In addition, maxime scibile can mean that which can be cognized with the greatest certainty. This cognitive-psychological, that is, subjective meaning, does not interest us here. The first objective categorial meaning of the maxime scibile shows that the *ens* presents something *ultimate*, *highest*, which cannot be further analyzed.[2] {215/157}

This is also the *authentic philosophical meaning of the objective determinations* that are known in Scholasticism under the name "transcendentia." A transcendens is something that does not have a genus above it that could contain it. Nothing more can be predicated of it. This *character of ultimacy* of the ens as objectivity in general is the essence of a transcendens. That it applies to or can be predicated of many individual objects is accidental to it. These individual objects are not somehow also transcendentia because the concept of the *ens* is given along with

---

1. Primum objectum intellectus est ens, ut commune omnibus. Quaest. sup. Met. lib. IV, qu. I, 148a. Concedendum est, quod primum objectum intellectus non potest esse aliquid, nisi quod essentialiter includitur in quolibet per se intelligibili, sicut primum objectum visus non est aliquid, nisi quod essentialiter includitur in quolibet per se visibili, ut color in albo et in nigro. Cum autem quodcumque ens sit per se intelligible, et nihil possit in quocumque essentialiter includi nisi ens, sequiter quod primum objectum intellectus erit ens. Quest. sup. Met. lib. VI, qu. III, 336a.

Experimur in nobis ipsis, quod possumus concipere ens, non concipiendo hoc ens in se vel in alio, quia dubitatio est, quando concipimus ens, utrum sit ens in se vel in alio, sicut patet de lumine, utrum sit forma substantialis per se subsistens vel accidentalis existens in alio sicut forma; *ergo primo aliquid indifferens concipimus* ad *utrumque illorum et utrumque illorum postea invenimus ita primo, quod in isto salvatur primus conceptus, quod sit ens.* Quest. sup. Met. lib. IV, qu. I, 148b.

2. Maxime autem dicuntur scibilia dupliciter: vel quia primo omnium sciuntur, *sine quibus non possunt alia sciri*; vel quia sunt certissima cognoscibilia. Utroque autem modo ista scientia [scil. Metaphysica] considerat maxime scibilia ... Maxime scibilia primo modo sunt *communissima*, ut est ens inquantum ens et quaecumque sequuntur ens inquantum ens. Quest. sup. Met. Prologus, 4b.

them. *Only what is convertible with the ens can, in a strict sense, be counted among the transcendentia.* Hence, *convertibility* can be considered the criterion for deciding what else is to be regarded as belonging to the transcendentia besides the *ens.*[3] Within the elements that constitute an object, it circumscribes the ultimate domain, the one that stands highest in the *logical* hierarchy.

The remaining transcendentia such as *unum*, *verum*, and *bonum*, which can be considered quasi properties of the *ens*, are manifestly not primordial in the same sense as the *ens* as objectivity in general. Among themselves, however, they do not permit a hierarchization, such that one of them would be more original with regard to its object constituting character than the others. None of the transcendentals can be exhibited (manifestari, *not* demonstrari) without moving in a circle. Every time and as long as we decide something only about these ultimates as ultimates, that is, think of them as objects in themselves, {216/158} all the elements constitutive of an object in general are given with them.

The transcendentia as such cannot be the object of one science. Their essence precludes it. For they are encountered in one science as much as in another, where objects are everywhere present for treatment. Hence, when one seeks to trace the manifold individual objects back to their ultimate theoretical structural elements, they [that is, the transcendentia] must superfluously be treated *repeatedly.*[4]

Apparently, nothing more can be said of the *ens* as "something in general." Everything ends here as though with some ultimate. Or, in the final analysis, have we not yet exhausted its signification after all? But there can be nothing objective [Gegenständliches] above the object tout court that could be asserted of it in general. The "general" loses all sense here. And yet we can predicate more of the *ens*. Only, we may not restrict the predication one-sidedly and without warrant to subsumption. However, with the other predications, we enter into the *circular movement of thought* previously noted. That is not a defect insofar as this unavoidable "misfortune" (*Hegel*) is not due to us but due to the *object in general* and *as such*. Consequently, we must accept this as absolute. Furthermore, we should note that although we move in a circle with successive

---

3. *Transcendens*, quodcumque nullum habet genus sub quo contineatur; sed quod ipsum sit commune ad multa inferiora, hoc accidit. . . . Non oportet ergo transcendens ut transcendens dici de quocumque ente, nisi sit *convertibile* cum prius transcendente, scil. cum *ente*. Op. Oxon. I, dist. VIII, qu. III, 598a sq., n. 19.

4. Quaecumque autem rationes transcendentes, quae sunt quasi passiones entis, ut verum, bonum, etc. sunt posteriores primo objecto; et quaelibet earum aeque per se est intelligibilis, nec una magis habet rationem subjecti intellectus quam alia. Quaest. sup. Met. lib. VI, qu. III, 336a.

predications, each time we stand, as it were, at different positions on the circumference of the circle.

We say, the something is *a* something,* and seemingly do not rise above the object with this alleged triviality. And yet there is a productive moment in this sentence—that of *relation.* The object is referred back {217/159} to itself. To what extent is the something *a* something? Because it is not another. It is a something and, in being something, [is] not-being-another. "Something is what it is only in its limit," says Hegel.[5] Duns Scotus recognizes this relation in an object in general down to its ultimate elements: *idem et diversum sunt contraria immediata circa ens et convertibilia.*[6] The one and the other are not given immediately with the object in general in the same way. The *"heterothesis"*—not the one [das Eine] and still less the number one [die Eins] in contrast to two, but rather, the one *and* the other—is the true origin of thought as an appropriation of objects [Gegenstandsbemächtigung].

A modern thinker recently presented these primitive and seemingly empty conditions once again in all their clarity in an investigation that has all the more depth and subtlety because it arose from a transcendental-philosophical foundation.[7] This investigation illustrates the fundamental distinction between the "one" [dem "Einen"] and the "number one" [der "Eins"]. Put otherwise, it demonstrates that number is not a purely logical construct and is as yet not given at all with the object in general. In what follows, it will become clear how deeply Duns Scotus (who, we may note as an aside, was "passionately" engaged in mathematical studies)[8] was concerned with the distinctions in the concept of the *unum.* Such a distinction is not foreign to Scholasticism at all—otherwise, *Rickert* could hardly have begun his important investigation with a sentence from *Meister Eckhart.*

Idem et diversum sunt contraria, quia idem est quoddam unum et diversum quoddam multum.[9] The "quoddam" is striking. We are all too easily tempted to think

---

*Here and in what follows, Heidegger uses *etwas* (something) as a proper noun (*das Etwas*). We translate usages with the indefinite article (*ein*) as "a something," but what is primarily important for Heidegger here is the emphasis that "the something" is "one thing" or "one something."

5. G. W. F. Hegel, *Science of Logic,* ed. and trans. George di Giovanni (Cambridge: Cambridge University Press, 2010), 100; Heidegger cites *Wissenschaft der Logik* (Nuremberg: Johann Leonhard Schrag, 1812), 1:62.

6. Quest. sup. Met. lib. V, qu. XII, 293a.

7. See Heinrich Rickert, "Das Eine, die Einheit und die Eins: Bemerkungen zur Logik des Zahlbegriffs," *Logos* 2 (1911–1912): 26ff.

8. See Maurice de Wulf, *Geschichte der mittelalterlichen Philosophie,* trans. Rudolf Eisler (Tübingen: J. C. B. Mohr, 1913), 329n1.

9. Quest. sup. Met. lib. X, qu. VII, 634a.

immediately of something numerical in relation to the *unum*. Duns Scotus seeks to preclude this through the "quoddam." {218/160} He is aware of the problems inextricably linked with this concept of the object; otherwise, he would not explicitly point them out, which he seldom does.[10]

Before we can examine the "heterothesis," idem et diversum, more closely, we must counter an objection. One might suspect that in a philosophy oriented toward the substantial and thingly, as Scholasticism appears at first glance to be, the idem et diversum would only hold of real things. As such it would have a quite *limited* field of application and could not be brought without further ado into relation with the *ens commune* as the primordial category of the objective in general. Duns Scotus grants that the idem et diversum is probably primarily asserted of substances (of real things), meaning that these represent its most proximate domain of application. This admission hence concerns the frequency of application within a specific field of objects and *not* the extent of the "domain" within which the distinction holds sway. It is valid of qualities, quantities, relations, indeed of negations and privations as well; in other words, of everything and anything of which we can be conscious as something.[11] Duns Scotus also explicitly remarks in a passage that the term *"res"* need not remain restricted to natural reality. {219/161} Rather, it can mean everything that is not simply *nothing*. Whatever entails a contradiction (for example, a circular rectangle) is nothing. Hence, everything that does not entail a contradiction is a *res*, whether it be an *ens reale* or an *ens rationis*.[12]

Consequently, whatever we determine about the idem et diversum in what follows will be of a primordial objective character.

---

10. Notandum, quod haec questio de ente et uno habet tot difficultates. Quest. sup. Met. lib. IV, qu. II, 165a.

11. Dicendum, quod *idem et diversum* sunt contraria, quia idem est quoddam unum et diversum quoddam multum . . . Sed intelligendum, quod quia substantia est radix omnium generum, et quia omnia, quae habent rationem entis ad substantium attribuantur, sicut *quod quid est* principaliter in substantiis, per posterius in accidentibus, sic *identitas et diversitas*, sive *idem et diversum* principaliter insunt substantiis et per attributionem aliis generibus. Et non solum extenduntur ad aliqua alia genera, sed etiam ad negationes et privationes, inquantum rationem entis participant *et ideo omne ens comparatum enti est idem vel diversum* sibi. Quaest. sup. Met. lib. X, qu. VII, 634a.

Omne ens omni enti comparatum et idem aut diversum; ergo identitas *non est tantum in genere substantiae sed in omni* genere. l. c. lib. V, qu. XII, 294b. [Idem et diversum] in *omni genere* reperiuntur. l. c. n. 6.

12. Non . . . nomen *rei* secundum usum loquendi determinat se ad rem extra animam. Et isto intellectu communissimo *ens vel res* dicitur *quodlibet conceptibile,* quod non includit contradictionem. Quodlibet. qu. III, n. 23.

There are three moments in the heterothesis: the relation and the [two] members of the relation (relata). The relation is only a relation qua existing between the relata, and they are relata qua *founding* the relation. Relation and relata are, in a certain respect, correlative. The one and the other are the relata "between" which the relation exists. What kind of relation?

We most surely gain information concerning it when we set out from the relata that found the relation, thus when we initially set out from the one. The *unum* is predicated equivocally: it can mean the unum, which is *convertible* with the one, or the unum as the *principle of number*.

The unum *through* which every object is *an* object means something other than the unum *as number*.[13] Something similar holds of the multitudo. Not every "plurality" (or more precisely, not every manifold or multiplicity) justifies a number. Just like the unum as a transcendens, the manifold in itself has a wider domain of validity than number. Multiplicity only requires objects *distinguished in general*, and its concept does *not* yet entail anything *quantitative*.[14] {220/162} What has been said here in a merely preliminary sense about the unum and multum as transcendentals will first become fully clear by contrasting it with the quantitative, that is, with the domain of number.

The unum *qua* convertible with the objective in general holds of every object. Everything that is, *is* (an object) as long as it is *one*.[15] How should we think of being-an-object and being-one? How do the ens and the unum relate to each other? Certainly, as convertible the unum is nothing quantitative. Indisputably, the unum also means something distinct from the ens. With each object, which is necessarily *one* object, does it not follow that we have *two* objects?

Duns Scotus says that the unum (ens) does not add a new object to the ens—as being-white, for example, is added to substance. Every object is *one* object in and of itself. The unum is rather immediately given along with the What [Was] as its form (determination, determinacy). Convertibility does not imply an absolute

---

13. Unum est aequivocum ad unum, quod est convertibile cum ente et ad unum, quod est principium numerorum. Quaest. sup. Met. lib. IV, qu. II, 158a.

Sciendum est, quod alia est natura unius, *qua* substantia cuiuslibet rei est una, alia autem unius, *quod* est principium numeri proprie dicti.

et est [unum] in genere quantitatis, et est unum, quod convertitur cum ente. De rer. princip. qu. XVI, 566.

14. Multitudo absoluta est in plus quam numerus. Sicut enim unum absolute acceptum (unum transcendens) est in plus quam unum, quod est principium numeri, sic multitudo absolute accepta est in plus quam multitudo, que est numerus. Quaest. sup. Met. lib. X, qu. XIV, 644a.

15. Omne quod est, tamdiu est, quamdiu unum est. De rer. princ. qu. XVII, 593b; see Oxon. II, dist. III, qu. IV, 112a sq., n. 20.

distinction between two objects, but only a distinct perspectival aspect, a determinate aspect of the same content. If, by contrast, an *object* were *an* object only through the addition of a new object, we would have to inquire further into what makes this object one object—resulting in a *processus in infinitum* even in respect of the primordial object of thought. What is designated as an object simultaneously means *one* object; the What is *a something.* The *unum,* however, is not what is primarily meant. Rather, in itself it bespeaks a *privation* insofar as an object is *not* the *other.* Thus, it does not add any *positive content* to the concept of the object. {221/163} The *convertibility* of the unum with the ens hence cannot refer to the *substantial* [*inhaltliche*] *essence* of the object. Were that the case, a "plurality," for example, could not be *an* object insofar as a plurality *qua* plurality is precisely not a "unit"-y. But the fact that every plurality is *a* plurality clearly indicates that the unum does not affect the What of an object, but rather is necessarily added to it as an essential determination. Every What occurs in the form of the *unum*—it remains the *one identical determination* for all objects, irrespective of how different they are in terms of content.[16]

The character of the unum transcendens as determination already manifests from the way Duns Scotus opposes it to the unum as number. The unum transcendens is something *pertaining* to an object, something *through which* an object becomes *an* object, a moment that determines objectivity in general. By contrast, the unum as number is *itself an object,* a quite specific instance of objectivity.[17] {222/164}

---

16. Tale unum, quo res dicitur una et convertitur cum ente, non dicitur *rem aliquam super substantiam* rei ut albedo supra subjectum. Et ita substantia cuiuslibet rei est una per se, non per aliquam rem additam super ipsam: ut sic sit verum dicere, quod omnino eadem est ratio *realis rei et unius rei* sicut *hominis* et *unius hominis,* sicut dicitur in elenchis, quod eadem est ratio propositionis et unius propositionis. Huius rei est aperta ratio, quia, si res esset una per aliquod additum super eam, iterum de illa quaererem, utrum sit una per se vel per aliud etc. et erit processus in infinitum. De rer. princ. qu. XVI, 567b.

Intelligendum, quod illud, quod per se significatur per *ens,* illud dat unum intelligere, non tamquam principale significatum, sed significat privationem per se, et privatio non est nisi in natura, ideo dat intelligere naturam ex consequenti. Quaest. sup. Met. lib. IV, qu. II, 159a.

Dicendum, quod concedit [Avicenna] converitibilitatem non essentialem vel essentialiter, sed quod idem sunt subjecto non secundum essentiam; quia si sic, multitudo secundum quod multitudo non esset ens, quia multitudo secundum quod multitudo non est una, ita quod sit essentialis praedicatio, sed *unum* accidit multitudini; convertuntur ergo non tamen essentialiter vel secundum essentiam; l. c. 162a.

Nec eius [scil. unius] *ratio variatur per se propter diversitatem subjectorum, quibus inest.* l. c. 164a.

17. See above, p. 22, n. 14.

How should we understand the unum transcendens more closely as determination?

The concept of form plays a decisive role in Aristotelian philosophy as it does in transcendental philosophy. It is indispensable to scientific thinking and particularly to philosophy. That is not to say that it is clearly and, above all, unambiguously grasped. As the concept of form will decisively influence the following investigation, particularly concerning the doctrine of meaning, let us make some general and preparatory remarks concerning it here, where it explicitly manifests for the first time.

Form in Aristotelian philosophy possesses, above all, metaphysical meaning as the formative principle of physical, psychic, and metaphysical realities. But it in no way plays a subordinate role in the area of logic. Kant first raises the concept of form to a decisive position of power in the domain of logic. Since then, it has become an indispensable instrumentarium logicum. It is in this sense that we shall subject it to a preliminary examination here.

Everything that is experienced "over against" ["gegenüber"] the I is *grasped* somehow. The "over against" is already a specific *respect* (a respectus), a *relational context* that exists in regards to the object. One may not, however, think in terms of spatial distance and proximity here. The expression "over against" is borrowed from natural reality and used to characterize the nonsensory relation of *consciousness*. Consciousness is a unique relation. Just as an identical moment—pure opposition—is preserved in the "over against" despite the fact that everything confronting me in natural reality changes the instant I change my location, so it occurs in experience, in [my] being conscious. This relation of the I to the not-I is preserved as originally proper to me, even when I change, as it were, my "location," that is, perceptively encounter other objects. {223/165}

The concept of determinacy is already at work when something in general (ens) is consciously given to me, that is, when I make something the object of my consciousness. Whatever is an object already stands in a certain clarity, even if only in the hazy kind of clarity that lets us behold nothing more than something objective in general. Where this initial moment of clarity is absent, I still would not have absolute darkness. For inasmuch as I have it, this [darkness] itself stands, once again, in a certain clarity. Rather, one must say: I have no object at all; I live blindly in absolute darkness; I cannot rouse myself intellectually, rationally; thought stands still. With the ens I gain the first determinacy and, insofar as every ens is an unum, the *first order* among the manifold fullness of the objective sphere. *Determinacy is therefore something that institutes order in relation to the given, making it graspable, cognizable, comprehensible.*

Even though the unum does not add anything new to the object, it nonetheless lends greater clarity to the object, endows it with order. The determinacy of the unum is not equiprimordial with the ens. Rather, it is based on it. "Object" means something positive, absolute. The unum is no longer original, for it already presupposes the ens. The unum endows the object with a certain manner of comporting itself (quendam modum se habendi). A certain relational context exists with regard to the object in virtue of the unum. This relational context is not positive but negative, or more precisely, *privative*. As a privative determinacy, the unum does not exclude the positive, otherwise it could not be predicated of God, who is the absolute.

We know that the unum stands in contrast to the multitudo, to multiplicity. To what extent is the multitudo a privation and the unum, consequently, the *privation of a privation?*[18] {224/166}

In clarifying this peculiar relationship, Duns Scotus proceeds from general considerations that will concern us more closely later in relation to the doctrine of meaning. Often, we predicate something of objects as a positive meaning that, in terms of its content, is privative. Thus, "corporeal" designates something privative in terms of its content, while "incorporeal" (intellectual) designates something positive.[19] As material reality is initially closer and more familiar to us than the incorporeal and as in addition we are given positive meaning before privative ones, we often grant what is more familiar a positive meaning and what is less familiar a privative meaning. Hence, because it is initially closer to us, we grasp the reality of the created with a positive meaning, even though it is finite and limited and consequently, in its content, not positive in relation to divine Being. By contrast, we grasp what is positive in its content with the *privative* meanings "infinite," "unlimited." The privative forms of meaning express a positive content.

We have now derived the concept of the unum from the form that holds together the parts of an object (the formative principle). In a certain respect, the unum is something undivided, simple, just as the multum, contrariwise, is divided, manifold.

---

18. Est tamen sciendum, quod licet *unum* non dicat rem absolutam super ens sive per substantium rei, tamen unum istud dicit aliam rationen et *alium modum significandi ab ente* . . . Modus enim significationis [entis] imponitur enti a ratione simpliciori quam modus significationis unius; ita quod, quamvis ens et unum idem significent, tamen significatio unius praesupponit significationem entis. Ens enim imponitur ab actu essendi absoluto et positivo. Unum autem in suo significato includit rationem entis cum *determinatione*, non dico cum determinatione addente *rem* supra rationem entis, sed addit *quendam modum se habendi*. Ille autem modus quem addit, non est positivus sed privativus solum, non privando aliquod positivum, alioquin unum non diceretur de Deo, sed privat aliquid negative tantum. De rer. princ. qu. XVI, 568a sq.

19. In the interest of understanding, it should be noted here that this train of thought is based on the belief that the reality of the spiritual is genuine and of higher value than the material.

The manifold thus arises from out of its difference with "unit"-y and hence bespeaks the privation of unity. {225/167} Even though the multum is now grasped in its positive meaning (as divisum), nonetheless, in terms of its content, it is a privation. Contrariwise, the unum is uttered in its privative meaning. In its content, it expresses a positing, something positive that excludes the privation that lies in the multitudo. Thus, the unum expresses something positive regarding its content, while with respect to its mode of meaning (modus significandi), it means a privation. The unum is a *privation of a privation* that lies in the *multum*. For its part, the multum is a privation of the unum. Consequently, the unum is defined through the multum, and vice versa. It should have become clear by now in what way the unum adds to the object. *It endows it with determinacy through its privative mode of meaning.* An object is *an* object and not another.[20] {226/168}

---

20. Ut igitur videamus, quid est privatio importata per hoc nomen *multitudo*, quam quidem privationem de suo significato privat hoc nomen *unum* ut convertitur cum ente, est sciendum, quod (ut patuit ex. 8. Metaphysic.) nullus potest imponere nomen rei, nisi qui novit rem ... Nunc autem aliquando contingit, quod nominaliter aliquid multis positivum est, quod secundeum veritatem est privatio, quamvis significetur nomine positivo, quia habitus sibi contrarius dicit naturam positivam. *Corporeum dicit* secundum rem privationem, *incorporeum* positivum; et cum notiora sint corporea naturaliter quam incorporea, in compositis ex materia et forma, *unum* secundum veritatem habitus quidam est a forma rei partes continente causatus; et ille habitus significatur nomine *unius*. Divisio autem secundum eorum veritatem est privatio illius habitus et significatur nomine *multitudinis* ...

Ex quo patet, quod cum multitudo surgat ex diversitate unitatis et compositionis, *multitudo* dicit privationem habitus importatam per unitatem et compositionem. Et quia (ut dixi) secundum quod res novimus eis nomina imponius, ideo cum compositiones, causae et partes sint nomina magis nota, ideo etiam illud, quod importatur nomine multitudinis, etiamsi dicat privationem respectu illius, quod importatur nomine *unitatis*, quia nomina positiva magis sunt nobis nota, ideo illud significamus nomine positivo, quod est *divisio*; et illud quod significatur nomine compositi seu *unius*, quia est nobis minus notum, significamus nomine privativo per indivisionem; quia multitudo est quaedam divisio, unitas autem est quaedem indivisio, sicut iam dixi: quia substantia incorporea dicit habitum positivum respectu substantiae corporeae, et haec respectu eius dicit privationem. Etenim, quia substantia corporea est nobis magis nota quam incorporea, illam nominamus per modum positivum, aliam per modum privativum ...

Patet igitur ex dictis, quod *multum* etsi significetur nomine positivo, quod est *divisio*, dicit tamen privationem *realiter* illius habitus, qui causatur a forma totius, quod partes continet. Unum autem etsi significetur nomine privativo, quantum ad modum significandi, quod quidem nomen est *indivisum*, realiter dicit positionem, quae positio de ratione sua privat illam privationem, quae importatur nomine *multitudinis*; quia *indivisio* est negatio divisionis, divisio autem est privatio positionis. Sic forte caveatis

We now have a sufficiently secure foundation in order to decide the question concerning the nature of the relationship between the idem and the diversum. It may seem as though this detailed treatment of the unum and the multum was not needed. The idem and the diversum are different. The utterly irreducible relationship of *difference*, which has its simplest expression in the "*not*," exists between them. However, the other cannot be conjured up merely by negating the unum *qua* something. "Negation turns something only into a not-something or the nothing. It lets the object in general, so to speak, disappear. Similarly, alterity or difference can never arise from non-identity."[21]

By now, it is evident that the nature of the opposition between the idem and diversum is not clear without further elucidation. We therefore need to investigate the individual kinds of opposition and decide which one of them is applicable in this case. We already indicated that mere negation does not suffice to characterize the relation in question. What is contrasted with an object by means of the "*not*" as a member in a relation, forms an opposition, {227/169} but it does not posit anything (nihil ponit), that is, it does not create *another* object. Neither does it require a subject as privation does. Namely, one can say that the "nothing" does not see, just as a stone does not see.[22] Duns Scotus succinctly expresses the peculiarity of this opposition, of this contradiction, as follows: Contradictio salvatur in ente et non ente (This opposition is retained in the domain of the existent and the nonexistent).[23]

Although the existent and the nonexistent are opposed to each other, they are not different. Difference exists only in the domain of beings, for difference is not mere negation (separation) but also combination. Something like difference is possible only where there is a perspective or a higher unity, against which what

---

totum, et ideo indivisionis ratio, quam includit unum, est ratio privativa, non privativa afirmationis, quia tunc unum non diceretur de Deo, sed privativa privationis: et sic secundum rem unum significat positivum, secundum vero modum significandi, qui sequitur modum intelligendi, significat privationem. Et quia *unum* dicit privationem privationis importatae per multum, *multum* dicit privationem habitus importati per unum, habitum est quod unum definitur per multa et e contrario. *Unum* enim est, quod est principium multitudinis, multitudo item quae numeratur per unum. Quia enim privatio cognoscitur per habitum, cum unum sit privatio multitudinis secundum rem, et multum sit privatio unius secundum modum, ideo *unum* habet per alterum definiri et e contrario. De rer. princ. qu. XVI, 568b sqq.

21. Rickert, "Das Eine, die Einheit und die Eins," 36.

22. Quod enim contradicit alii, opponitur sibi, sed nihil ponit, nec subjectum requirit; potest enim dici, quod non ens non videt et quod lapis non videt. Quaest. sup. Met. lib. X, qu. XI, 639b.

23. l. c. qu. V. 630b sq.

is to be distinguished can be measured. Negation, as it manifests in contradictory opposition, belongs within "subjective logic." "Not-human" can be said of an ass, that is, of an existent object, but negation, insofar as it is grasped purely as negation, exists [ist ein Seiendes] only in the understanding, that is, through a subjective positing. Negation does not have *objective* existence in a contradictory opposition. Not-white, insofar as it is opposed to white, is not black. Rather, its meaning encompasses every existent and nonexistent with the exception of white.[24] {228/170}

The one and the other, however, are transcendentals, primordial determinations of the object, and as such are convertible with the object. Both refer to something objective. *Consequently, the contradictory relation does not apply to them.*[25]

How do matters stand regarding privation? Privation exists only in the domain of beings and thus has a more restricted domain of application than contradiction. Nonetheless, privation appears the fitting expression for the relation that prevails between the unum and the multum, because like them, it exists only in the domain of the ens. It appears all the more relevant when we reflect on the characterization of the unum and multum given above, which defined the one as the privation of a privation (that is, of the manifold). Nonetheless, even privation must be excluded as an unfitting relation. Although it exists in the domain of beings, it too does not posit an object. The same thing holds of it as was asserted of

---

24. Ens et non ens contradicunt et tamen non differunt nec sunt diversa, quia diversitas est differentia *entis* et differentia similiter . . . concedendum, quod contrarietas et relativa oppositio essent, intellectu non existente, non autem privativa oppositio nec contradictio; quia alterum extremum in illis oppositionibus, puta negatio et privatio secundum quod est extremum relationis, est tantum ens secundum rationem; quod de negatione patet, quia, licet illa dicatur de aliquo ente, ut non-homo dicitur de asino, tamen secundum rationem, qua contradicit homini non est ens nisi rationis. Per hoc patet, quod licet contraria maneant, non existente intellectu, non oportet contradictoria manere, secundum quod sunt contradictoria; quia negatio albi prout contradicit albo non est in nigro, quia ut contradicit, est dicibilis de ente et de non ente. Si dicatur, quod ad nigrum saltem sequatur negatio albi ut contradicit albo et ita contradictoria sunt, si contraria sunt; dico, quod non existente intellectu non est consequentia. Similiter privatio, licet sit negatio habitus in subjecto, tamen tantummodo opponitur habitui ratione negationis, et illa non est ens nisi tantum secundum rationem. Quaest. in lib. Praed. qu. XXXVIII, 523a sq.

25. Neutrum [nec unum nec multum] dicitur de non ente, cuius probatio satis plana est de *uno*, cum convertatur cum ente. Sed quod multum dicatur de ente videtur, quia quaelibet pars multitudinis oppositae uni, quod convertatur cum ente, dicitur solum de ente . . . non potest dici multum nisi de qualibet parte eius possit dici, quod sit unum, sed unum non de ente; igitur multum non reperitur nisi in entibus. Quaest. sup. Met. lib. X, qu. V. 631a.

contradiction. It too is a certain kind of contradiction insofar as pure negation is effective in it, albeit with a specific orientation toward a precisely circumscribed object of the negation, the "*habitus.*" It is distinguished from contradiction in that it does not let the object disappear into nothingness {229/171} but precisely requires an object to bear the determination that is to be excluded through the privation (subjectum habitus). That is why neither the nothing (because it is not an object) nor a stone (because the capacity of sight does not apply to it), but only a living being inherently capable of vision, can be called *blind*.[26]

Because contradiction causes one member of the relation to disappear into nothingness, and because privation, while remaining within the domain of the ens, does not posit any object as a member of the relation, both relations are inappropriate to characterize the true relationship between the unum and the multum. The unum and the multum, taken in themselves, are absolute.[27]

The sole relation that characterizes the relationship between both members is *contrariety*. It is characteristic of the members of its relation that each posits an object whose content is otherwise.[28]

It is superfluous to further discuss the theory of opposition, particularly the relations of the three kinds of opposition and their logical hierarchy. This does not imply that the theory of *opposition* is not *fundamentally significant* for every philosophy. *Value philosophy*, a school of thought that has rightly attained respect and preeminence today, works with the concept of opposition in decisive places.

For the present investigation, the only significant insight is that the unum qua transcendens, as a primordial determination of the object, requires the multum equiprimordially, such that the "heterothesis" is the genuine "origin" of the thought of the object. {230/172} "The logical beginning must already be . . . the one and the other, since there is no object if the one and the other do not exist, and the subject cannot even begin to think logically if it does not, with its first step, think the one and the other 'at one stroke.'"[29]

We already said that the unum is an equivocal expression. On the one hand, it means the unum transcendens as a determination of the object convertible

---

26. Privatio non salvatur nisi in ente, nullam tamen naturam ponit. l. c.

Privatio autem alii contraponitur, tamen naturam nullam ponit et igitur non est in genere; subjectum tamen habile requirit et ideo nec non ens, quia non est subjectum, nec lapis, quia non est aptus, possunt dici *caeca*, sed solum animal. l. c. lib. X, qu. XI, 639b; see above, p. 28, n. 24.

27. Unum et multum in se accepta sunt absoluta . . . non igitur opponuntur privative nec etiam relative. l. c. qu. V, 631b.

28. Utrumque extremum *aliam* naturam ponit. l. c. qu. XI, 639b.

29. Rickert, "Das Eine, die Einheit und die Eins," 37.

with the ens. On the other hand, it means the unum as the *principle of number*. Until now, however, there was no reference to number in what we settled about the unum transcendens. From this, we may conclude that something new must emerge with the unum as the principle of number. In other words, number *is not already given with the object in general and does not exist from the very beginning. The other means only a multiplicity, and not* "both: the second in quantity, the other in quality."[30]

Number is a logically posterior construct to the object in general. In what follows, to let the distinction between the unum transcendens and the unum as number—in modern terms, the distinction between the "one" and number "one"—appear and simultaneously to characterize the "one" more precisely in its peculiarity we shall examine the unum *qua* principle of number. The simplicity of the relationships prevalent in the "beginnings" of the domain of logic can be characterized less by positively delineating the contours than by comparing the phenomena in question.

The unum as principium numeri in Duns Scotus's sense is not limited to pure number, that is, to the mathematical. {231/173} Here, too, the word unum should be taken right away in the wider sense of *encompassing the objects counted*—and once again, this is the case in multiple respects. Consequently, corresponding to the polysemy of the expression *numerus*, the unum as principium numeri forms a title for *diverse* investigations.

It is indisputable that pure number logically precedes the counted objects. Because we seek to show that, with the unum transcendens, nothing numerical is given as yet, we shall begin with the treatment of pure number before any considerations about counted objects and their associated problems. Simultaneously, the contemplation of pure number and the counting undertaken in respect of objects takes us further in the general direction of the investigation, which aims at a division of the domains of reality. At first glance, it may appear more consistent and purposeful to introduce the treatment of the other transcendentia—*verum* and *bonum*—once the treatment of the first transcendens is exhausted, and only then take up the special task of characterizing the individual domains of reality. The order chosen here, however, preserves the conceptual relation between the individual transcendentals and the different domains of reality more distinctly and securely. This will become clear with regard to the unum and the verum, which we shall treat next. The lack of a logically structured overview of the whole, which I do not mean to discount here, will be remedied with a corresponding summary at the end of this section.

---

30. Paul Natorp, *Die logischen Grundlagen der exacten Wissenschaften* (Leipzig: Teubner, 1910), 61.

As yet, the unum and the multum are not numerical. One could grant this and yet point out that number is implicit in them. The one [das Eine] is one [eins], and the other is one [eins]; one and one [eins und eins] make two. If I take the two as one [das Eine] and add another, then I arrive at three. In this way, one could proceed arbitrarily far in the numerical series. {232/174}

Yet this interpretation projects something onto the concept of the one and the other that cannot in fact be found in it. When I say "the one and the other," I am not counting yet. I do not determine "how much." Number first exists when I say "*this much*." Duns Scotus expresses this as follows: the *ratio mensurae*, the concept of measure, must be added to the unum transcendens and to the multum transcendens.[31] The multum in the domain of numbers is not simply the other, the multiple [Mehrerlei]. It is more than this. It is even more than a set. One could grant that this derivation of number from the one and the other projects too much onto the primordial definition of the object, and one could still wish to emphasize that with the one and the other and another, a manifold, a plurality is posited—a quantum, out of which even the simplest quantum, the one, can now be gained.

However, this attempt at a derivation also necessarily fails. Certainly, a manifold is given with the unum and the multum. Duns Scotus, however, emphatically asserts: *Non omnis multitudo causat numerum simpliciter.* As the primordial determination of an object, the one is beyond the limited and unlimited. The thought of measurement and quantitative determination cannot arise here at all.[32]

With the concept of the manifold, we have not yet attained pure number. It is essential to the set that it does not have any determination and, even more distinctive, that it does not know an *order* among the objects that constitute it. It is, as it were, only a heap, a random collection. Pure number, Scotus says, does not possess unity or determinacy through mere heaping up—for example, like *a heap of stones*.[33] {233/175} The set, therefore, is still outside the domain of mathematics. The circumstance that there nonetheless exist mathematical disciplines today that explicitly concern themselves with manifolds and sets, or more precisely, with "cardinalities," is only seemingly evidence

---

31. Unum principium numeri nihil addit super unum transcendens *nisi rationem mensurae* . . . Sic multum quod est numerus, nihil addit super multum transcendens nisi rationem mensurati. Quaest. sup. Met. lib. X, qu. V, 631a.

32. De rer. princ. qu. XVI, 588a.

Conceptus unitatis transcendentis generalior est, quia *ex se indifferens est* ad limitatum et non limitatum. Quaest. sup. Met. lib. VI, qu. II, 167a.

33. Numerus non solum est unus aggregatione sicut acervus lapidum. De rer. princ. qu. XVI, 589a.

against what we just said. For when one calculates with sets, specifically with "infinite" sets, and shows that the cardinality of the totality of rational numbers *is not equal* to the totality of real numbers [der reellen], these calculations are possible because determinations of a quantitative nature have crept into the concepts of set and class. The justified objections against deriving cardinal numbers from the apparently even more elementary concept of class are based on this fact. We cannot address the doctrine of the manifold further here, even though it is not only interesting but also highly significant from a philosophical perspective. We need only confirm in every respect the statement concerning the *non*mathematical character of the manifold given with the "idem et diversum."

Just as the one is not yet the number one, so also the manifold is not yet a so-much, a number. A manifold only requires *objects* that are *distinguishable in some way*. Numbers, however, are distinct in a highly *specific respect*. Not only that, but this distinction is *unique* to number.[34] For numbers to be distinguishable in a highly specific respect, they must, as it were, occur in a specific "medium." They require an element in which they can live, which gives them constancy and preserves them in it.

We already said that every number means a *this much* and that the aspect of measure must be added to the unum transcendens {234/176} for the one to generate the *number one*. In general, this can now be expressed as follows: the *medium for the numerical is quantity*.[35] Duns Scotus calls quantity the *"mistress"* [Herrin], the ruler [Beherrscherin] of measure.[36] The mathematician can only move within the medium of quantity. Quantity is the *relational context* that must necessarily obtain among all his objects; it is *the condition of possibility* of mathematics. It is not an object of mathematics *itself*.

But quantity nonetheless belongs among the ten categories that are valid of *natural reality*. More precisely, it is an accidens, a property. Mathematics, however, is not a natural science, and is concerned as little with the accidental, as the *independent* domain of numbers shows.

Quantity is not an object of mathematics such that we can say it inheres in substance, sed quasi *medium supponitur*. Mathematics does not dispose over substances just as it does not dispose over natural reality in general. In mathematics,

---

34. Multitudo vel replicatio unitatum differentiam specie vel genere *numerum non constituit*. l. c. 589; see Quaest. sup. Met. lib. X, qu. XIV, 644b.

35. See the text of note 37.

36. Quantitas est *domina* mensurarum. Quaest. sup. Met. lib. X, qu. I, 623a. Mathematicus omnia per *rationem quantitatis* ostendit. l. c. lib. VI, qu. I, 315a.

quantity has a completely different significance and function than it does in natural reality.[37]

The mathematician, says Duns Scotus, does not have a concept of the accidens at all. Everything that is decided about mathematical objects occurs "as if" they exist for themselves.[38] {235/177}

A science is mathematical not just insofar as its objects turn out to be *abstract* and *nonsensory*—this is also the case with the objects of logic—but rather because it contemplates its objects under the aspect of *measure*, of *quantity*. And this concept of the quantitative proves to be still free of the concept of motion. Thus, the nonsensory domain of mathematics is not mixed up with that of natural reality. Mathematical judgments are valid whether or not motion exists. They are independent of the existence [Realität] of natural reality.

The nonsensory character of mathematics also manifests itself in the fact that, in his preoccupation with pure numbers, the mathematician is not concerned with whether the corresponding quantity of counted objects exists in natural reality. Likewise, from his perspective, it is irrelevant for the theory of a circle whether or not the radii are actually drawn. What is decisive is the ideal equidistance of all points on the circumference from the center.[39] We can hardly express the nonempirical being of the nonsensory objects of mathematics more clearly.

It has thus become clear that pure number is a formation that only occurs on a *specific* ground. Quantity is the constitutive category of the domain of numbers.

---

37. Dicendum, quod *falsum* assumit, *quod quantitas sit subjectum mathematicae,* sicut dictum est in solutione quaestionis, quia tamen quantitas non ostenditur inesse substantiae corporeae, sed quasi *medium supponitur*; et de substantia corporea non ostenditur aliquid in Mathematica nisi per naturam quantitatis, tamquam primae passionis, ideo videtur esse quasi ratio propria subjecti illius scientiae et quasi ponitur subjectum, licet sit ibi passio, quia includitur in subjecto priori, ut ibi dictum est. l. c. lib. VI, qu. I, 314b.

38. Mathematicus non habet verum conceptum de accidente, quia imaginatur de eis, *ac si essent res per se existentes.* 1. c. lib. I, qu. VII, 390a.

39. Sicentia [aliqua] dicitur Mathematica, non quia est de rebus abstractis aut insensibilibus, sed quia est de rebus *secundum rationem mensurae et mensurabilis* et quia ratio mensurae et mensurabilis est impertinens ratione motus, ideo dicitur, quod Mathematica est de separatis a motu ad istum sensum. l. c. lib. II, qu. VI, 539a.

De definitione numeri Mathematicus non curat, an sit aggregatio vel non, sed sufficit sibi, quod numerus sit multitudo unitatum vel ex unitatibus. Consimiliter de definitione circuli Mathematicus non curat, utrum illae lineae [radii] ducantur vel non, sed sufficit sibi, quod omnes illae lineae sunt aequales, quarum unus terminus esset sicut centrum et alius sicut circumferentia circuli. l. c. 541a.

It circumscribes a specific region of objects that, as became clear, is *of a nonsensory nature* according to its form of reality. The unum as *pure number* no longer has the wide, all-encompassing domain {236/178} that the unum transcendens has as a determination of the object as such.

The uniqueness of the domain of number just mentioned already suffices to prevent an identification of the one with the number one. But our characterization of the domain of number is not yet complete; indeed, what *gives* number its *genuine determinacy* still remains obscure.

The unum as number should be principium numerorum. There are thus many numbers and also a beginning, a "principle." The manifold of "the one and the other" is, as it were, without a rule. For each one, there are indiscriminately *many others*. The one does not contain a prescription about which [of these] must be *its* other. *Every* other can become the other to the one.

In order to clarify this situation by means of an image, albeit an *image* only, let the one be some point in space. I can proceed from this point to another in arbitrarily many directions. Not so in the domain of numbers, where we encounter a highly specific, unambiguous, and singular *direction* of progress. If the point now signifies the number one, then there is only a highly specific "path" to two, three, et cetera, a path that is fixed by the determinacy of these numbers. We must now present this peculiar form by which every number becomes this utterly particular number and each is distinguished in a highly specific respect from every other. Thereby, we will also see how the essential moments of the domain of mathematics that we just demonstrated—quantity as "medium" and the nonsensory character—attain to their right and *manifest* themselves as the *conditions of the possibility of the determinacy proper to numbers.*

To identify the form that confers this determinacy, Duns Scotus begins at a point where the problem immediately reveals itself most clearly and, correspondingly, lets itself be identified easily. It cannot do so in the abstract domain of the pure number. But in relation to "real numbers," that is, in relation to counted objects, the question easily arises: How is it that {237/179} *ten* objects, for example, although they are not *one* but *several*, nonetheless make *one* specific number? What is the moment that endows the indisputably present plurality with *thisness, unity, determinacy*? Duns Scotus grants that the investigation into this is not easy and that opinions about the nature of this moment differ.[40] We strictly follow the

---

40. Difficultas, in qua discordant diversi, est de unitate et forma specifica numeri ... Hoc autem difficile est invenire in numero, quia secundum Avicennam 3. Met. cap. 5, *multitudo inquantum multitudo non est una,* numerus essentialiter autem est multitudo; ideo difficile est videre, a quo numerus habet unitatem specificam, et ideo circa hoc sunt opiniones diversae. Reportata lib. I, dist. XXIV, qu. unic. 272a.

philosopher's reasoning here. First, he critically discusses three different theories, in order to then present his view, which shows that the problem *can genuinely be resolved only in the domain of pure number.* For number does not first *arise* through counting, but the other way around: counting is first possible on the basis of pure number.

Thomas Aquinas holds the view that a number derives its determinacy and thisness from its *last unit,* specifically, in such a way that this unit does not confer determinacy absolutely *qua unit,* but rather, on the basis of its specific *distance* from the first of the units that comprise the number. The determinacy of a number emerges in accordance with this distance, that is, the distance of the last unit from the first of the respective number. These different distances characterize numbers as specifically distinct from each other.

The respective last unit can perform the function of conferring form and determinacy either because it is this unit, or because it has a definite distance from the first. Duns Scotus sharply rejects both possibilities.

Anything that is to serve as the form of an object must pervade the material of the whole object, imprint its determinacy on the matter as {238/180} a whole just as the soul as the essential form of man determines and enlivens all parts of the body. However, the last unit of a number does not extend its determinacy, insofar as it is this unit, across the preceding units of the number. It leaves them, as it were, untouched and does not have any determining function in relation to them.

Furthermore, we should note that the last unit of a number itself belongs to those units that constitute the material awaiting determination. Otherwise, the number four, for example, if its last unit were not the matter but rather the form of the number, would have to become the number three. Therefore the last unit as such, qua belonging to the material, does not have priority over the others, such that determining the preceding [units] in their totality, it could legitimately appear their form.

But neither is the *function of conferring form proper* to the *last unit* of a number in the second respect, that is, in its distance from the first unit. The distance from one unit to another—which should be understood neither spatially nor temporally—is at any rate a relation. Were the determinacy of a number founded on such a relation, then number would not be a specific quantum at all but a relation, a perspective.

Further, if we accept this distance as the form of the number, how should it live up to its character as form and extend itself, as it were, across all units, since qua relation only affects the last and the first members, but not those in between? Simultaneously, it is not evident to what extent the last unit has priority over the first in this distance, just as in general, each of the units that constitute the respective number could stand in the first as much as the last position, or in some other position. If the last unit is the form of the number as a whole, the stated equality of the individual units would be impossible.[41] {239/181}

The second of the theories Duns Scotus lists, whose author remains anonymous, takes for granted that number is a discrete phenomenon distinct from the continuum. Just as in a continuum the *specific* continuity constitutes the form of unity—for example, just as each time we encounter a specific form of continuity in a line, a plane surface, or a body—so also *number* gains its determinacy and unity, each time, from specific discrete moments. Just as the parts of the continuum represent the material for the form of continuity, so also the units of a number represent the material for the different *discrete moments* {240/182} through which the individual numbers first become specific species. Given this interpretation of the determinacy proper to number, it is also comprehensible why a number is not comprised of *numbers* but of *units*. One specific species

---

41. Quidam dicunt, quod numerus suam habet unitatem specificam ab ultima unitate, non autem absolute ab unitate inquantum unitas, sed secundum quod habet determinatam distantiam ad primam unitatem et secundum talem distantiam ad primam unitatem distinguuntur numeri specifice secundum diversas distantias, unde talis distantia distinguit specifice numeros.

Sed contra, ultima unitas alicuius numeri, si det formam et speciem illi, aut igitur inquantum haec unitas est, aut inquantum distans a prima? Non inquantum haec unitas, quia illud, quod est forma et species alicuius totius, oportet perficere totam materiam totius, sicut anima quae est forma hominis perficit totam materiam et omnes partes corporis hominis. Sed ultima unitas non informat omnes unitates praecedentes in numero; igitur non potest esse forma totius numeri inquantum unitas talis est.

Praeterea, haec unitas, quae est ultima, est materialis, sicut et aliae unitates, aliter ternarius esset quaternarius, si ultima unitas quaternarii non esset pars totius materialis sed tantum forma praecedentium; non igitur inquantum haec unitas est magis forma totius numeri quam alia unitas. Nec potest dici, quod sit forma totius numeri secundo modo, quia distantia unius unitatis ab alia formaliter est relatio; igitur si numerus sortiatur suam unitatem specificam ab unitate propter illam distantiam a prima unitate, sequitur, quod numerus non sit quantitas, sed relatio sive respectivum.

Praeterea contra hoc, cum illa distantia ultimae a prima tantum sit in ultima unitate vel in illis duabus unitatibus ultimate distantibus, et non in mediis, sicut distantia, qua disto a pariete, tantum est in me vel in me et in pariete et *non* in aere medio, sequitur, quod illa distantia non potest esse forma totius numeri, cum non sit forma cuiuslibet partis numeri, et per consequens ab illa distantia non poterit numerus habere suam unitatem specificam, cum illa distantia sit in uno distante vel solum in duobus, et non potest esse in *omnibus unitatibus ut forma.* Reportata lib. I, dist. XXIV, qu. unic. 272b sq.

Si prima unitas fiat ultima et ultima prima, nulla fiat differentia in substantia numeri, quod non staret, si ultima unitas esset forma completiva et specifica numeri. l. c. 273a sq.

cannot be potentially part of *another* specific species. Qua determinate, every number has its own *discreteness*, which differs from that of the others and hence represents a different species. Other species cannot be present in one and the same species as parts.

The criticism of this view begins with a general consideration. Parts that do not have a greater unity and determinacy when united into a whole as compared with when they are not part of a whole are *not* parts of a whole that is a unit in itself. But this is the case with the units of numbers if discreteness is the form that confers determinacy on them. If the units were not united into *one number*, each would be distinct and separate from the other. But according to the theory just cited, this is how they are related in a number. For qua discrete, they are countable and thus constitute the number. Consequently, number is not *one in itself*, a unity, but only through an aggregation (aggregatio) of units. In other words, *discreteness* is not a form that confers determinacy.

If number is to receive its unity through discreteness, then qua real component, it belongs among the counted objects. *Six* stones constitute a different quantity than *seven* stones; the one reality does not differ from the other only *in thought*. But it is impossible that an absolute form, such as numerical determinacy represents, can supervene on the material without altering it. If one more stone is added to the six stones, the six stones cease to be in the form of the number *six*. Through the number *seven*, they attain a form differing from the previous one in a determinate respect. But if this new absolute form does not change the six real stones in themselves, the form of {241/183} seven—and, in general, the form of determinacy of every number—cannot be *a real component* of the quantity. Discreteness is thus excluded as the form of determinacy.[42]

------

42. Alia opinio est, quae videtur esse secundum intentionem Aristotelis magis quam prior, quod sicut continuitas est forma et per se unitas continui et partium eius, a qua habent suam unitatem in toto . . . et partes in continuo, est *discretio*, ut sicut continuitas est unitas continui, ita discretio est unitas discreti sive numeri; et sic per aliam et aliam continuitatem est alia et alia species continui, ut patet in linea, superficie et corpore, ita secundum aliam et aliam discretionem est alia et alia species; et sicut partes continui sunt materiales respectu continuitatis, quarum omnium continuitas est forma, . . . et per talem discretionem habet numerus esse in determinata specie et secundum aliam et aliam discretionem unitatum est alia et alia species numeri.

Secundum hoc etiam patet, quod numerus non componitur ex nuermis, quia una species completa non est pars potentialis alterius speciei. Cum igitur numerus ex hoc quod habet certam discretionem unitatum sit completa species in unitate sua specifica, stante sua discretione, quae est opposita discretioni alterius speciei numeri, non poterit esse pars eius, cum habeat oppositam discretionem et in eadem specie numeri non possunt complete et actu esse oppositae discretiones, sed tantum unitates

We shall note only a few points and their clarification by Duns Scotus regarding the *third*, less interesting theory—that of Henry of Ghent. It states that number arises from the continuum and has the latter's unity. But how should number be distinguished from the continuum? The difference lies in the arrangement of the parts, {242/184} which are combined in the continuum under a uniform aspect; that is, the continuum does not manifest any gaps. This absence of gaps is lacking in number as a discrete quantity. Consequently, number is a species of quantity by itself. It is distinguished from the continuum by the lack of an absence of gaps. Apart from the fact that number is not *positively* distinguished from the continuum in this way and privation does not constitute a new species, Duns Scotus remarks that he cannot understand how number is supposed to attain unity and determinacy from the continuum, when it has been characterized precisely by its *lack* of continuity, and hence negatively. But because the determinacy of number is something positive, it must be found elsewhere.

According to the theory under discussion, number has the same essential form as the first unit, that is, ultimately, the same form as the continuum from which it is, as it were, cut off. Numbers differ only *in an accidental respect*, in that they distinguish themselves through their differing *distance* from the first unit. But this distinction does not lie in the nature of the units that constitute number, because the number is unchanged when the first unit replaces the second, and vice versa.

We can show that this account does not justify a specific difference between numbers as follows: "many" and "few" relate to each other in a discrete quantum the same way that "large" and "small" relate to each other in a continuum. "Large" and "small," however, are not specifically different, and hence neither are "many" and "few." Just as a small magnitude grows steadily by addition without changing specifically, numbers are not specifically differentiated from each other when their distance from the first unit is changed, that is, becomes greater or smaller.

---

sunt partes numeri et sic numerus componitur ex unitatibus et non ex numeris . . .
Sed contra: partes, quae non habent maiorem unitatem in toto quam haberent, si non
essent in toto, non sunt partes alicuius totius, quod est per se unum . . . igitur unitates
prout habent discretionem, non sunt partes alicuius unius per se; igitur sequitur, quod
numerus non sit aliquid per se unum sed tatnum *aggregatione*.

Item secundo sic: impossibile est formam absolutam advenire alicui sine sui
mutatione, quamvis hoc dicatur esse possibile de forma respectiva; sed si lapidibus
facientibus senarium numerum addatur unus lapis per generationem sive creationem,
lapides priores desinunt esse sub forma senarii et incipiunt esse sub forma septenarii
et ab illa forma habent unitatem aliam specificam. Si igitur forma numeri septenarii
sit ab aliqua forma absoluta et illi sex lapides in nullo mutantur per hoc, quod de novo
generatur alius lapis, sequitur quod forma numeri septenarii non sit alia forma absoluta
extra animam in illis septem lapidibus. l. c. 273b sqq.

We can understand this argument concerning "large" and "small" and "many" and "few" in two ways: first, insofar as magnitude and plurality are *types of quantity*, and second, insofar as they signify properties. In the first respect, {243/185} it is true that magnitude and plurality do not change specifically in the continuum or the domain of number. But if "large" is contrasted with "small" and "many" with "few," that is, if these determinations are conceived as properties, then it is correct that, just as the former is a determination of the continuum, the latter is a determination of the discrete domain of number. But we may not conclude from this that "many" and "few" are determinations of numbers of the same species the way "large" and "small" are determinations of magnitude of the same kind. Continua vary only with respect to the distinct aspect of *divisibility*, but "large" and "small" are unaffected thereby. By contrast, the determinations "many" and "few" vary with the type of *discreteness*. However much a magnitude increases in the continuum, the genus of the continuum remains the same. But when a unit is added to a specific number, the number changes essentially, that is, it becomes another number. Consequently, "many" and "few" in the domain of number signify a difference in kind. Continuum and domain of number are hence essentially distinct, thus demonstrating the untenability of the theory in question.[43] {244/186}

---

43. Alia est opinio Gandavensis . . . ponentis quod solus numerus accidentalis non est nisi multitudo ex unitate profusa per divisionem continui . . . Secundum hoc igitur, omnes numeri de genere quantitatis vel profluunt ab uno continuo, . . . , quantum est ex parte materiae et formae continuitatis et hoc quantum ad naturam numeri in se. Sed quomodo se habet illa unitas continuitatis ad numeros? Dicit quod partium numeri sive unitatum eius non est alia forma essentialis quam sit forma continuitatis in prima unitate, a qua discinduntur sive natae sunt discindi.

Hoc autem quantum ad unitatem specificam numeri; sed si non sit alia forma absoluta in numero a forma continuitatis, quomodo ergo differt numerus a continuo? Respondet quod non est differentia inter continuum et discretum, nisi secundum respectum quendam et ordinem partium aliter se habentium inter se in continuo et aliter in discreto, quia in continuo partes copulantur ad terminum communem, in discreto autem non; et hoc non convenit discreto ex natura alicuius positivi, quod super continuum addat, sed potius ex natura privativi, in quo deficit a continuo. Numerus enim non habet *esse* nec *intelligi*, nisi ex privatione continui . . . sic numerus sive discreta quantitas nihil addit super continuum nisi rationem negationis aut respectum partium ad invicem, ex quibus habet aliam rationem mensurandi quam habet quantitas continua et est altera species quantitatis quam continua. . . .

Quod non est alia forma numeri essentialis a forma continuitatis primae unitatis sed tantum alia forma accidentalis [respondet Gandav]. Quod probat primo per hoc, quod species unius numeri non differt nisi propter aliam distantiam ad primam unitatem, quia enim ternarius aliter distat a prima unitate quam binarius, ideo ternarius differt a binario. Sed talis distantia ad primam unitatem est accidentalis numero, quia non

So far, we have only made a negative decision about what can be considered the form that endows number with determinacy and unity. We must now find a positive answer to this question. {245/187}

Above all, we must understand that the unity of ten *counted* objects is not a *reality* added to the objects, but rather an *ens rationis*, an intelligible *form*, with which *consciousness* unites the given objects.[44]

The objects given are as such incapable of constituting the unity of a number. They are this object and this object, that is, as objects the one and the other. Their sum merely possesses unity through *consciousness*. Number possesses pure and true "existence" only as a *nonsensory object*; it is then applied as such to the objects

---

est ex natura unitatum, quia si prima fieret secunda, non variaretur et hoc idem probat secundo sic: sicut *magnum* et *parvum* se habent in continuo, ita *multum* et *paucum* in quantitate discreta; sed *magnum* et *parvum* non distinguunt specie quantitatem continuam, igitur nec *multum* et *paucum* quantitatem discretam; igitur sicut aliqua magnitudo parva cresceret secundum additionem et fieret continue maior et non esset alia magnitudo specie, ita cum numeri crescunt secundum unam distantiam, numerus parvus, secundum se non differt specie a magno nisi accidentaliter propter distantiam ad primam unitatem et sic numerus non habet aliam formam essentialem a continuitate primae unitatis. Reportata I, dist. XXIV, qu. unic. 275a sqq.

Illa praedicta [de magno et parvo, multo et pauco] possunt accipi dupliciter: uno modo secundum quod magnitudo et multitudo sunt species quantitatis et alio modo secundum quod sint passiones. Primo modo verum est, quod sicut magnum et parvum se habent in continuis ita multum et paucum in discretis; et ideo sicut magnitudo est alterius rationis in continuis, ut in linea et superficie et in corpore, ita multitudo in numeris variatur secundum species diversas. Si vero accipiantur secundo modo, prout sunt passiones, sic accipiuntur ut magnum opponitur parvo, et multum pauco, et sic verum est, quod sicut isto modo magnum et parvum sunt passiones continui, ita multum et paucum sunt passiones discreti. Si tamen ex hoc concludatur, quod sicut magnum et parvum sunt passiones magnitudinis eiusdem speciei, quod ita multum et paucum erunt passiones eiusdem numeri secundum speciem, *dicendum, quod non est simile*, quia continua non variantur, nisi penes aliam et aliam rationem divisibilitas; magnum vero et parvum non variantur penes aliam et aliam rationem discretionis; multum vero et paucum variantur per discretionem prout opponuntur. Unde quia forma numeri est magis praecisa, quia omnino indivisibilis . . . non autem sic forma continuitatis, ideo quantumcumque augmentetur magnitudo, non variatur eius species propter magnitudinem, sed addita unitate variatur species numeri essentialiter; ideo non stant multum et paucum in eadem specie numeri. l. c. 279a sq.

44. Numerus nullam unitatem realem habet aliam a rebus numeratis sed solum unitatem *rationis*, quam mens concipit. De rer. princ. qu. XVI, 585a.

to be counted. Just as there are real and nonsensory relations, so also there is real and nonsensory *quantity*.[45]

When we inquire into *pure* number, we are not interested in the things that we count as one, two, three, et cetera, but in what first makes counting meaningful and possible, that is, in the *form of number itself*. Pure mathematical number is that number *with* which we count real objects and objects in general. The objects to be counted *are counted*, brought into an order. In contrast, pure numbers *count themselves*. They possess a determinacy in themselves that does *not* supervene on them from without. They themselves determine the progression from one to the other. *As pure quantum, number measures itself (per aliquid sui).* It has a specific position in relation to others, that is, numbers constitute a {246/188} *series* and are subject to a *law of series*, which they themselves generate for their totality. Numbers are not *indiscriminately* thrown together like a *set*.[46]

We can now answer the question of the form that endows the number with unity and determinacy definitively. Because pure number is not a real formation belonging either to bodily or psychic reality, but rather exists among the *non-sensory*, the form that grants it unity must also be drawn from the nonsensory. What is the nature of the domain of reality of mathematics? Earlier, we said that quantity is the constitutive category of the domain of mathematical objects. If this is so, the form that endows determinacy must also become intelligible on its basis. This requires that we study its essence more closely.

As something ultimate, it cannot be defined perfectly. We can only describe, indicate (notificari) its essence. The quantum is the *how much* and can therefore be determined as a *so much*. This occurs through *measurement*. *Mensurability* thus appears as the fundamental moment of quantity.

---

45. De quantitate nihil est extra animam, nisi quantitas continua, cuius partes divisae extra animam non possunt habere unitatem numeri, nec unum numerum constituere, sed tantum sunt haec, haec, haec, non habentia aliquam unam formam numeralem. . . . solum numerus habet suam unitatem ab anima. . . . Reportata, l. c. 279b.

Intellectus primo mensurat *intellectualiter* aliquam multitudinem intellectam, quam postea applicando ad alia discreta, quae sunt extra, mensurat illa multitudine intellecta, a qua ut sic quantitas numeri habet suam unitatem sicut ens formaliter in anima. l. c. 280a.

46. Numerus mathematicus dicitur multitudo aggregata ex rationibus unitatis ut participant quantitatem; ut ternarius numerat tria quanta, sive sint ferra sive lapides sive ligna vel albedines vel quaecumque quantitatem participant: et hic est numerus *quo* numeramus. Numerus naturalis dicitur multitudo aggregata ex ipsis rebus, quibus convenit ratio unitatis; quae sunt ipsae res numeratae ut tres lapides, vel tres albedines: et iste est numerus *qui* numerat per numerum mathematicum. De rer. princ. qu. XVI, 580a.

Diversa enim ad se invicem *numerantur*, numeri autem *numerant* se *ad invicem*, aut per numerum aut per unitatem. l. c. 590a.

Duns Scotus rejects this view. Mensurability is only a *property* of quantity. It does not signify its proper essence. More precisely, it is a property of what exists under quantity. Quantity itself is nothing quantitative. The essence of quantity exists, rather, in *divisibilitas in partes eiusdem rationis.* "Divisibility," determinability {247/189} through "making cuts," division into parts having the same *identical nature,* constitutes its essence. This determinability in respect of the same—in modern terms, with a view to the *law of series* that governs the pure quantum—is not quantity itself but flows, as it were, from it. The nature of quantity is such that it makes such determinability possible. Mensurability is only a consequence of this primary determinability, that is, of *progression* in quantity from one to another according to a particular aspect (*quantitas domina mensurarum*). The pure continuum that enables discreteness is not first composed through the discrete quanta. It precedes everything discrete as *something identical* that first of all enables determinability according to an identical aspect. It is simply the *lawfulness of the series itself. Divisibilitas in partes eiusdem rationis* means nothing other than this.[47]

The determinacy of number is thus cognized through the law of series. By occupying (situ distinguitur) an adequately determined position (situs) within the series, number is also sufficiently determined as this *one* identical number. The "one" is therefore the same in kind as the numbers it measures. The individual numbers are only distinguished by their *position* in the series (*situ* recte distinguitur propter maiorem vel minorem replicationem talium unitatum). No two numbers are an equal number of steps immediately distant from the number one. Thus 2 times 3 is not *the number six,* but yields 6, that is, the result of the multiplication can be equated with the number {248/190} *six,* which, as such, is only present once and attains its determinacy from its position in the series.[48]

Consequently, Duns Scotus *himself* seems to *adopt* the concept of distance that he had rejected as *inadequate* to the task of determining number in his critical

---

47. Ratio mensurae . . . magis inest discretis et continuis non nisi inquantum *participant* quantitatem discretam. Quaest. sup. Met. lib. V, qu. IX, 251a.

Ratio mensurae est *passio* quantitatis et sic non propria ratio quantitatis . . . dicendum . . . quod propria ratio [quantitatis] est *divisibilitas* in partes eiusdem rationis . . .

Divisibilitas fundatur in quantitate et dicit habitudinem ad divisionem, et cuicumque inest divisibilitas in partes eiusdem rationis, hoc est per quantitatem . . . Quantitas notificatur per proximam passionem eius et non definitur . . . l. c. 252a sqq.

48. Dico igitur, quod ratio *indivisibilitatis* in numero uno sicut quaternario vel ternario, sub qua uniuntur unitates, utpote quae inter se sunt divisae, sub qua etiam uniuntur numeri materiales constituentes unum numerum ut sex, quatuor, decem; illa dico ratio indivisibilis et una quae est ratio formalis unius numeri, *est identitas in specie unitatum replicatarum,* illum numerum constituentium, ut sic dicamus, quod quaelibet species numeri ex eo est una, quia constat ex uno et uno eiusdem rei usque ad certum numerum replicationis talis numeri; ita quod una species numeri ab

discussion of Thomas Aquinas's theory. This is in fact the case—as a later remark shows—but, he says, the concept of distance is *not the primary aspect* from which numbers attain their determinacy. We can first speak of distance when the object concerned already has a specific position, which number attains from the law of series.[49] The number one and the numbers that follow it in the series are identical in *kind*. A *uniformitas* reigns in the domain of number. Numbers are not composed of random units or objects of a heterogenous nature. They occur in a homogenous "medium" represented, as should have become clear by now, by pure quantity (unum et numerus sunt unigenea). {249/191} Heterogenous objects at all times exclude unity and determinacy of the sort proper to the pure numbers.[50]

If we now compare the unum transcendens, the one, and the unum as principium numeri, the number one, their distinction should be apparent. Simultaneously, it is clear that the number one cannot be derived directly from the one. Rather, new conditions are required for this, new moments that are not yet given with the one. *Quantity* and the *homogenous medium* first make number possible and make it into a highly specific phenomenon. The one and the other are distinct only in general, but the number one and the number two are distinct in a highly specific respect (ratio). This *respect* is constitutive of the domain of number and directs it into specific boundaries, that is, makes it into a domain of objects that is specifically distinct from other domains. The unum transcendens is valid of every object, regardless of the domain of reality to which it belongs. It is also valid of numbers. The number one is meaningful only in the domain of the quantitative.

In previous discussions, I repeatedly emphasized that we must distinguish between pure numbers and counted objects. The form of unity of a particular sum

---

alia *situ recte distinguatur* propter maiorem vel minorem replicationem talium unitatum. De rer. princ. qu. XVI, 587b.

Bis tria non sunt senarius sed quae *habent* bis tres unitates, *habent* senarium et est denominativa praedicatio. Quest. sup. Met. lib. V, qu. IX, 257b sq.

Duae species numerorum ... non possunt se habere per aequalem immediationem ad unitatem. De rer. princ. l. c. 572a.

49. Quando arguitur, quod numeri distinguuntur per aliam et aliam distantiam ad primam unitatem, dicendum, quod, licet illa distantia diversa necessario *concomitetur* numeros distinctos, non tamen est *prima ratio distinguendi eos*, ut probatum est, unde non potest esse forma primi numeri, *sed concomitatur certam discretionem numeri*. Reportata I, dist. XXIV, qu. unic. 278b sq.

50. Haec et illa non faciunt unitatem binarii, *sed una praecise distincta a se invicem*. Quaest. sup. Met. lib. V, qu. IX, 257b.

Unum quod est eiusdem speciei est mensura unitatum integrantium numerum et est uniformitas unitatis specificae in eis. De rer. princ. qu. XVI, 587b.

Unum et numerus sunt unigenea, quia numerus nihil aliud est quam plura una. Quaest. sup. Met. lib. X, qu. I, 624a, b.

of objects is not a real piece of the objects themselves, something that might belong to the same domain of reality as the objects themselves. *Consciousness* adds the form of unity to objects. I simultaneously showed that the form of unity and determinacy in question can only exist in the nonsensory, mathematical domain due to this domain's special constitution, characterized by quantity {250/192} and a homogenous medium. Then again, it is a fact that numbers, albeit nonsensory, are used to determine and count objects that are of a sensory nature, that is, that lie outside the domain of mathematics. How is this possible?

As we trace the thread of number and its form of unity, we arrive in the sphere of natural reality in order to study the forms found there and their *distinction* from the pure mathematical form.

Form is a correlative concept. A form is the form of a material, and every material exists in some form.[51] Matter, further, always occurs in a form appropriate to it. In other words, form always derives its meaning from matter. Thus, if we want to grasp the form of unity in the sphere of the real world, we find ourselves referred to the material that is to be combined into a unity, which has, as it were, the power to decide which specifically constituted form is capable of unifying it. The focus of our interest thus shifts to an investigation into the categorial constitution of reality, both sensory and supersensory. In this way, the fulfillment of our real task—dividing the domains of reality—takes a significant step forward by rendering intelligible the form of unity dominant in the world of the real.

The real objects of natural reality attain a preliminary delimitation from other object regions from their characterization as *entia extra animam*. For now, we shall leave it undecided whether this provides a sufficient criterion of reality. Someone could immediately question whether *psychic* reality is not just as real as physical reality. At any rate, the criterion "extra animam" says nothing decisive as long as *psychic reality* {251/193} *itself is not sufficiently determined in a positive sense*. This is not an easy problem. Even today, when psychology is on course to constitute itself as an independent science, the problem has not been satisfactorily answered. When one recalls that the delimitation of the psychic over against the domain of the logical has contributed not a little to a sharper characterization of the former's unique reality [Eigenwirklichkeit] and made it much easier to raise the question of its essence more precisely and without fatally confusing regions, it appears advisable in the present case also to first settle the question of the nature of the psychic world when treating of *logic*. For now, we shall concern ourselves with physical reality as one of the areas belonging to the real world. Of course, if we interpret the word "*anima*" to mean "*consciousness*," then "*extra*

---

51. Materia non potest intelligi nisi sub habitudine ad formam. Sup. lib. II, anal. post. qu. VI, 333b.

animam" points to a reality that transcends consciousness and includes not only the psychic and the physical within itself but also the supersensory reality of the absolute being of *God*. Irrespective of how these problems are to be settled more precisely, we know what counts as reality sufficiently well, albeit without sharp, conceptual determinacy.

Intelligendum est . . . quod *esse existere* non consequitur essentiam primo, sed primo consequitur *individuum. Individuum enim per se et primo existit, essentia non nisi per accidens.*[52] With these sentences, in relation to a problem much debated at the time, Duns Scotus formulates in all clarity a thought of wide-ranging significance. What really exists is an individual. The concept of the individual does not intend an *indeterminate* object of a determinate species. "Being-individual" [Das "Individuelles-Sein"] does not coincide with being-an-object-in-general. Hence we may not think that the concept of the individual is already exhausted by the unum transcendens, which distinguishes one object from another. {252/194} Individual means: determinacy as this unique [thing], otherwise encountered never and nowhere else, which, in its very essence, resists subdivision into independent qualitative moments. The individual is an *irreducible ultimate*. It means the real object κατ' ἐξοχήν prout includit existentiam et tempus. Two apples on the same tree do not have the same *"regard"* toward the sky; even if they are otherwise fully identical, each is already distinguished from the other by its *spatial* determination.[53] Everything that really exists, is a "such-here-and-now."[54]

---

52. l. c. qu. IV, 329b.

53. The decisive function of temporal determination in characterizing the individual is particularly manifest in historical science's concept of time. I analyze its categorial structure in my essay "Der Zeitbegriff in der Geschichtswissenschaft," *Zeitschrift für Philosophie und philosophische Kritik* 161 (1916): 173–88. See GA 1, 415ff.

Tr.: See Thomas Sheehan, trans., "The Concept of Time in the Science of History," in *Becoming Heidegger: On the Trail of His Early Occasional Writings, 1910–1927,* ed. Theodore Kisiel and Thomas Sheehan (Evanston, IL: Northwestern University Press, 2007), 63–76; Harry S. Taylor, Hans W. Uffelmann, and John van Buren, trans., "The Concept of Time in the Science of History," in *Supplements: From the Earliest Essays to Being and Time and Beyond,* ed. John van Buren (Albany: SUNY Press, 2002), 49–60.

54. Expono quod intelligo per *individuationem* . . . non quidem unitatem indeterminatam, secundum quam quodlibet in specie dicitur unum numero, sed unitatem *signatam ut hanc,* ut est *haec* determinata. Oxon. II, dist. III, qu. IV, 33a, n. 3; see l. c. dist. II, qu. I–VII.

Accipitur individuum substantia et simul totum stricte, prout includit existentiam et tempus ut *hic* homo *existens* et hic lapis existens. Quaest. in Met. lib. VII, qu. X, 215b, n. 76.

Singulare dicit gradum distinctum naturalem unius individui a gradu naturae alterius individui eiusdem speciei, eo quod . . . numquam natura generat duo individua

The form of individuality (haecceitas) is called on to deliver a primordial determination of existent reality. This reality constitutes an "unsurveyable manifold," a "heterogenous continuum." This peculiar aspect of the immediately given has been sharply emphasized in the present above all by Rickert, who makes it the basis of his fundamental methodology.[55] {253/195}

The problem is now, How can one count within this unsurveyable manifold? The number has its determinacy through its position in the series (situs). The series is a series only through a law of series. This implies something about the sequence, the distance, the reciprocal determination of neighboring members of the series. Numbers have their fixed, determinate position. They do not arise and pass away and are absolved from all change. Is there something of this nature in existent reality? When I say "four trees," do I thereby indicate a specific position in a specific series? Or is it the other way around: is "four trees" determined by a position in the series? After all, I can put "four trees" together in many ways. How must I progress, and toward which of the trees present, in order to reach "five trees"? How can I count the trees at all, when each is already distinguished from the other through its local determination, to say nothing of other differences in growth such as the leaves, flowers, fruit, growing conditions, et cetera? *Each is after all an other.* It is not at all grounded in the individual trees to be, for example, the fifth in the count. But they are counted nonetheless.

Earlier, we showed that the "homogenous medium" is the vital element of number. However, empirical reality, to which the individually distinct trees belong, is anything but homogenous. Rather, its absolute diversity is precisely its most prominent characteristic.

Consequently, if counting is to be possible in existent reality, that is, if number is somehow to gain constancy and be applicable, this is not possible without

---

eiusdem speciei secundum eundem modum et gradum participantia illam speciem, sicut nec duae species umquam aequaliter participant naturam generis. De rer. princ. qu. XIII, 501b.

Duo poma in una arbore numquam habent eundem aspectum ad coelum. l. c. 502a.

Hic et nunc quae sunt conditiones concernentes *rationem singularis.* l. c. 511. See esp. part II, chapter 2.

55. Besides Rickert's main work, *Die Grenzen der naturwissenschaftlichen Begriffsbildung,* 2nd ed. (Tübingen: Mohr, 1913), see the especially instructive essay "Geschichtsphilosophie" in *Die Philosophie im Beginn des zwanzigsten Jahrhunderts (Festschrift für Kuno Fischer),* 2nd ed., ed. Wilhelm Windelband (Heidelberg: C. Winter, 1907), 321–422.

Tr.: See Heinrich Rickert, *The Limits of Concept Formation in Natural Science: A Logical Introduction to the Historical Sciences,* ed. and trans. Guy Oakes (Cambridge: Cambridge University Press, 1986).

homogeneity. If I observe this tree only according to its individuality as having never existed before and never recurring again and another tree *in just the same manner*, I could never count them. {254/196} I could only say: the one and the other. In contrast, they can only be called "two" if the one and the other are, as it were, projected onto a homogenous medium through a projection that retains only the *universal determination of being-a-tree*. Consequently, such projection onto a homogenous medium means: the objects are observed in a *specific respect and in this respect only*.

In each instance, then, these *respects* circumscribe a specific domain of a homogenous kind, and they are in a certain sense its hallmark. Through this respect, the heterogenous discrete quantum is *annulled*. It is not a priori evident that such respects actually exist. We can only read them off from empirical reality, insofar as this reality is distinguished by a categorial structure that enables them. Hence, we must now characterize this more precisely. When we say empirical reality manifests a specific categorial structure, this means that it is formed, determined, ordered. Where order exists, be it of the simplest kind, there already we can no longer speak of an absolute manifold. Grasped as an absolute manifold, empirical reality is therefore a limit concept, such that every doctrine of categories must necessarily hypostatize it.

The natural environment and, simultaneously for medieval man, the *supersensory* world, of which he is no less constantly and poignantly aware, are already categorially determined. The sensory and supersensory worlds along with their reciprocal relationships occur within an order. In an anticipatory manner we may specify the main trait of this order: it is *dominated by analogy*.[56] We have not encountered this concept yet. We only know the homogenous continuum and the {255/197} absolute manifold of the heterogenous continuum. *With analogy, we face a new character of order*. By highlighting the constitutive elements of this concept, we will open up an insight into the peculiarity of the categorial structure of the existent sensory and supersensory reality.

Initially, two forms of *analogy* can be distinguished. A word has a meaning. In its application to different domains of reality, however, this meaning undergoes a peculiar differentiation of meaning deriving from these domains. Thus, there is something common in the words "principium" and "causa," namely their primordial meaning, that they refer to something from which something else arises and from which this latter thing gains its constancy. This general meaning is

---

56. Illa ratio a qua imponitur ens non est una sed aequivoca in diversis sicut et ens. Quaest. in lib. Praed. qu. IV, 449b.

Apud Metaphysicum vel Naturalem, qui non considerant vocem in significando sed *ea quae significantur secundum id quod sunt*, [vox entis] est analoga. l. c. 447b.

differentiated in the domain of logic into the meaning "reason" and in the domain of existent reality into the meaning "cause." The two are not interchangeable. "Principle" is thus used *analogously* as "reason" and as "cause."

Further, the meaning of a word can be applied to an object that has a certain similarity to the object actually intended by this meaning.[57]

However, *none* of these forms of analogy is proper to the categorial structure of existent reality.[58] *The analogy that {256/198} governs the world of the real is that of per attributionem.* The analogues occur here in a specific relationship of co-belonging. *Something that stands in an analogy is neither totally distinct nor totally identical.*

The constitutive elements of analogy are: a certain *identity* of meaning and, yet, a *distinction* depending on the domain of application. Insofar as we can call the identity of meaning—the uniformity of perspective—a homogenous element found in all analogues, it is the element of the analogy that justifies the order. Insofar as the "commune" in the different domains is experienced as *different*, the *manifold* is also preserved in the analogy. Hence, if analogy reigns in the fundamental structure of existent reality, this means that homogeneity and heterogeneity are *entwined* in a unique manner in this domain. The manifold is preserved despite a certain *unity* of perspective; for its part, this manifold is such that it does not exclude the *identity* of the respect. What results is a peculiar unity in the manifold and a manifold in the unity.[59] {257/199}

---

57. Ponitur analogia in voce … quia significat unam rationem primo, quae *existendo* diversimode convenit duobus vel pluribus, quae dicuntur analogata: sicut hoc nomen *"causa"* et hoc nomen *"principium"* … significant unam rationem primo, tamen illa est in diversis secundum ordinem.

[Alio modo] quia vox uni imponitur proprie et propter aliquam similitudinem ad illud, cui primo imponitur, transfertur vox ad significandum aliud … et hoc secundum significat solum propter aliquam similitudinem eius ad illud, cui primo imponitur. l. c. 446a sq.

58. Sed qualitercunque sit de modo ponendi analogiam, *nullus istorum modorum videtur convenire enti respectu decem praedicamentorum.* See Quaest. in lib. Physic. lib. I, qu. VII, 388b. Sec. Op. sup. lib. Periherm. qu. I, 584a.

Concedo quod ens non dicatur univoce de omnibus entibus, non tamen aequivoce, quia aequivoca dicitur aliquid de multis, quando illa de quibus dicitur non habent attributionem ad invicem, sed quando attribuuntur, tunc analogice. Quia ergo [ens] non habet conceptum unum, ideo significat omnia essentialiter secundum propriam rationem et simpliciter aequivoce secundum Logicum; quia autem illa quae significantur inter se essentialiter attribuuntur, ideo analogice secundum Metaphysicum realem. Quaest. sup. Met. lib. IV, qu. I, 153a.

59. Quaedam sunt nomina penitus univoca: et illa sunt, quorum ratio substantiae eadem est et nomen idem. Quaedem sunt nomina, quae proprie dicuntur aequivoca: ut illa, quae actu plura significant sub propriis rationibus; et illa sunt, quorum nomen

This is the basic hallmark of the "genus metaphysicum" that encompasses the sensory and supersensory world. The relationship between unity and the manifold will change depending on the difference in the "*attributio.*" If one interprets unity and the manifold as analogous to the domain of number, the difference in the attributio can be expressed in terms of the difference in the way the manifold proceeds from a unity. Correspondingly, the manifold is measured differently in relation to unity. This measurement presumably cannot be purely quantitative, because this is possible only in the nonsensory domain of mathematics. We shall see that this measurement has the character of an *evaluation and a determination of value.* Unity is the *measure* of the manifold arising from it: the *type* of measurement is as distinct as the unity.

The "*monas*" potentially contains a plurality, which somehow emerges from it; it is in some sense the starting point. First, it can be the "*source*" of plurality vis-à-vis the *form* and essence of the objects that constitute the plurality. Second, with respect to the substance and the material, it itself coconstitutes the material that enters into number.

The "monas" can be the source of the plurality of the objects according to its essence in turn in two ways. First, as an active creative principle. The "*unitas Dei*" is of such a nature. The plurality of the created does not proceed from the *unitas Dei* through division, for the latter would then be destroyed as absolute unity. The "*number*" of the created realities comes to be "*per sui communicabilitatem.*" {258/200}

Second, unity can contain plurality "passively" in itself. *The unity of the "genus metaphysicum" is of such a nature.* Pluralities arise from it not through *division* into homogenous pieces, but through *division "in partes subjectivas."*

---

est idem et ratio substantiae diversa; et aliqua sunt nomina analoga, quae significant primo aliquod commune, sed tamen illud commune diversimode reperitur in diversis. Sicunt "infinitum" significat illud cuius non est terminus; sed hoc diversimode reperitur in magnitudine, in numeris et in continuis et discretis; quia ergo huiusmodi nomina significant aliquid commune, ideo proprie non dicuntur aequivoca, et quia illud commune diversimode reperitur in diversis, ideo talia nomina non dicuntur proprie univoca sed dicuntur proprie *analoga*; quia ergo huiusmodi nomina significant aliquid commune primo, ideo per immediate adjunctum contrahi possunt. Huiusmodi autem nomina sunt "multum" et "album": nam multum primo significat excessum in quantitate: et ideo contrahi potest. Similiter "album" primo significat aliquid faciliter movens sensum; sed hoc diversimode reperitur in diversis, scilicet in colore et in voce quia in colore est albedo, et id etiam in voce reperitur, sumendo albedinem pro alta et elata voce et huiusmodi, et ideo potest contrahi. Quia ergo multum et album significant aliquid commune ideo per immediate adiunctum contrahi possunt. Aequivocum autem inquantum aequivocum nihil commune significat et ideo contrahi non potest. Quaest. sup. lib. elench. qu. XIII, 17b sq.

In the division of the unity of real magnitudes such as an extended body, unity itself constitutes the *material* (the *substance*) of the individual pieces. In this "divisio in partes integrales," the parts are such that the original unity can be regained through "integration." Because it is based on real quantity (extension), this unity is accidental to natural objects. They are not such unities *in themselves*, but through the extension that befalls them.[60] {259/201}

Only the first two types of unity—the "unitas Dei" and the "unitas generis metaphysici"—are relevant for the present inquiry. The hierarchical character of

---

60. Constat in omni genere semper imperfectum et diminutum oriri ab illo, quod est perfectum simpliciter in illo genere . . . Cum ergo quaelibet res et quidquid est in rebus, quocumque modo *esse* vel rationem entis participet, aliquo modo sit imperfectum et admixtum, oportet, quod omnis res secundum illud totum, quod in ea est, a *primo et perfecto* ente oriatur: hoc autem ens non est neque intelligi potest, nisi unum solum infinitum. Ab hac igitur unitate oritur totus numerus et omnes unitates creaturarum, non per huius unitatis *divisionem*, ut de ipso uno fiant duo, et pereat eius unitas ex hoc, quod unitas et numerus exoriantur, sicut in divisione quanti, ut jam dicetur; hic enim numerus qui procedit ab uno in quantis, multiplicatur, quia unum *fit* duo; sed ab ista unitate oritur numerus et unitates, ut ab ipso principio calidi omnium primo procedit primum et item secundum et iterum tertium et sic deinceps usque ad infimam creaturam. . . . Sed praedicta mediatio . . . debet intelligi, quoad mediationem *in genere dignitatis*, quia primum causatum immediate participat divinitatem, secundum non ita immediate . . . Et sic patet quod universalitas rerum est numerus quidam constans ex unitatibus particularitatis in essentiis, eaeque omnes ortum habent ab unitate prima Dei, quae non est participata, sed quam omnis creata unitas participat, per quam dat imitationem, quae totum rerum numerum et eius unitates virtute continet et potentia activa; quae unitates oriuntur ab ipsa . . . per *sui communicabilitatem* . . .

Alia est unitas, a qua oritur numerus et omnes [eius] unitates, quas ipsa continet potentia et virtute, quasi modo specificato et ex ista oritur tota multitudo non per sui communicabilitatem, ut dixi de unitate divina, sed per sui *divisionem*, non quidem in partes quantitativas, sed in partes subjectivas. Et ista unitas est unitas *generis metaphysici, cuius communitas* consistit *in analogia*; ita quod res importata nomine talis generis, per se principaliter et veraciter dicitur solum de uno; de aliis per quandam attributionem ad illud . . .

Alia est unitas continens numerum, qui ab ea oritur et eius unitates secundum substantiam et naturam, ita quod per divisionem illius unitatis, non in partes subjectivas *sed integrales*, oritur numerus ab illa unitate. Et isto modo unum magnitudine habet in se omnem numerum, qui per divisionem magnitudinis potest inde procedere. Et quia talis unitas, quae est quantitas, *accidit rebus*, quae sunt de genere substantiae per ipsam quantitatem, quae est accidens substantiae, ideo etiam talis divisio . . . accidit rebus aliorum praedicamentorum, quibus accidit quantitas. De rer. princ. qu. XVI, 570b, 571a sq., 572a, 574b.

analogy proper to the domain of existent sensory and supersensory reality can be extracted from them.

We said that the moment of homogeneity, the *identity* of the *respect* lies in analogy. In the present case, in which the real world is at stake, this means: *each and every thing possesses existent reality. Only God* is real in the strictest and absolute sense. He is the absolute that *is existence, that exists in essence and "essences [west]"* in existence. Natural reality, the *sensorily real,* exists only qua created. It *is* not existence like the absolute; rather, it *has* existence through the "communicabilitas." Although both creator and created are real, they are so in *different* ways. Here we encounter the moment of heterogeneity in the analogy. The *difference lies in the degree of reality.* As absolute reality centered in itself, the *"unum infinitum"* is the *most valuable,* the ultimate measure of all reality.

The created real is likewise not consistently real to the *same degree.* Within the sensorily real world, in which the familiar ten Aristotelian categories are valid, real existence in the genuine sense belongs to substance. Accidents possess reality only insofar as they are attached to substance, insofar as they *participate* in its reality. {260/202} Accidents are *"entia per attributionem ad subjectum."* Analogous to the absolute, substance is a "genus metaphysicum." The same relationship of analogy continues in the domain of accidents, among which there is one— *quantity*—that can become an accident "for itself," whereas the rest can only belong to substance through it.[61]

Hence, order in the real domain is *not* that of a purely generic [gattungsmäßigen] generalization, in which the meaning of the genus applies *synonymously* to each of the "subcases," as occurs, for example, in taxonomy, in zoology and botany.

The character of the analogous enters the domain of the real through the aspect of *evaluation* of the degree of reality. Every individual object of natural reality has a specific valuation, a degree of being real. The more intensively the object

----

61. Et isto modo ens communissime sumptum, est genus metaphysicum ad creatorem et creaturam; et eius unitas dividitur in ens, quod est in se *esse,* et in ens *habens* esse, sive cui convenit esse ens . . . quod est genus commune metaphysicum et dividitur in decem praedicamenta. Et prima divisione dividitur in ens, quod est per se secundum quod "per se" opponitur ei, quod est "aliter se habere," et in ens quod est alicuius, quod continet novem praedicamenta accidentis. Et similiter ens, quod est alicuius, est genus metaphysicum et dividitur in ens quod est alicuius per se, ut est quantitas; et in ens, quod est alicuius per aliud, qualia entia sunt omnia accidentia alia a quantitate, quia mediante quantitate insunt substantiae naturaliter. Et quodlibet genus praedicamentorum, quae sunt decem, dividitur per subalterna genera et sic usque ad individuum; et sic causatur numerus ex divisione unitatis, non in partes quantitativas sed subjectivas. De rer. princ. qu. XVI, 572a sq.

participates in absolute reality, the more its degree of reality increases.[62] This *"esse divinum"* is distinguished from the *"esse creaturae,"* above all, *by the fact* that it *cannot* be further specified in terms of genus and species, as holds for the sensible world. If we can at all speak of categories in the absolute, they must receive a completely different order and a completely different structural arrangement, {261/203} that is, a meaning *corresponding* to absolute reality.[63]

Thus, the concept of measure that determines quantities in mathematics does not reign in the real world. If this concept is also to apply to reality, then its hierarchical character, which includes heterogeneity, must be destroyed and it must be considered solely *as if* homogeneity prevails. Moreover, the "mensura perfectionis"—the judgment of objects according to their degree of reality—is unique to reality.[64]

It thus seems that *number* and *measurement* must be granted a preeminent place in the totality of knowledge. A contemporary logician holds that "all power of knowledge, all possibility of logically determining the sensory seems comprehended in the thought of number."* "The highest postulate, which makes all knowledge into knowledge, is fulfilled in number. For, number is a universal aspect through which we posit the sensory manifold as uniform and homogenous in the concept."** This is not the place to critically evaluate the theoretical views underlying these statements. Although we cannot measure the previous discussions critically against modern logic, this much may have emerged from them: remarkable differences exist between "unum" and "unum"; above all, pure number is incapable of comprehending empirical reality and, furthermore, the *historical*, in its *individuality*. Not even serial systems, whose common "intersection" is supposed to be individuality, suffice for this. Because the series and a fortiori

---

62. Omne aliud ens ab ente infinito dicitur ens per *participationem*, quia capit partem illius entitatis, quae est ibi totaliter et *perfecte*. Quodlibet. qu. V, 229b, n. 26.

63. Esse divinum non potest esse contractum nec ad genus nec ad speciem; esse cuiuscumque creaturae potest ad utrumque esse contractum. De rer. princ. qu. VI, 335b.

64. Quaedam est mensura *mensurans per replicationem*, quae aliquoties sumpta reddit totum et talis est propria quantitatis. Alia est *mensura perfectionis* sive secundum perfectionem. Quaest. sup. Met. lib. V, qu. IX, 251a sq.

*Ernst Cassirer, *Substanzbegriff und Funktionsbegriff. Untersuchungen über die Grundfragen der Erkenntniskritik* (Berlin: Bruno Cassirer, 1910), 35. Our citation; Heidegger does not provide one in his text. See Ernst Cassirer, *Substance and Function and Einstein's Theory of Relativity*, trans. W. C. Swabey and M. C. Swabey (Mineola, NY: Dover, 2003).

**Cassirer, *Substanzbegriff und Funktionsbegriff*, 93, 252. Heidegger paraphrases and combines passages.

serial systems only exist in a homogenous domain, {262/204} such attempts at representing the individual are hopeless from the outset. Mathematical, natural scientific knowledge is not *the* knowledge.

This kind of categorial characterization of the real sensory and supersensory world of objects leads to a most unique *insight* into the sphere of reality, in which aspects of evaluation have attained the power of determination. The purely logical (and, in the medieval sense, equally metaphysical) fragmentation of the totality of objects by the "unum et diversum" appears, vividly overpainted, to have been brought to a unity, albeit of a peculiar kind. If one introduces the transcendental-philosophical approach, it becomes clear that medieval realism—whether naïve or critical—which holds on to the tangible character of natural reality, far from naturalism, is, rather, a *spiritualism*. The hierarchical character of existent reality, grounded in analogy, is intended to overcome the problems that confront every dualism, without sinking back into an impossible monism.

Consequently, the fact that the inherited Aristotelian categorial system cannot encompass the totality of the categories must be traced back to the prevalence of the thought of transcendence in medieval intellectual life. They are hierarchical forms for only a specifically delimited area peculiarly inserted into the whole of the metaphysical world-picture.

A comparison with the modern scientific approach to natural reality reveals that this approach must transform the unsurveyable manifold of empirical reality completely into a homogenous domain to apply theoretical physics as a research tool. This transformation also occurs in some sense in medieval "physics" because of the prevailing meaning accorded the concept of motion. But it is not hard to understand that {263/205} the categorial forms of modern science are more varied and complex and stand, above all, in service of completely new questions.

One might suppose that the previous ordering of existent reality aimed at a cultural scientific investigation. But this is not so. The concepts of "personality" and the spiritual individual are not totally alien to Scholasticism (consider the doctrines of the trinity and angels or its anthropology). But medieval intellectual life is only aware of the complexity of historical personality—its unique essence, its contingency and its manifold effects, its interwovenness with its environment, the thought of historical development and its associated problems—in completely insufficient conceptual determinacy.

And yet it would be misguided if we were to declare as absolutely worthless this insufficiency in the categorial characterization of existent reality for work in the individual sciences.

Apart from the valuable perspectives for the treatment of metaphysical problems concerning *God* and the *world*, the previous categorial characterization provides, above all, insight into the structure of the domain of empirical reality that is yet to be scientifically analyzed. When we consider that the words of language or, more accurately, their meanings first *transform* empirical reality in that only specific "aspects" of it enter into meaning, while existent reality, as their material, also determines meanings and their forms in some sense, then we can easily understand that a doctrine of the forms of meanings such as should become perspicuous in the course of this inquiry must relate to empirical reality if we are to understand the individual forms.

Consequently, when we turn to the *doctrine of meanings*, we shall have to return to this aspect of the *doctrine of categories* and possibly other areas also, {264/206} but it is also possible that none of them will suffice *completely* to understand the *forms of meaning*.

But before we turn to this, we must complete our characterization of the remaining *transcendentals* and the domains of reality attainable thence by *specifying their meaning*.

TWO

—∿—

THE VERUM

Logical and Psychic Reality

EARLIER, WE IDENTIFIED CONVERTIBILITY WITH the object as one of the hallmarks of the transcendentia. Accordingly, at the outset of this chapter, we must inquire into whether convertibility is proper to the "verum."

Every object is *one* object. Every object is a *true* object. What must it possess that we can call it *true*?

Among the many problems relating to the concept of the "unum," Duns Scotus touches on the question whether the "unum" represents an object distinct from the "ens"—a "res"—or whether it only means a specific way of "presenting itself [Sich-gehabens]" (quendam modum se habendi). He also remarks that this problem extends to all the *remaining* transcendentia, thus also to the "verum."[1] Accordingly, is the "verum" an object alongside the object [called true] or only a specific *manner* in which the latter presents itself? Just as the "unum" reveals itself to be a primordial form of the object in general, so also the "verum" must be interpreted as a *relationship of form*. With respect to cognition, the object is a true object. {265/207} Insofar as the object *is an object of cognition, it can be called a true object*. In it, we can see the "fundamentum veritatis."[2] Transcendental philosophy

---

1. Quarta [difficultas est], an [unum] aliquam rem dicat ab ente? Et hoc est *commune dubium de omnibus transcendentibus vero et bono* etc. Quaest. sup. Met. lib. IV, qu. II, 165a. (*This* inquiry does not consider the bonum, as it is only interested in *theoretical* objectivity.)

2. Primo quia sui manifestativa quantum est de se, cuicumque intellectui potenti manifestationem cognoscere. Secundo quia assimilativa intellectus assimilabilis . . . Tertio quia facta manifestatione vel assmiliatione res in intellectu est sicut cognitum in cognoscente . . . si nullus esset intellectus, adhuc quaelibet res secundum gradum suae

55

has found the sharpest expression for this: the object is an object only as an object of cognition; cognition is only cognition as cognition of the object. No object [Objekt] without the subject, and vice versa. Certainly, it would be an overinterpretation if we were to interpret the "verum" of Scholasticism in this sense. In principle, however, the verum expresses nothing other than the relationship of every object to cognition. From the fact that the object *somehow* enters cognition, is affected by it, it becomes a *true* object, that is, one present in cognition.

Duns Scotus has not left this relationship to cognition completely indeterminate. He characterizes the object in terms of *three* potential relationships to cognition that represent progressively increasing degrees of the unity of object and cognition. Initially, every object confronts cognition as *determinable by it*. The determinability can be limited to the minimum that all we can say of the object is that it is an object of cognition. The greater or lesser extent and complexity of determinability, as a question of *actual cognition*, does not belong among the purely theoretical problems we shall treat here. In order to be determined, whatever is now determinable in some way must {266/208} *"conform"* to the cognizing subject. The determinable object undergoes a *formation* through cognition. The form, after all, is the factor that endows determinacy. Determinability is *"affectability [Betreffbarkeit]"* through form (Lask). Determinacy is *"being affected [Betroffenheit]"* through form. In this manner, something befalls the object from cognition. Viewed from the object's perspective, it assimilates itself to this cognition. Something contradictory, such as the "four-cornered circle," resists such assimilation. Cognition does not know what to do, as it were, with such an object. The determinability of this object can be reduced to the observation that, while it is an object, it is an "impossible object."

Hereafter, the object that has gone from determinability to determinacy itself stands in cognition. The object is now in the cognizing subject, just as what is cognized is in the one cognizing. The X of the conformity to cognition [Erkenntnisgleichung] is dissolved; the object has entered into cognition.

The "verum" thus does not add anything *substantially [sachlich]* new to the object; it only endows it with a peculiar index and says that every object has a potential relationship to cognition, in which alone we can first genuinely speak of truth. *Every object is an object and is as such related to cognition.*

---

entitatis, esset nata se manifestare; et haec notitia est, qua res dicitur nota naturae, non quia natura cognoscat illam, sed quia propter manifestationem maiorem vel minorem nata esset quantum est de se, perfectius vel minus perfecte cognosci. Esse autem assimilativum dicit rationem activi respectu assimilabilis et sequitur naturaliter esse manifestativum vel disparatum est non habens ordinem ad ipsum sed semper assimilativum. l. c. lib. VI, qu. III, 337a sq.

Just as the "unum" indicates the domain of mathematics and the real domain of counted objects, so also the "verum" indicates the domain of *cognition as such*.[3] We must now grasp it in its unique nature and its distinctiveness from everything else.

In view of the three basic forms of cognition, we can speak of a "verum in intellectu" in a twofold sense. The contrary of the truth of the "simplex apprehensio," the simple possession {267/209} of an object,[a] is not falsity but *nonconsciousness*, *noncognition [Unkenntnis]*. In a certain sense, even simple re-presentation [Vorstellen], the [act of] bringing something to its givenness, can be called *false*, insofar as it comprehends the object in a determination that does *not* apply to it. This meaning, although false in itself, can nevertheless attain consciousness. Even if it does not permit any objective fulfillment, it is still something objective, a "quid nominis," a meaning free from the character of judgment.

Because the given becomes an object every time as this given, pure and simple re-presentation is always *true*. Measure and measured coincide here. Truth culminates in givenness and does not extend beyond it. We will later have to settle what kind of *constancy* is proper to it.[4]

Judgment is a cognition whose truth has *falsity* as its contrary. Judgment is what may be called *true* in the *authentic* sense. Every cognition is a judgment, every judgment is a cognition. We earlier said that the "verum transcendens" indicates a domain of cognition that is as yet unknown. We now know in relation to which formation of this domain we must study its peculiarities: in relation to

---

3. Veritas aut accipitur pro fundamento veritatis in re aut pro veritate in actu intellectus componente aut dividente. Oxon. I, dist. II, qu. II, 408b, n. 8.

[a] First edition of 1916: See Edmund Husserl, *Ideas for a Pure Phenomenology and Phenomenological Philosophy. First Book: General Introduction to Pure Phenomenology*, trans. Daniel O. Dahlstrom (Indianapolis: Hackett, 2014), 12 [*Husserliana*, vol. III (Den Haag: Nijhoff, 1950), 15]; Heidegger cites Edmund Husserl, *Ideen zu einer reinen Phänomenologie und phänomenologischen Philosophie. Erstes Buch: Allgemeine Einführung in die reine Phänomenologie* (Halle: Max Niemeyer Verlag, 1913), 11.

4. Verum autem in intellectu duplex est secundum eius duplicem operationem [simplex apprehensio . . . propositio] . . . Est autem inter istas veritates differentia una, quod primae falsitas non opponitur sed ignorantia tantum; et sic intelligitur illud de anima, quod *intellectus circa quod quid est semper est verus* sicut sensus circa proprium sensibile; et hoc est intelligendum praecise circa conceptum simpliciter simplicem; nam intellectus *simplex* circa conceptum non simpliciter simplicem, licet non possit esse formaliter falsus . . . *apprehendendo aliquid sub determinatione sibi non conveniente* . . . ratio in se falsa, non solum de aliquo falsa . . . simplici apprehensione intelligibilis est, sed illa non includit vel exprimit aliquod quid, nisi forte *quid nominis*. Quaest. sup. Met. lib. VI, qu. III, 338.

judgment. Not without justification, it has recently been called the "cell" of logic, its primordial formation. {268}

The circumstance that judgment manifests an *articulation* (compositio) does not signify a fall away from its character as a primordial formation, {210} which one likes to imagine as completely simple, unarticulated. The composite nature of judgment (complexum) separates it from the concept (incomplexum). To be sure, concepts are also composite, but in a different way than judgment. The judgment's composite nature can only be found in it, and indeed, in such a way that it is closely connected with the character of the judgment's reality.

The structure of judgment must manifest itself in how the components of the articulated whole are connected.[5] That which we encounter as the moment in the judgment that endows it with contexture and unity, that which actually first makes it a judgment, must also simultaneously let us recognize how this domain in which judgments have their existence is constituted. If judgment is to represent an articulated unity, the components (*extrema*) to be combined into a unity cannot be completely disparate and unrelated. Rather, the circumstance that these components *require* each other is grounded in their content. Qua *belonging together*, they demand the unity of the judgment. The "*nota compositionis*," the relation that establishes unity, forms the "*est*" in the judgment. But the "*est*" does not mean "*to exist*," to be real in the manner of sensory and supersensory objects. *Rather, what is meant is the mode of reality* ("esse verum"), for which *the felicitous expression "to be valid [Gelten]"* is available *as a characterization today.*

As little as the "est" of the copula coincides with "to exist," so little should its meaning be restricted to the relationship of subsumption, which is commonly presented as the relationship of judgment taught by Scholasticism. Correctly recognizing its peculiar meaning and function, Duns Scotus interprets the copula as generally as possible. The {269} relationship "to be valid" and hence the peculiar {211} mode of reality remains *unaffectedly* the same in every judgment.[6] Indisputably, we can find differentiations with respect to the relation between

---

5. Alia est materia complexi et incomplexi. Propria materia autem complexi sunt dictiones per se significativae; sed materia incomplexi sunt syllabae et litterae non per se significativae. Differunt etiam ex parte formae, nam forma complexi consistit in *unione dictionum* quae per se significant. Quaest. in lib. elench. qu. XIX, 28b.

6. I undertake this *objective*-logical interpretation of the sense of the copula in my dissertation (GA 1, 177ff.) cited earlier (p. 10, n. 10). Geyser's interpretation is more along the lines of a "*subjective* logic": he defines the copula as an "intention toward the object." See his *Grundlagen der Logik und Erkenntnislehre: eine Untersuchung der Formen und Prinzipien objektiv wahrer Erkenntnis* (Münster: Heinrich Schöningh, 1909), 142ff.

the subject and the predicate, but they make themselves known through a *determination* implicit in the content of the respective judgment.

The relationship of validity of the copula, the "esse" as a relationship between the subject and the predicate, reveals itself to be the genuine bearer of truth. The judgment is *valid*; it is true and is "made" true for the subject through the acts by which the subject takes a stance toward it.[7] Judgment as true cognition simultaneously signifies cognition of an object. The object enters into the judgment and is thus grasped in its What and its That [seinem Was und Daß]. For the judgment, this implies *being bound to the object*. According to Duns Scotus, conformity with the object cannot simply be thought of as a *"representation,"* as a repetition of what "lies in the things," as though the relationship of judgment were also to *exist* qua *ontological*. The meaning content of the objective material that has attained givenness is taken up along with the form of reality peculiar to it into the judgment. Better expressed: the content in question undergoes {270/212} a *formation* through the judgment and thereby becomes valid cognition. The true is constituted in cognition.[8]

Objects only contain *"virtualiter,"* that which fuses in the judgment into a unified totality of sense. The relationship of judgment is not a "similar sign" of *states of affairs* found in the world of objects in different domains, but an *equivocal* [sign]. Duns Scotus uses the relationship between a barrel hoop hung outside a tavern and wine to illustrate this. *As a sign for a tavern, the barrel hoop signifies wine.* It itself is *not similar to wine.* For the connoisseur, however, it is a true sign that wine will be served. By contrast, it would be a false sign for the distribution of milk and such things. Consequently, judgment, as a valid sense formation [Sinngebilde],

---

7. Verbum *"est"* potest notare *qualemcumque* unionem extremorum et non oportet quod *semper* notet praedicatum esse superius subjecto; sed ad exercendum illud, quod signatur, hic oportet addere ad compositionem huius verbi "est" aliquam determinationem. Quaest. in lib. praed. qu. XIII, 475a.

Esse enim, quando praedicatur tertium, praedicat unionem extremorum, quae necessaria est substantiae ad substantiam sine existentia extremorum. Quaest. in lib. I. periherm. qu. VIII, 554a.

[Compositio] est actus comparativus unius conceptus simplicis ad alterum ... hunc autem, necessario sequitur vel concomitatur *relatio rationis* in utroque extremo ad alterum, quam habitudinem videtur signare hoc verbum, "est," ut est nota compositionis ... esse uno modo significat *verum*, hoc est habitudinem rationis inter extrema, quae nata est esse vera [esse verum = "to be valid"]. Quaest. sup. Met. lib. VI, qu. III, 344a.

8. Verum non est prius actu intelligendi ... patet quia intellectus facit rationem veri. De anima qu. XX, 607b.

Res non est causa praecise veritatis in intellectu *sed intellectus componens praedicatum cum subjecto.* Quaest. sup. Met. lib. VI, qu. III, 334a.

differs both in terms of its reality and in relation to its structure from the objects of which it is valid as cognition.[9]

Duns Scotus unmistakably struggles to find the expression to present, in all its clarity, the heterogeneity between the judgment and the objects cognized in and through it as he has become aware of this heterogeneity. How far he has advanced in recognizing the intrinsic value [Eigenwertigkeit] of the judgment's content as valid sense can be seen from its delimitation from the *act of judgment*. Rather than regard the latter "*objectifyingly*," that is, as an existent psychic reality, he regards it in terms of its "functional sense," which the act first {271/213} receives from the sense of judgment (*mediante veritate habitudinis verus est actus*). Without an act of judgment as its activity, the cognitive subject could never bring itself into possession of cognition. The act mediates between the valid sense and the subject that receives and acknowledges this [sense] as cognition. In becoming aware of the conformity of the act of judgment (its functional sense) with the relationship immanent to the members of the judgment, the one judging becomes aware of the truth of the judgment.[10]

An insurmountable difficulty appears to bar the way here. If I compare the relationship of judgment, its sense A, with the real state of affairs B, this comparison itself posits a further relationship C. How should I recognize the truth of C? Through another judgment? This results unambiguously in a regressus in infinitum. We could never consciously attain true cognition in this manner. Further, if I am to cognize the truth of judgment A through its relationship to the real state of affairs B, surely this too must be cognized. Through which judgment is this possible? If it is the same as A, I have a tautology. If it is another, D, then I have two judgments about the same real state of affairs.[11]

---

9. Ista habitudo rationis conformis est rei, non quod oporteat in re esse relationem aliquam inter extrema ut in re similem istius rationis, quae est inter extrema *ut intellecta, imo ut ab intellectu invicem comparata* . . .

Habitudo correspondet rei, quando est talis, qualem res virtualiter continet, sive qualem res de se nata esset *facere in intellectu*, si faceret habitudinem illam, sive quae est *signum non simile sed aequivocum*, exprimens tamen illud quod est in re, sicut, circulus non est similis vino, est tamen verum signum vini, falsum autem lactis vel huiusmodi. l. c. lib. VI, qu. III, 344a sq.

10. Haec igitur correspondentia praedicta huius habitudinis ad id quod est in re formaliter, est secunda veritas [veritas compositionis] et ita illa habitudo, quae dicitur compositio expressa per "est" vera est immediate et *mediante illa verus est actus comparativus secundum illam habitudinem*. l. c. 344b.

11. Contra hoc quod superius dictum est, quod veritas complexi cognoscitur per hoc, quod intellectus apprehendit conformitatem actus componendi entitati extremorum istius complexi, arguitur: quoniam quando comparo actum

Duns Scotus unearths a difficulty that confronts every conscientious "theory of representation," {272/214} that operates with [a concept of] cognition as representation [Vorstellen]. It is simply impossible to compare the sense of judgment with real objects [Objekten]; for I once again know of real objects precisely through cognition, judgment. An object that is not recognized is not an object for me. We cannot advance from the content of judgment to real objects themselves. The theory of representation poses an insurmountable difficulty. Quite consistently, Duns Scotus abandons this theory and chooses the thought of immanence. He does not thereby "dispute the reality of the external world" and "take sides with" "subjectivism," "idealism," and whatever else the other epistemological specters are called. Correctly understood, the thought of immanence neither annuls reality nor dissolves the external world into a dream. Rather, *precisely by* [granting] *the absolute primacy of valid sense, the thought of immanence shatters all physiological, psychological, and economic-pragmatic epistemological theories and irrevocably* founds the *absolute validity of truth, genuine objectivity* [*Objektivität*].

Accordingly, the functional sense of the act of judgment orients and measures itself directly against the meaning content of the members (extrema) that enter into the judgment, which contain the relationship of judgment virtualiter. The meaning content of what is given, the state of affairs simply apprehended, is the measure of the sense of the judgment. The latter derives its objective validity from it. One could also say, the sense of judgment is the logical form of reality and the structural form of the elements that belong together, which the content presents.[12] {273/215}

A promising scientific theoretical outlook is only possible when the individual sciences have attained the peak of a conscious application of the methods peculiar to them. This presupposes a certain maturity of intellectual-historical

---

compositionis A rei B, hoc facio actu compositionis C; quomodo sciam istam secundam compositionem C esse veram? Si per aliam compositionem, erit processus in infinitum, antequam cognoscatur veritas compositionis A et ita nunquam cognoscetur ... Item si debeo cognoscere A esse veram per collationem ad rem, oportet igitur rem cognoscere; quo ergo actu? Si eodem qui est A, idem cognosco per C, si alio ut ipso D, ergo duo actus simul de eadem re. l. c. 339a sq.

12. Dico quod illam complexionem cognosco esse veram, cognoscendo conformitatem eius ad illam habitudinem virtualiter inclusam in extremis. l. c. 341b. ... objecta conceptus complexi, quae sunt extrema, *aliud esse habent* quam ut sunt in conceptu non complexo et prius naturaliter in se, ut simplicia sunt, secundum quod esse prius, mensurant illum conceptum complexum, cui esse priori conceptum complexum conformari est verum esse, difformari est falsum esse; hoc *"esse"* est habitudo virtualiter inclusa in extremis naturaliter, antequam extrema comparentur a ratione. l. c. 340b sq.

development and, often, the decisive influence of genial personalities (for example, Galilei's in physics). We can genuinely speak of a theory of science only after Kant. Before this, individual questions in this direction may have arisen, but without systematic connection to the logical problems raised previously. But when the individual sciences stand only at the beginning and the method peculiar to each does not yet present itself in the necessary plasticity and sharpness and does not proceed along a secure path, all conditions for scientific theoretical work are lacking. Not only that, the very spur that drives us to intuit these problems as problems in the first place is lacking. This is how matters stand regarding Scholasticism.

Consequently, Duns Scotus too could not advance beyond the *universal theory* in his doctrine of judgment. He did not recognize any limit therein and, indeed, could not recognize such a limit, because he could not know anything of the structural complications of the sense of judgment in the different sciences corresponding to the specifically structured state of affairs and objects underlying them.

Someone could object here that we earlier pointed out a division of the different domains of reality. But these domains indicate, in general, a general classification [Artung] and its sphere, in which the individual sciences that deal with them operate. A *treatment in the sense that has developed today is, however, lacking.* And it is first in the treatment, that is, in recognizing and solving the problems found in the different object regions, that *the modification of the sense of judgment reveals itself.*

The lack of scientific theoretical research is not due to Scholasticism as such. The reasons for it {274/216} are of a scientific and intellectual-historical nature. We should not overlook the fact that transcendental philosophy has encouraged and made the recognition and comprehension of such problems much easier. But even today, in many areas of the theory of science, we have not advanced beyond general programs and statements of the problem.

Compared with the interpretation and solution of logical problems from a *psychologistic perspective,* which has lately been on the backfoot, Scholastic thought, even though it often limits itself to general hints, reveals a *maturity of insight into the unique nature and intrinsic value of the* logical *domain that we should neither ignore nor underestimate.* Precisely because the battle against psychologism has sharpened and deepened our knowledge of logic's field of validity, it is not uninteresting to examine the extent to which *a delimitation over against the psychically real* already *breaks through* in Duns Scotus.

This consideration should simultaneously lead us further in our cognition of the logical sphere of sense, while permitting us to distinguish it still more clearly from the heterogenous continuum of empirical reality and the homogenous continuum of the mathematical. We shall also have to clarify the question of the meaning of "extra animam," which we earlier left open. The "ens rationis" is contrasted with the real sensory and supersensory world (ens naturae). Existent reality is such that it does not depend on the soul (cuius esse non dependet ab anima). The "ens rationis" is therefore an "ens in anima." Logical reality belongs to the "soul." How is this belonging to be thought more precisely?[13] {275/217} Should we interpret "ens rationis" in the sense that it belongs to the soul like a memory that suddenly arises in psychic life or like feelings such as sadness and joy that shake us from within—events that arise momentarily and then disappear? Does judgment exist "in anima" in the sense that the psychic power of understanding passes judgment, whereafter it subsides and makes way for other psychic events? But how would matters then stand with the truth of judgment? The judgment would be true only as long as the performance of the act of judgment lasted. If the psychic activity of judging is [what is] "true," truth could not exist. Consequently, when the "ens logicum" is described as an "ens rationis" or an "ens in anima," it cannot mean that logical reality is a *piece*, a segment of *psychic reality*.

Moreover, the "ens logicum" is characterized as an "ens *diminutum*." It means a *diminished* kind of being vis-à-vis existent natural reality, and hence it does not belong to the object region of metaphysics, which is indisputably a science of the real. As an aside, it is not uninteresting to compare the characterization "ens diminutum" for the logical with the modern characterization: Rickert calls logical sense the "*unreal*." Indeed, Duns Scotus explicitly states that logical being does not have the reality of real existence, and hence the category of *causality* is not applicable to this domain either. This category makes no sense in the logical domain. In other words, what is at stake in this domain is not an *occurrence, coming to be and passing away*, not *processes*, occurrences—in short, *natural realities* are not at stake here.[14] {276/218}

---

13. Ens est duplex, scil. naturae et rationis. Ens autem naturae inquantum tale est, *cuius esse non dependet ab anima*. Quaest. sup. lib. elench. qu. I, 1b.

Quaecumque scientia quae non solum vocatur *realis*, sed etiam quae vocatur *rationis*, est de re sive de *ente*. Quodlibet. qu. III, 114b, n. 2.

14. [Ens verum] est ens *diminutum* et est ens *logicum* proprie. Quaest. sup. Met. lib. VI, qu. III, 346a.

Ens secundum quod abstrahens a *sensibili* et insensibili est voce proprium objectum intellectus. l. c. n. 22.

Ens reale est perfectius ens quam ens, quod est tantum rationis. Oxon. I, dist. VIII, qu. IV, n. 10.

Ens rationis est ita diminutum, quod non potest esse perfectio entis realis. Quodlibet. qu. I, n. 4.

Ens autem diminutum ... non habet esse realis existentiae; ergo nec inquantum tale potest esse causa propria alicuius entis realis. Oxon. I, dist. XIII, quaest. unic. 893b sq., n. 7; see l. c. III, dist. VIII, n. 19.

Certainly, psychic reality is not an "ens diminutum." On the contrary, it is the *essential form* of man; it first endows man with his existence as man. Not only that, but for Duns Scotus, the soul is, "as individual, something primary that constitutes a substance in itself, that is, apart from its union with the body, and hence is not first individualized through incarnation."[15] *Indeed, we earlier defined the individual as what exists in the genuine sense.*[16]

One can easily understand that on the grounds of the theory of reciprocal causality the *psychic is governed by the category of causality.*

These considerations force us to conclude that the characterization "ens in anima" for logical reality cannot refer to psychic reality. Rather, the expression must mean what we today express with the words "noematic sense": that is, the circumstance that intentionality, as a correlate of consciousness, is inseparable from consciousness and yet not contained in it as real [reell]. The "in" character-izes the completely unique relationship that exists when we are conscious of something: the fact that whatever has meaning or value is linked to spiritual life, [and] not, for example, that it belongs to it the way a piece can be a part of a whole.

The "ens rationis" thus means the *content*, the *sense* of psychic acts; its being lies in contemplative, thinking consciousness; it is the *"ens cogitum,"* that which is thought or judged. We must distinguish this from what is "subjective in intel-lectu." The activity of understanding and knowledge acts are in the soul in *this latter* manner, namely, as real psychic faculties. {277/219} Simultaneously, both fall under the category of quality, a category of existent reality. By contrast, under the "ens in anima," we should understand the "secundo consideratum," thus not the objective [das Gegenständliche] in objective cognition of reality and intention [Gemeintheit]—*non tamquam primo consideratum sed tamquam ens in primo considerato inquantum consideratum.*[17] One could hardly state more

---

15. See Hermann Siebeck, "Die Anfänge der neueren Psychologie in der Scholastik," *Zeitschrift für Philosophie und philosophische Kritik* 94, no. 2 (1888): 167, 178ff.

16. See above p. 45f.

17. Ens rationis hoc est praecise habens esse in intellectu *considerante*. Quodlibet. qu. III, 114a, n. 2.

Dicendum, quod universale est in re, ut in subjecto, quia illum denominat, non intellectum; sed in intellectu est veluti in *efficiente et ut cognitum in cognoscente.* Sup. Qu. Porph. qu. XI, 136a. (Psychic reality, which is subject to causality, is distinguished most clearly from *intentional content* here. See part II, chapter 1, p. 88–89).

Ens diminutum, quod scil. est ens cognitum. Oxon. I, dist. XIII, 893b, n. 7.

Nec intelligo hic ens rationis . . . quod est tantum in intellectu subjective. Oxon. IV, dist. I, qu. II, 100b, n. 3.

clearly that what is intended here is the *content* separated from cognitive activity, from judging: that is, the *sense of judgment* in its function of presenting, of cognitively constituting real objects [Objekte]. This content is what is *valid*, of which we can say that it is *true*. Through the individual psychic acts of judgment—which, strictly speaking, are neither true nor false but only either exist or do not exist—the sense of judgment is given each time to the cognitive subject as conscious and, in a certain respect, as "real"; it is taken up into individually real spiritual life.

Bolzano, whom Husserl first discovered and whose significance for contemporary logic Husserl first brought to light, thinks that we can find the idea of a purely logical content separated from psychic reality already among the Greeks:

> Later, I shall set out the reasons that lead me to surmise that the concept of
> a *truth in itself* was not entirely unknown to the *Greeks*. From this it may be
> gathered that they also sometimes connected the concept given above with
> the word proposition (πρότασις, ἀπόφανσις, λόγος ἀποφαντικὸς). For a truth
> in itself is also a proposition in itself. {278/220} The fact that they generally
> defined propositions as a kind of *speech* (λόγος), however, does not justify us in
> concluding that they only looked on propositions expressed in words as genuine
> propositions. For it is possible that it was only the sensible nature of language
> that hindered them from expressing themselves as abstractly as they wished to
> be understood by their readers.[18]

In my view, the logic of *Scholasticism* must likewise be considered from the same perspective if we are at all to endow its logical theories with potential sense.

But we can also consider the peculiarity of the domain of logical validity from another perspective. In this way, we shall bring its constancy, which is independent of every existent reality, to unmistakable clarity.

In natural life, thought, and cognition, our consciousness is directed toward the real objects [Objekte] found in immediate reality. Scholasticism characterizes this natural attitude with the expression "prima intentio." Through a unique redirection of our gaze, thought can be attuned to its own *content*, "secunda intentio." Everything existing in the metaphysical, physical, and psychic world of objects [Objektwelt], including mathematical and even logical objects, is taken up into the domain of the "secunda intentio." In it alone are we aware of the existence of objects [Objekte]. The most cardinal distinction of the modes of reality is that

---

18. Bernard Bolzano, *Theory of Science*, trans. Rolf George and Paul Rusnock (Oxford: Oxford University Press, 2014), 1:63; Heidegger cites Bernard Bolzano, *Wissenschaftslehre* (Sulzbach: J. E. v. Seidel: 1837), 1:83. *Hauptwerke der Philosophie in originaltreuen Neudrucken*, vol. IV, *Werke Bernard Bolzanos*, ed. A. Höfler (Leipzig: Felix Meiner, 1914).

between consciousness and reality, or more precisely a mode of reality whose nature is *not* that of validity, [but] which, for its part, is always and only given through and in a context of sense that is of the nature of validity [geltungsartigen Sinnzusammenhang].

Duns Scotus defines the absolute dominion of logical sense over all the worlds of objects [Objektwelten] that can be cognized and are cognized as the *convertibility of the "ens logicum" with objects.* {279/221} Whatever is an object can become an "ens diminutum." Whatever is cognized, whatever we pass judgments about, must enter into the world of *sense*, in which alone we cognize and judge. *Only in that I live in the domain of validity am I aware of existing things.*[19]

While distinguishing the domains of existent reality from mathematical objects, we particularly highlighted the difference in their categorial constitution. How do matters stand with regard to this in the domain of logical validity? Do we also encounter something like order, hierarchy here? Are there also different *degrees* of existence here as in the real sensory and supersensory world corresponding to the modes of being characteristic of God, of the created, of substances, and of accidents? We spoke of the convertibility between the real domain and the logical; an overlap, as it were, between the former and the latter. The real objects [Objekte] are taken up into the sphere of logical sense; this taking up would be completely unintelligible if someone sought to grasp the "ens logicum" as psychic reality.

Reality can enter into sense only because it is somehow *interpreted [aufgefaßt]* through the logical, because something is pried loose from it, and thereby distinguished, delimited, and arranged. That which creates order is a *form-like* thing. The forms are determined in their meaning by the material of the world of objects [Objektwelt] and hence are in turn applicable to the latter. The form of ordering of the logical in general is *the judgment.* Subjectively, this can be expressed thus: it is essential to logical content "to be predicated" (praedicari). This is possible only because it is valid. {280/222} The real that is characterized, that is, "meant" (praedicari est intentio) in a unique way in the logical domain—namely, through the judgment—occurs and exists in the real domain.

We cognize through judgment. The categories are the individual components of this form of order. They are not taken from the domain of real objects as mere *copies.* The real provides, as it were, only the *impulse* (occasio); it offers the *starting*

---

19. Convertitur tamen [ens logicum] cum ente aliqualiter, quia Logicus considerat omnia ut Metaphysicus, *sed modus alius considerationis, scil. per quid reale et per intentionem secundam, sicut convertibilitas entis simpliciter et diminuti,* quia neutrum alterum excedit in communitate; *quidquid enim est simpliciter ens, potest esse ens diminutum.* Quaest. sup. Met. lib. VI, qu. III, 346a.

point for creating ordering relationships that have no adequate correspondent in the real.[20]

The character of being valid of the domains of objects [Objektbereiche] to be cognized (sunt applicabiles) is proper to judgment as sense and the categories that comprise it. They "encompass" the material encounterable in its givenness; get it, as it were, in their power. *Intentionality*—that is, *validity* or *expressability*—is the moment that determines order and characterizes the logical domain. *Unlike the real, the logical domain is not analogous, but univocal.*[21] {281/223}

---

20. Ens est duplex, scil. naturae et rationis. Ens autem naturae inquantum tale est, cuius esse non dependet ab anima. Sed ens rationis dicitur de *quibusdam intentionibus*, quas adinvenit ratio in ipsis rebus, cuiusmodi sunt genus, species, definitio et huiusmodi. Ens autem dictum isto secundo modo aequiparatur secundum communitatem enti priori modo dicto. *Non enim est aliquod ens naturae, quin possit cadere sub ente rationis et quin super ipsum fundari possit aliqua intentio, ut puta generis vel speciei vel differentiae vel proprii vel individui vel saltem causae vel causati.* Quaest. in lib. elench. qu. I, 1b.

Quia ergo Logica est de huiusmodi intentionibus, quae *applicabiles sunt omnibus rebus*, ideo Logica dicitur ex communibus procedere. l. c. 2a.

Dico, quod res *non* est *tota causa* intentionis, *sed tantum occasio*, inquantum scil. movet intellectum, ut actu consideret, et *intellectus est principalis causa*; ideo minor unitas sufficit in re, quam sit unitas intentionis; quia sufficit intellectum ab aliquo extrinseco moveri ad *causandum multa per considerationem, quibus non correspondent aliqua in re simpliciter.* Quaest. in lib. praed. qu. III, 443a.

21. Dici potest quod hic [in libro de praedicamentis] consideratur de decem praedicamentis, *inquantum aliquid a ratione causatum eis attribuitur, quia aliter non possunt a Logico considerari*; et illo modo non habent tantum unitatem analogiae sed etiam *univocationis*; et illud univocum istis . . . *est aliquod intentionale*, quod est hic primum subjectum et illud potest nominari praedicamentum vel generalissimum; quia omnes proprietates, quae per se de istis determinantur hic, determinantur de eis, inquantum habent rationem generalissimi vel praedicamenti. Quaest. in lib. praed. qu. II, 441a.

Quae Metaphysicus per se considerat, hic per accidens consideratur, quia hic per se consideratur *aliquid intentionale applicabile eis*, quae Metaphysicus per se considerat. l. c. 442a.

Dico . . . quod scientia realis est de universali primo modo, quod est *res*, sed *Logica* est de universali secundo modo, quod est *intentio*. Quaest. sup. Porph. qu. VIII, 121b.

Oportet diere, quod maior est unitas [praedicamentorum] *in aliqua proprietate ab intellectu causata, quam inquantum sunt entia*; et ita cum haec scientia [scil. Logica] *non sit una unitate analogiae*, oportet assignare aliquod intentionale, quod sit istis *commune* et primum subjectum, quia de solo *tali* per se considerat Logicus. Quaest. in lib. praed. qu. II, 440b.

Univocum apud Logicum dicitur omne illud, *quod per unam rationem devenit apud intellectum*, secundum quam dicitur de multis. l. c. qu. VII, 455a sq.

Aliquid intentionale univocum applicari potest rebus omnium generum; quia *diversitas* in rebus primae intentionis inter se non impedit ipsas ab intellectu posse concipi *per eundem modum concipiendi*; intentiones autem omnes eis attribuuntur,

The noematic, the content of psychic acts, is an objectivity of a unique kind. "While objects simply (understood in an unmodified sense) stand under fundamentally diverse supreme genera, all the senses of objects and all noemas whatsoever, however diverse they may otherwise be, intrinsically belong to one sole supreme genus."[22] The *univocity* of the domain of logical sense in contrast to the ordering through *analogy* in the world of real sensory and supersensory objects that Duns Scotus asserts expresses this very thought.

The logical domain is a *homogenous domain*. We said the same thing of the mathematical domain. {282/224}

The logical domain is a *nonsensory domain*. The same is true of the mathematical domain. Do the two domains then coincide? Is logic mathematics, or is mathematics logic—or is neither of these views correct?

Deciding these questions would not only exceed the circle of our tasks, [but also] it cannot at all be resolved with the means of *Scholastic ideas*. One thing, however, can be decided on the basis of what was previously said: the two domains in question, even if they are both nonsensory in character, cannot be identical. The homogeneity, which attains its unique character from the unity of the *respect*, is distinct in both worlds. The homogeneity of the mathematical domain is grounded in *quantity*. The homogeneity of the domain of logical validity is based on *intentionality*, the character of being valid of [something]. As distinct as intentionality and quantity are, just as much do logic and mathematics differ from each other.

Intentionality is the "regional category" of the logical domain. Therein, we once again see that the "ens in anima" *cannot* mean psychic being. Intentionality can exist only where there is something endowed with sense and meaning, not in realities. The latter can at most be *affected* by sense and meaning, but not vice versa.[23]

---

inquantum ab intellectu concipiuntur et ideo intentiones eaedem specie possunt diversis rebus attribui. l. c. qu. II, 442b sq.

Sciendum est, quod, *cum praedicari sit intentio*, est intentionum per se, rei vero per accidens. *Esse* vero est rei per se. Aliud sciendum, quod esse in rebus primae intentionis illud exercet, quod praedicari signat in secundis intentionibus. Quaest. sup. Univ. Porph. qu. XIV, 178a.

22. Husserl, *Ideas I*, 254 [*Husserliana* III, 314]; Heidegger cites Edmund Husserl, "Ideen zu einer reinen Phänomenologie und phänomenologischen Philosophie," *Jahrbuch für Philosophie und phänomenologische Forschung* 1, part I (1913): 256.

23. Dico quod intellectus dicitur perficere sensum in sua cognitione [interpretation of the object that exists actualiter] eo quod cognitio sensitiva praecise consistit in apprehendendo illud, *quod est verum*, non *ipsam veritatem* [this, consequently, is nothing sensory] et quia talis cognitio potest perficere, ut id, quod cognitum est inquantum verum, solum cognoscatur inquantum habet raionem veritatis, quod fit per intellectam. De rer. princ. qu. XIII, 519b sq.

H. Siebeck locates "the beginnings of contemporary psychology" in Duns Scotus.

> For, it is not Thomas Aquinas, but Duns Scotus, who is epochal in medieval philosophy. The Thomistic codification gave the substance of the medieval worldview an enduring {283/225} stability and the power to serve the clerical world for centuries as the foundation for their opposition to new systems and methods. But the characteristic traits of the new epoch itself, and the first confident steps in its direction, are to be found in the radical and incisive critique that Duns Scotus untiringly leveled against the content of the transmitted system.[24]

He first rediscovered the psychic world of the objects [Objektwelt] of inner experience for "independent inquiry."

Given Duns Scotus's sharp eye for the individuality and uniqueness of empirical facts along with the clear insight into the world of logical validity, we might suppose that he also expressly separated the fields of research of logic and psychology from one another. Then again, we should not be surprised that the logical interest strongly predominates when considering "higher" psychic life. At first glance, this could appear a disadvantage, and one might arrive at the thought that has been expressed so often: Scholastic psychology is worthless because it operates only conceptually, without a genuine attunement toward empirical facts.

But this predominance of the logical perspective, which in fact is present, only needs to be correctly evaluated.

Rather than consider cognitive acts objectifyingly as psychic realities, we shall consider them with regard to their function, their achievement. Regarded thus, they actually no longer belong in the area of psychology as a real science of the psychic, but rather to *logic*, provided that one does not want to assign them to the utterly unique field of *phenomenology* (specifically, a phenomenology that is preferentially oriented toward "noesis").

Thus, thought is characterized as that psychic activity, which grasps truth as truth. {284/226} Consciousness may be attuned to "the true" through its mere givenness, but it first becomes conscious of it as true, valid sense through judgment. Inasmuch as the act of thinking, on the basis of this its *activity*, is now distinguished from sensation and perception and valued higher, it is no longer considered merely as a psychic reality that comes to be and passes away, but rather, [it is considered] in respect of its content.[25] And only thus can it be

---

24. Siebeck, "Die Anfänge der neueren Psychologie in der Scholastik," 161, 163.

25. Heinrich Rickert, "Vom Begriff der Philosophie," *Logos* 1 (1910): 28. "Insofar as it grasps the truth, cognition is unreservedly a sense concept, the product of an interpretation proceeding from logical value" (30). Further, see *Der Gegenstand der Erkenntnis: eine Einführung in die Tranzendentalphilosophie*, 3rd ed. (Tübingen: Mohr Siebeck, 1916), chapters 3 and 4.

fully grasped. Rickert, who, along with Husserl, in the present points out most emphatically this manner of considering acts, says, "We can only make headway into the subject and its acts proceeding from values." He emphasizes that an inquiry that is attuned toward thought in this manner operates not with *factual concepts* but with *sense concepts.*

Duns Scotus says that the subject, qua psychic reality, may evoke or cause real psychic acts. However, in relation to its objective content (circa tamen objectum) it does not cause the emergence of a reality; rather, it permits the sense to become conscious through its activity. If the current knowledge is annulled, that is, if the subject does not think and judge, then it is also not aware of the content: the content is currently no longer conscious. But this does not mean that the content was also destroyed when the act of judgment disappeared, or that it loses its mode of reality—that of being valid (scibile in potentia)—when the act loses its own [mode of reality], namely, existence.[26]

Consequently, we can subject the act of judgment to a twofold consideration. First, we can consider it insofar as it is a psychic reality with {285/227} whose aid a judgment can be effected currently. This consideration belongs to psychology. But then we can focus initially on the content of the judgment, the sense, and thereafter on its unique connection with the act of judgment. Duns Scotus says that the logician presupposes the psychologist's work, the investigation of the *activity of thought* through which these functions are carried out. We can justifiably dispute whether it is in fact necessary that we undertake a consideration of the logical content only after a fundamental investigation of the activity of thought. If that is so, we cannot engage in logic even today with a clear conscience. However we decide about *this* relationship between logic and psychology, it is irrelevant for the present case. It is significant that Duns Scotus does not just tacitly keep logical and psychological considerations apart in his investigations but *explicitly* emphasizes their difference.[27]

---

26. Intellectus enim licet in se causet actum suum, circa tamen objectum non causat realitatem absolutam, sed tantum ens rationis. Reportata lib. I, dist. XXIV, qu. unic. 272a.

Destructa scientia in actu destruitur *scitum in actu.* Sed destructa scientia in actu non destruitur *scibile* in potentia. Quaest. sup. Met. lib. V, qu. XII, 298a.

27. Patet enim ex dictis, quod [verum] vel est mentis aliqua passio realis ... et tunc illa sicut et prima veritas pertinet ad *considerationem libri de anima.* Ex natura enim actus intellectus cognoscitur, quomodo est fundamentum talis relationis; vel est *relatio rationis* fundata in actu intelligendi aut magis in habitudine rationis quae est inter objecta comparata per actum intelligendi ... et tunc est mentis aliqua passio *originaliter,* sed *formaliter* pertinet ad considerationem Logici ... *Praesupponit tamen Logicus considerationem de actibus intelligendi, quibus secundae intentiones formantur.* Quaest. sup. Met. lib. VI, qu. III, 345b.

As Scholastics investigate the psychic, particularly where it is a matter of the activity of thinking and willing, it is *much more* than what we today grasp in the natural sciences as the psychically real. The Scholastics simultaneously contemplate the sense endowing [sinngebende] function, the "act character" of the psychic. Consequently, Scholastic psychology must be judged and evaluated bearing in mind this attitude. Much of what it taught, particularly concerning the physiology and psychology of sensory activity, may be incorrect or, at the very least, insufficient today. But the doctrine of acts undoubtedly offers much that is {286/228} interesting and valuable. To my knowledge, a detailed and thorough investigation of the Scholastic concept of the act—both intellectual and emotional acts—does not yet exist. I can only point out the problem here. By contrast, our task is a universal separation and corresponding characterization of the individual domains of reality. This task has possibly been fulfilled.

The "transcendent" determinations of unum and verum apply to every object. All domains of reality, insofar as we seek to cognize them and, indeed, do cognize them, *can be affected by nonsensory logically valid structures of sense [Sinngebilden]*. As regions of the cognizable, we encountered the sensory (physical and psychic) domain of natural reality, the reality of the supersensory, that is, the region of metaphysical objects and, alongside the logical domain previously mentioned, the nonsensory domain of the objects of mathematics.

A necessary conclusion results from this: A doctrine of categories that restricts itself to the ten Aristotelian categories that have been handed down will reveal itself to be not only incomplete but also hesitant and inaccurate in its determinations. It will be the latter because a consciousness of the difference between the domains and, correspondingly, a consciousness of the difference in meaning between the categorial forms that are conditioned by the nature of the domains escapes it.[28]

Duns Scotus is clearly aware that the ten inherited categories only hold for existent reality. Undoubtedly, the domain of *intentions* requires other forms of order, {287/229} because it represents an object region in itself. Intentions can be cognized and defined by themselves. Logic itself thus requires its own categories. There must be a logic of logic.

Duns Scotus goes even further: even the "non ens" is an object of cognition, enters into judgments, and is grasped in meanings and characterized by words.

---

28. Tantum sunt decem generalissima rerum, *quorum distinctio non sumitur penes aliquid logicum tantum sed penes ipsas essentias.* Ipsa enim intentio *"generalissimum"* est tantum variata numero in istis, unde quoad id, quod est difficultatis, quaestio est magis metaphysica quam logica; ideo sufficienter hic scitur *"quia ita est,"* quamvis forte Metaphysicus debeat vel possit scire *"propter quid."* Quaest. sup. lib. praed. qu. XI, 468a.

As we can make judgments about the "non ens," a most universal concept of the "non ens" must exist—a category that cannot occur among the ten categories of the real. The same thing holds of fantastic creations that do not belong to natural reality (figmenta), and of privations.

Someone could object that fictions and privations attain their universal formal determinacy from a reduction and abstraction of natural reality, *whose* fictions and privations they are. Specific categories for them are therefore superfluous. But when I judge, "blindness is a privation," a universal concept of privation as such is always presupposed. Furthermore, the distinction between "ens" and "non ens" does not lead to this or that specific "non ens" but rather to the concept of *"non ens" in general.*

Accordingly, fictions and privations are, like intentions, objects of their own kind and require corresponding "generalissima," that is, categories.

Indeed, the ten categories of the real determine only real objects [Objekte] and not any arbitrary object of cognition (non quodlibet intelligibile). Logic regards the categories in general with respect to the intentional character of their validity vis-à-vis the material. Hence, the categories of the nonreal must necessarily become visible to the logician, as is indeed the case in Duns Scotus.[29] {288/230}

---

29. Intentiones sunt per se intelligibiles, quia definibiles et in eis manifestum est esse aliquid superius et inferius, igitur aliquid supremum; illud non habet superveniens genus aliquod istorum, quia ens secundum se dividitur in haec decem [generalissima]; est igitur ens in anima, igitur est unum generalissimum intentionum praeter haec omnia. Item contingit intelligere non ens quia et significare . . . et in eis est ratio superioris et inferioris; ergo aliquid supremum, *illud non continetur in aliquo istorum decem; quia nullum istorum de illo praedicatur*; ergo est distinctum generalissimum non entium, *et ita plura genera quam decem.* Item figmenta concipiuntur ab intellectu et in eis est superius et inferius, ergo supremum; ergo aliquod generalissimum. Item de omnibus istis scil. intentionibus, non entibus, figmentis sic potest argui: intellectus componens facit compositiones de eis, quarum veritatem vel falsitatem judicat, ut patet, igitur et intellectus simplex ea concipit, igitur sub aliqua ratione concipiendi, non singularis; igitur universalis . . . igitur est in eis generalissimum.

Diceretur ad hoc, quod concreta, intentiones, non entia, privationes, figmenta et quaevis huiusmodi, sunt in genere per *reductionem ad abstracta et primae intentionis entia, quorum* sunt figmenta et privationes, quia cum communiora intelligantur prius minus communibus, oportet generalissima esse primo intelligibilia: haec autem non sunt intelligibilia nisi per attributionem ad illa, ad quae dicta sunt habere habitudinem, ideo non possunt poni generalissima, sed ponuntur in genere per *reductionem* . . . Contra hoc: in omnibus istis est per se praedicatio superioris de inferiori, ergo sub ratione alicuius universalis, quia praedicari proprie est proprium universalis non alterius quam generis. Arguatur de singulis sicut supra argutum est de concretis:

Thus, what was just said shows once more that Duns Scotus has a clear awareness of the tasks of the doctrine of categories. Simultaneously, the reference to "figmenta, privationes" and "non entia" suggests that the number of domains of reality listed so far is, in the end, not yet exhausted. {289/231}

igitur si non sit in infinitum procedere in eis, erit aliquod genus non habens supraveniens genus, igitur generalissimum ... illud nulli istorum decem est idem, quia ron habet easdem species, quia nec de eidem praedicatur per se primo modo, igitur *est aliud generalissimum ab istis decem* ...

Ad omnia objecta de istis quinque: concretis, intentionibus secundis, privationibus, non entibus et potentiis posset responderi, quod licet haec possint intelligi sub aliqua ratione intelligendi et praedicari inter se sub ratione alicuius universalis et statum esse ad aliquod universalissimum, quod inquantum attribuitur ei ista intentio, est diversum ab illis decem; tamen stat tantum esse decem generalissima *rerum quia non quodlibet intelligibile, sed ens secundum se dividitur in haec [5. Metaph.]; et ita nullum istorum est ens secundum se, distinctum ab illis decem.* Quaest. sup. lib. praed. qu. XI, 466a, b, 467a, b.

THREE

LINGUISTIC FORM AND LINGUISTIC CONTENT

The Domain of Meaning

THE "ENS LOGICUM," THAT IS, the sense, as well as the components encounterable within it—the meanings—have proven to be their own world vis-à-vis real being, and this in two ways. One, concerning their "existence," or better, their mode of reality (Thatness), and two, with respect to the content of their essence (Whatness). A peculiarity of these formations has intentionally not been considered thus far, namely, the fact that meaning and sense attach to words and complexes of words (sentences). Sense and meaning are *expressible* through linguistic formations. As formations endowed with sense and meaning, these linguistic forms become expressions in the widest sense of the word.

This coexistence of logical content and linguistic form leads to the question: how far are the latter to be integrated into logic? Is this mysterious coexistence ultimately so essential and indissoluble that logic must also integrate the linguistic formations and their structure into its domain of problems? Does not every grammatical element have "in" itself a logical element, and vice versa? What is Duns Scotus's position on these questions? Does he draw a boundary line between logic and grammar? And what is it? Further, one must investigate whether a regulation of the boundary results from his interpretation of the logical and of logic.

If linguistic formations as such demand their own science for their treatment, then they must enable a mode of consideration that sets itself apart from a logical investigation, just as conversely, logical problems must be soluble without bringing in linguistic moments as *evidentiary material*.

Above all, Duns Scotus emphasizes the independence of the logical, of the sense in judgment and in the nexus of judgments {290/232} (conclusions). *These logical formations have their own reality, even when they are not linguistically expressed.* They are "something prior" and do not require language for

74

their constancy, that is, ultimately for their validity. With reference to the words as such, they are that in which objective value inheres, the *content* (significatum).[1]

As a complex of sounds or a composite of letters, a word does not have intentional character. If it is used as an expression, it does not attain any new quality in itself. It does not actually carry the meaning within itself, otherwise a Greek [speaker] would also have to immediately *understand* a Latin word on hearing or reading it.[2] Precisely because he makes this radical division between linguistic formation and logical content, Duns Scotus succeeds in seeing the further distinctions in all their clarity.

In the words as such there is no context, no order. They are merely conglomerates that stand next to each other without obvious relationship as something devoid of sense and meaning. Only when they are considered as endowed with sense and meaning does the possibility of a distinction and thus an articulation open up.

Considered merely as a finite sequence of words, a sentence is a singularity. The *content* of the sentence, however, the *judgment*, can be singular or universal. The distinction between {291/233} "incomplexum" and "complexum" too can be understood only from the content of its meaning. Primarily, it is the concept—in a wider sense, also the *meaning*—that is simple in comparison to the judgment. In a derivative manner, words and sentences can also be understood as simple or composite. One cannot say in itself whether a sentence is true or false. At most it is written or spoken, or it is not. Truth and falsity can only be predicated of the *sense* inherent in the sentence and of this, in turn, *not* insofar as it is the content of a sentence, but only insofar as it *has objective value*. Thus, the *written sentence*, "man is a living being," is not false, even though the word "man" and the word

---

1. Iste liber [de Praedicamentis] non est de decem vocibus ut de primo subjecto, *nec aliqua pars logicae est de voce,* quia omnes passiones syllogismi et omnes partes eius possunt sibi inesse secundum esse quod habent in mente, etiamsi non proferantur ... sed est de *aliquo priore,* quod respectu vocis significative tantum habet rationem significati. Quaest. in lib. praed. qu. I, 438a.

2. Quod impositio ad significandum nullam qualitatem voci tribuit, concedo, nec aliquam intentionem nec aliquem conceptum. Unde nihil valet quod dicunt aliqui, quod vox significativa continet in se conceptum rei, quem causat in anima audientis. Si hoc esset verum, tunc vox significativa audita movere posset intellectum audientis secundum illam intentionem, inquantum scil, est sic significativa; et tunc vox latina significativa moveret intellectum Graeci audientis eam ad conceptum, quem exprimit, quod falsum est. *Unde per hoc quod est significativa,* nulla qualitas rei sibi imprimitur nec aliquem conceptum in se continet. Oxon. II, dist. XLII, quaest. IV, 472b, n. 17.

"living being" are *distinct*. But it is just as little true, because true and false are predicated of that which inheres in the sentence, of the *judgment*.[3]

Both formations, sentence and sense, word and meaning, however unusual and close their connection may be, belong to different domains of reality. The linguistic elements are *sensorily* (visually, acoustically, mechanically) perceptible. They belong to {292/234} the world of the really existent; they endure in time, [and] arise and pass away. By contrast, sense and meaning withdraw from all sensory perception. As such they are not subject to change. They are timelessly identically the same.

Irrespective of the differences in sound formation in individual languages, the identity of the domain of sense remains untouched in its validity, even if its content is "grasped" and brought to understanding in the most varied forms of words and sentences.[4]

---

3. Dici potest quod, licet in genere vocis *non sit aliquis ordo*, inter voces significativas tamen inquantum significant conceptus, *inter illas est ordo*; sicut omnis propositio in genere propositionum est singularis, tamen aliqua est singularis, aliqua universalis *ratione conceptus significati*. Quaest. in lib. praed. qu. I, 439b.

Passiones conceptus insunt voci significativae sicut incomplexum et complexum, significare verum vel falsum ut signo per naturam significati. l. c. 438b.

Significare verum et falsum convenit enuntiationi, sed non ut est vox significans conceptum, *sed ut conceptus significet rem*. l. c. 439a.

Absoluta confirmatio vel negatio non est antequam denominatur ad rem, quia ante illud quodlibet de quolibet enuntiatur ut solum signum de signo. *Signum autem inquantum signum nec verum nec falsum dicitur nisi in comparatione ad significatum.* Quaest. in lib. periherm. (op. 2) qu. I, 584 b.

Veritas et falsitas sunt in sermone ut in signo; ergo enuntiatio prolata illud significat, in quo est veritas et falsitas, illud est compositio intellectus . . . haec propositio: "homo est animal" *scripta* non dicitur falsa, licet haec vox "homo" non sit haec vox "animal" et hoc, quia litterae non significant voces ut sunt aliquid in se, sed *ut sunt signa aliorum*; et ita in omnibus his semper oportet recurrere ad ultimum significatum. Quaest. in lib. periherm. qu. II, 542.

4. Vox repraesentatur sensui, significatum intellectui; vox enim est signum et signum se offert sensui, aliud *derelinquens intellectui*. Quaest. sup. lib. I, anal. post. qu. I, 201a.

Passiones inquantum sunt signa et res inquantum sunt significata sunt eaedem apud omnes; nam eadem passio in anima apud quoscumque concipientes repraesentat eandem rem, quia eadem similitudo in anima semper est eiusdem repraesentativa, sicut est similitudo sensibilis in sensu litterae et voces in se eaedem non sunt eaedem apud omnes inquantum sunt signa; quia nec eadem littera apud omnes repraesentat eandem vocem, sed vel aliam vel nullam, nec eadem vox apud omnes significat eandem passionem sed vel aliam vel nullam. Ex hoc patet, res et passiones signa esse naturaliter, quia apud omnes uniformiter significant et significantur; et quod est a natura, est idem

Even the genetic, physiological-psychological mode of consideration is not unknown to Duns Scotus. He raises the charming objection: as a social being, man interacts with others and must make himself understood. The expressive means must necessarily be *bound* with the sense that is understood. Meaning and sense, accordingly, have an essential relationship to specific words and sentence formations associated with them and only with them. {293/235} However, Duns Scotus cautions that it is not the word endowed with meaning (vox significativa) that is the instrument of making oneself understood but the throat and lungs from which the word is formed in its physical existence. *Nature* provides these means for forming words. However, it does not follow from this that the unity of meaning and word also exists by *nature*. The linguistic formations that have naturally arisen are rather *"signa ad placitum."*

For its part, the genetic mode of consideration also shows how completely different the meaning appears from the word to Duns Scotus's gaze.[5]

A mindset for which the essence of the logical was still obscure could not carry out the consistent division of logical content and linguistic form starting from their fundamental moments. It can be executed only theoretically in all its precision. The question of the extent to which one can live entirely in logical content,

---

apud omnes; littera autem et vox non sunt signa a natura, quia non sunt eaedem apud omnes, inquantum significant aut significantur. Quaest. in lib. periherm. qu. IV, 546b sq.

In nominibus significativis haec vox "homo" quotiescumque prolata dicitur *una vox numero* et distingui ab hac voce "lapis" numero; cum tamen non possit eadem vox numero bis proferri, ita quod *quot sunt prolationes tot sunt voces distinctae numero*, et haec vox "homo" et haec vox "lapis" non tantum numero sed etiam specie distinguuntur; tamen quia ad finem vocis, scil. ad exprimendum conceptum per aequivalentiam sunt idem numero "homo" et "homo," "lapis" et "lapis," quotiescumque prolata, ideo dicuntur esse una vox numero respectu illius finis. Oxon. II, dist. II, quaest. VI, 333a sq., n. 9.

5. Vox significativa est signum naturale; ergo idem significat apud omnes. Probatio minoris: cuiuslibet virtutis naturalis est aliquod instrumentum naturale, sed virtus interpretativa est virtus naturalis homini, cum homo sit animal *sociale*, volens alii exprimere quod apud se est; ergo vox significativa quae est instrumentum illius virtutis, est signum naturale; ergo naturaliter significat. ... dico quod vox significativa non est instrumentum virtutis interpretativae in homine, sed *guttur* et *pulmo*, quae concurrunt ad formationem vocis; sicut si naturaliter homo velit fugere nociva, non sequitur omne illud esse naturale instrumentum, quo fugit nociva, puta vestimenta vel arma vel huiusmodi, sed tantum natura illa dedit ut instrumenta naturalia, quibus homo haec posset sibi praeparare ut manus; nam per manus homo potest illa per artem praeparare, et sic per rationem et instrumenta naturalia formandi vocem potest homo aliqua imponere, quae sunt signa ad placitum et non naturalia, sive conceptus. Quaest. in lib. periherm. qu. IV, 546b, 547b.

understand without linguistic supports, is a *factual question* that we leave to the psychology of thought processes. Whatever its solution turns out to be, it will change nothing concerning the validity of the division carried out above.

However necessary and valuable it may be to divide the region of the logical formations of sense and the region of the grammatical linguistic formations in order to {294/236} work out their heterogenous characters, this division must once again be suspended. It must be *forgotten*, as it were, *as soon as one lives in cognition and its presentation. In doing so, the alogical character of linguistic formations disappears.* They reveal themselves to be realities endowed with a completely unique function—*bearers* of meanings and sense formations, and, through these, that is, via their character of relating to objectivity, *"signs"* for objects [Objekte]. In this way, one could say that, for someone presently living in speech, the spheres of the existent grammatical and the valid logical that were so radically torn apart in the preceding sections are once again fused into one.

The linguistic formation is a sign of meaning, of sense. Meaning, in turn, is a "sign" of the object. Thus, in a certain respect, the following sentence is applicable: quidquid est signum signi, est signum signati.[6] For the relational context of the grammatical, logical, and objective spheres this implies that word and sentence, as formations endowed with meaning and sense, point to the objective region. Things are present in thoughts, and thoughts inhere in words and sentences.

If, following the preceding theoretical separation, we are to recognize the interpenetration of the domains mentioned, we shall have to make the *concept of the sign and of being a sign* into a problem.

But this theory of the *sign* can, at first, only be regarded as a preliminary analytic clarificatory inquiry. The questions that turn out to be decisive are as follows. What kind of signs are linguistic formations with respect to what is immediately signified, the logical content? Further, what does their character as a sign mean in relation to the mediately signified, the {295/237} objects? Depending on how the determinations of the sign-characters just mentioned turn out, the relationship between sign and signified will also undergo a corresponding interpretation. It may be that the relationships in question are not similar at all, with the result that the apparently so intimately unitary relationship of the three regions in living thought, cognition, and understanding will also turn out to be *distinctly constituted*. The difference of the structure, the unique aspects of the relationships, thus also requires treatment corresponding to its respective nature [Sachcharakter]. The domain of problems and how the problem is posed differentiate themselves

---

6. Quidquid est signum signi, est signum signati, ita quod signum intermedium non varietur in comparatione ad primum signum et ultimum signatum. Quaest. in lib. praed. qu. XXVIII, 504a.

essentially in adapting to the essential, [though] essentially distinct, contexts. Thus, it may turn out that in this field of investigation, seemingly so poor in terms of valuable eidetic content and richness of life, the ultimate and deepest problems have their reason and ground.

We must thus first clarify the concept of *"sign." Significare extensive sumitur pro dare intelligere.*[7] Something becomes objective to consciousness via the sign. The sign points away from itself to another object. The concept of the sign includes something that *contains a relation, a referential character.* Thus, the sign in itself is, as it were, the *fundament,* on which the function of reference is constructed, the point of departure for the cognition of the signified.

Relational character and *being a fundament* are the constitutive moments of the sign, and the kinds of signs can be demonstrated depending on how these moments are constituted.

First, the relationship between sign and signified can be *real.* {296/238} In this case, the real nature of the sign includes the reference to what it signifies. Thus, smoke is a sign of fire. Here, the difference between the relations is initially decisive. It is a separate question to ask, how *certainly,* with what degree of probability does such a sign refer to what it signifies?

Second, the relation can be *purely conceptual.* The sign as such does *not* already include a reference to a signified. That which serves as a sign—for example, the "monks' hand gestures" (the prescribed sign language of the monks during the required period of silentium)—can indicate many and varied things. What it ought to indicate is determined by an arbitrary convention.[8]

Duns Scotus therefore speaks of a "truth" in the sign, by which he understands what is announced through the sign. If the relation in the sign is a real relation, then the conformity between sign and signified is immediately given; the direction of the relation is unambiguously prescribed. The second type of relation includes different possibilities of the direction of relationship. We can

---

7. Quaest. in lib. praed. qu. VIII, 459b.

Significare est alicuius intellectum constituere; illud ergo significatur, cuius intellectus per vocem constituitur. Quaest. in lib. periherm. qu. II, 541a.

Significare est aliquid intellectui repraesentare; quod ergo significatur, ab intellectu concipitur. Quaest. sup. elench. qu. XVI, 22a.

8. Et cum signum hoc duo importet vel necessario requirat, scil. *fundamentum* et *relationem,* ex hoc sequitur, quod ex parte utriusque potest distingui. Ex parte autem relationis, quam importat signum, distinguitur signum primo in signum naturale, quod naturaliter significat et importat relationem realem ad signata; tum etiam in signum ad placitum tantum et non naturale, quod importat relationem rationis ut sunt voces et nutus monachorum, quia ista possunt significare alia, sicut ista, si placeret institutionibus. Reportata IV, dist. I, qu. II, 546a, n. 3.

now understand why signs of the first type were thought to be "truer" than those of the second.

What is meant with this truth, however, cannot be the same as the truth proper to judgment. To be sure, it has in common with the truth of judgment the fact that, considered πρὸς ἡμᾶς, with respect to the cognizing subject, it can trigger different degrees of security and certainty in the subject. To speak with Husserl, the "motivational context" between the {297/239} acts that interpret the sign and the signified is closer and more immediate among signs of the first kind.[9]

The following distinction is closely related to the distinction just stated. There are signs that always bear the signified "along with themselves." Thus, an eclipse, whether a solar or lunar eclipse, is a sign of the earth's position vis-à-vis the sun and the moon. Every time the sign occurs, the signified must also be there. The relationship is otherwise in the case of a judgment we express. There is no reason in it as such for the factual situation [Sachlage] expressed in it to also be given along with it. If we assume that the judgment is false, then nothing corresponds to it in the domain of the objective. Insofar as one interprets it as a sign, what the judgment ought to *signify* is lacking.

If we focus on the temporal moments in which sign and signified exist, we can once again distinguish the sign relation in this respect. The sign can *refer back* to something past or *point forward* to something that is anticipated, or a sign's reference aims at something present.

Furthermore, the sign can be the *cause* of what is indicated the way lightning is the cause of thunder; or vice versa, the sign is the *effect* of what is indicated the way smoke is an effect of *fire*.[10] {298/240}

If we regard the function of the sign as the *fundament*, we can identify distinctions in this respect insofar as signs can sensorily present themselves in different ways—as visual or acoustic entities. Different sensory organs can often work together in apprehending a sign.

---

9. Signum naturale verius significat quam signum ad placitum. Oxon. I, dist. XXII, qu. II, n. 5.

10. Alia est divisio signi in signum quod semper habet suum signatum secum quantum est ex parte sui, et tale signum est verum et efficax, sicut eclypsis est signum efficax interpositionis terrae inter solem et lunam et ita est similiter de aliis signis naturalibus. Aliud est signum quod non habet suum signatum secum: cuiusmodi signum est propositio quam proferimus, quia non est in potestate nostra, quod tale signum ut propositio secum habeat rem, quam significat; et hoc signum non est semper *verum*, sed aliquando falsum.

Tertia etiam est divisio signi in signum rememorativum respectu praeteriti et in prognosticum respectu futuri et in signum demonstrativum respectu praesentis. Reportata IV, dist. I, qu. II, 546a sq., n. 3. See Oxon. IV, dist. I, qu. II, n. 4.

What kind of sign is the word?

Can it somehow be categorized among the number of those just listed? The type of presentation is via the *senses. Vox repraesentur sensui.*[11] It is a sensory sign. As a complex of sounds it has an acoustic nature; as a written sign it has a visual nature. How should we determine the relation [of the sign] to the signified? Earlier, in the division of linguistic form and linguistic content, it was already underscored that words and complexes of words as such do not indicate anything. How do they nonetheless become signs?

Duns Scotus offers a clear hint: vox enim est signum et signum se offert sensui, *aliud derelinquens intellectui.*[12] It needs "an act that endows meaning" (Husserl). The act imparts something to the word (intellectus rationem voci *tribuit*), and thereby the word becomes an *expression* (dictio).

Expressions are thus unities of sign and signified of a quite unique kind.

The cloud-laden gray sky indicates rain; we also tend to say, it "means" rain. But the sky as such does not have any meaning, unlike the expression "heaven," for example. Expressions are "meaningful signs" (Husserl) in contrast to the "referential signs."

In every expression we can discover an act character, {299/241} an independent kind of act from which the word gains its content. Duns Scotus became aware of this act layer in its uniqueness. He did not consider acts in which one means something simply as psychic realities, occurrences, but rather as acts endowed with a *content.* They aim at this, at *meaning,* and originate *genetically* in the thinking subject. Their real existence is found in the subject; their content rests in the meaning.[13]

Can we somehow determine more precisely the phenomenon that inheres in the psychically real, meaning endowing acts? Can we find some property that permits us to view it henceforth as a phenomenon sui generis and to evaluate it accordingly?

Above all, we must ask, To which domain of reality should we assign the phenomenon "meaning"? We just said that meaning inheres in the psychically real,

---

11. Quantum etiam ad suum fundamentum potest signum multipliciter dividi. Potest enim hoc signum institui in uno sensibili unius sensus ut in re visibili aut audibili vel aliquo huiusmodi sicut in suo fundamento; vel in pluribus sensibilibus multorum sensuum . . . ut oratio longa, in qua sunt multa sensibilia et multae dictiones fundantes istam relationem importatam per huiusmodi signum, potest signum institui in uno sensibili vel pluribus ut dictum est. Reportata l. c. 547a, n. 5.

12. Quaest. sup. anal. post. I, qu. I, 201a.

13. *Rationes significandi non inducuntur per motum, sed sunt intentiones inductae per animam . . . potest dici quod . . . sunt in signo ut in termino et in anima ut in subjecto.* Quaest. sup. elench. qu. XV, 11a. See Quaest. in periherm. I, qu. II, 542a.

meaning endowing act, which always realizes itself when I wish to become aware of the meaning of a word. Because it "inheres" in this act, is given along with it and is connected to it, the view thus suggests itself that meaning also belongs to the domain of psychic realities.

Their real existence thus appears indubitable, all the more so as their mode of reality [Wirklichkeitsweise der Realität] can seemingly be presented from yet another side.

To do so, we must point to a new side of meaning that has not yet been considered.

Meanings, at least in the majority of cases, have, besides their *content*, the What, an object at which they aim and which is recognized through them. Let us suppose that such an object is a really existing object [Objekt]—for example, a tree. If the tree ceases to exist, then along with it {300/242} the meaning also appears to disappear into nothing. If that at which the meaning can aim and in which it gains a hold no longer exists, then it itself becomes illusory. Its reality stands and falls with that of the object. Consequently, object and meaning belong to the same domain of reality.

Is this argument appropriate to the matter [Sachverhalt]? Duns Scotus cautions that one must consider *how* the meaning refers to the object. It does not state something about it but *only represents it, only contains what a tree is and not that it is* (exists).

The meaning thus presents itself as freed of realities. Questions about the existence of the objects meant transcend the doctrine of meanings. Existence can be predicated only in a *judgment*. Something is always predicated of something else, that is, in every statement, a relation is given. By contrast, meaning *lacks* this character; it does not predicate something, it only *represents* something. *The sense of achievement specific to assertion is lacking in the character of the act of endowing meaning.*

Whether the object meant exists, changes, disappears, the meaning remains unaffected by this transformation. Were it really connected with the object, as was deduced earlier with apparent evidence, then it would itself have to become other along with the object.

Duns Scotus explicitly says that *it is completely foreign to meaning to exist* (res ut intelligitur, *cui extraneum est existere secundum quod significatur*).

This thought is essential and important enough that we must think it through to the end. Duns Scotus *teaches the freedom from existence of the domain of meaning.*

Insofar as the meaning endowing act presents an existent psychic reality, talk of meaning "inhering" in it cannot mean to imply a real connection. Through the meaning endowing act, I can {301/243} live in the meaning of the word, currently render present [vergegenwärtigen] its meaning to myself. But the meaning itself cannot first attain existence and being [Dasein] through the act, because it does not at all exist as real.[14]

The phenomena of logical content and linguistic form, initially presented in their complete alterity, ultimately revealed themselves to us in their quite unique interwovenness. We must now study this unity of word and meaning, which we have only referred to in a preliminary manner until now.

We must pursue what problems are possible in relation to it and why they are possible. {302/244}

---

14. Facta transmutatione in re, secundum quod existit *non fit transmutatio in significatione vocis*, cuius causa ponitur, quia res non significatur ut *existit* sed ut *intelligitur* per ipsam speciem intelligibilem; sed sive sit sive non sit, cum tam res ut intelligitur quam species sua maneant in transmutatae facta transmutatione in re ut existit quia per eandem speciem cognoscimus essentiam et eandem scientiam habemus de ea, quando existit et quando non existit … res ut significatur per vocem non transmutantur qualicumque transmutatione facta in re ut existit et per consequens *nec vox significans transmutabitur in significando* … concedendum quod destructo signato destruitur signum, sed licet res destruatur ut existit non tamen res ut intelligitur nec ut est signata destruitur …

Res ut intelligitur, *cui extraneum est existere … secundum quod significatur.* Quaest. in lib. periherm. qu. III, 545a sqq.

PART II

THE DOCTRINE OF MEANING

IN THE PRECEDING FIRST PART, we undertook an analysis and distinguishing characterization of the different object regions. At the end, the world of meanings emerged as a new, independent region. To begin with, we only tentatively postulated its existence and did not settle anything about its relationships to the other regions. Above all, we set aside all questions about its own potential structure.

Hence, in what follows we must first arrive at a decision about the questions that are, in general, possible about the domain of meaning and whether they constitute an independent group of problems that justify the demand for a discipline, the doctrine of meaning, that treats them. Fixing the *concept of a doctrine of meaning* and its task will then enable us to decide how far and to what extent philosophy must and *can* be concerned with "language," and moreover how the relationship of the doctrine of meaning to logic must be conceived. These questions will be treated with reference to the *general* portion of Duns Scotus's *Grammatica speculativa*.

The second chapter attempts to present and interpret the *doctrine of the forms of meanings*, which, as the theory of the *modi significandi*, constitutes the larger portion of this treatise.

85

Steinthal mentions the treatise and notes that "the famous Scholastic Johannes Duns Scotus" wrote it out of "an interest in logic."[1] {303/245} De Wulf considers it "the most perfect achievement in the area of speculative grammar."[2] In a brief review, Paolo Rotta mentions Duns Scotus's philosophy of language.[3] Karl Werner deals with it in greater detail in his essay "Die Sprachlogik des Johannes Duns Scotus."[4] This investigation is noteworthy because, along with an occasionally unsatisfactory description of its contents, it attempts to describe, mostly following Thurot,[5] the treatise's *historical position* in the grammatical doctrines of the Middle Ages as a whole. A more detailed *historical* characterization of the treatise vis-à-vis the systematic tasks of a doctrine of meaning is reserved for a separate investigation. In what follows, we are only concerned with a *theoretical understanding* of the theory it contains.

---

1. Heymann Steinthal, *Einleitung in die Psychologie und Sprachwissenschaft* (Berlin: F. Dümmler, 1871), 44.

2. Maurice de Wulf, *Geschichte der mittelalterlichen Philosophie*, trans. Rudolf Eisler (Tübingen: Mohr Siebeck: 1913), 339.

3. Paolo Rotta, *La Filosofia del Linguaggio nella Patristica e nella Scolastica* (Turin: Fratelli Bocca, 1909), 233–42.

4. Karl Werner, "Die Sprachlogik des Johannes Duns Scotus," *Sitzungsberichte der Philosophisch-historischen Klassen der Kaiserlichen Akademie der Wissenschaften* 85 (1877): 545–97.

5. Charles Thurot, *Notices et extraits de divers manuscrits latins pour servir à l'histoire de doctrines grammaticales au moyen-âge* (Paris: Imprimerie Nationale, 1868).

ONE

MEANING AND MEANING FUNCTION

The Principles of the Doctrine of Meaning

WE CAN INITIALLY SUBJECT THE organic totality of meaningful words (expressions) that we call "language" and that articulates itself in the most varied individual forms to the question: How did it *arise* in the first place—what factors played and still play a facilitating or retarding role in the development of language? {304/246} Moreover, we can study the genesis of language among particular individuals. It would be unjustifiably one-sided if someone were to dismiss the value of such investigations into language.

However, the far-reaching and in part deeply rooted sphere of influence that the idea of development has achieved within scientific thought in the present fosters a dangerous tendency to regard the presentation of the manner in *which* an object *has developed* as its explanation, and therewith as the *alpha and omega* of what can potentially be cognized of it. This absolutization of historical-psychological thought, however, overlooks the fact that a completely different— shall we say, practically contrary—mode of questioning is possible in relation to certain objects. Besides the question *How did language come to be?* another question is possible: *What ought it achieve?* Consequently, our cognition of an object is not completed with a genetic explanation. Furthermore, there is *teleological understanding.* Admittedly, regarded from the perspective of logic, this too is *not* the ground and keystone of our cognition of an object, but it is much more the *way* to the true "origin" than the genetic explanation.

We can read off the *aim* of an activity from the way we define its conditions of perfectibility. We call language—like its use—perfect when it is such that it can awaken in the consciousness of the one listening and comprehending the full sense of what the speaker intends with his speech. The activity of language thus aims at the complete communication of the sense of an utterance.

87

The overwhelming significance that accrues to linguistic *content* is immediately clear from this determination, for everything aims at expressing and communicating it. When someone uses a name perfectly, he does not just pronounce it, that is, realize it as a sound—even a trained bird can do that. {305/247} Rather, it means he uses it as a word *charged with meaning*, albeit not the way a Latin speaker pronounces a Hebrew word correctly without knowing what it means. The perfect use of a name requires the speaker to be *presently* conscious of its meaning.[1] This is true not only of everyday prescientific speech but also, and possibly even more, of the presentation of scientific insights, which after all is not possible without language. We can know something of objects and states of affairs only in and through contexts of meaning. Whatever its nature and however imperfect it may be, the domain of meaning pervades scientific speech and communication just as it pervades a systematically structured scientific train of thoughts.

It is therefore unsurprising that a deeper reflection [on language] runs up against the question of the extent to which language is capable of *expressing* intended objects and states of affairs, and letting them become present.

In demonstrating the complete alterity of *psychic* reality as compared with *physical* [reality], Bergson attained the insight that our language only succeeds to a very limited degree in expressing the fine points of psychological analysis: "In short, the word with well-defined outlines, the rough and ready word, which stores up the stable, common, and consequently impersonal element in the impressions of mankind, overwhelms or at least covers over the delicate and fugitive impressions of our individual consciousness."[2] "Breaking out of the *framework of language*," we could see our psychic life in a completely different light. {306/248} Above all it is Rickert, who has convincingly demonstrated vis-à-vis the problem of the limits of natural scientific concept formation that the word meanings do not attain the unsurveyable manifold of what is immediately given; rather, they already represent specific formations and transformations in comparison with it.[3]

This leads us to conclude that a formal content that enables this function must already be contained within meanings as such. Meanings are thus located under the aspect of *logical dignity*, an approach that appears unquestionably justified when we realize that all cognition, that is, judgments, are built up from meanings

---

1. Signum perfectionis constructionis est *generare perfectum sensum in animo auditoris*, De mod. sig. cap. LIV, 49b.

2. Henri Bergson, *Time and Free Will: An Essay on the Immediate Data of Consciousness*, trans. F. L. Pogson (London: George Allen Unwin, 1910), 132; Heidgger cites Bergson, *Essai sur les données immédiates de la conscience* (Paris: F. Alcan, 1912), 100; see also 10, 97, 99, 192.

3. Rickert, *Die Grenzen der naturwissenschaftlichen Begriffsbildung*, 31ff.

as their necessary components. Consequently, the guiding value for an investigation into meanings is *truth* as valid sense. Only cognition can be true, and cognition is always cognition of an object. If truth thus remains our guiding perspective, it is unavoidably necessary that we reach a decision about the relationship of the domain of meaning to the being of objects. This much to point out, preliminarily, the different problems concerning meanings.

We shall now have to show how far Duns Scotus was acquainted with these problems and how he provides a solution to them. In the first part of the investigation, I already pointed out how sharply Scotus distinguishes the sensorily perceptible *form* of the word from the nonsensory *content* of the word, the *meaning*. Likewise, with the sentence "Vox repraesentatur sensui, aliud *derelinquens intellectui*," he indicates that the meaning corresponds to a distinct act of consciousness. Duns Scotus clarifies what these acts achieve for meaning as follows: Intellectus *duplicem rationem* ei [voci] tribuit, scilicet rationem significandi, quae vocatur *significatio*, per quam efficitur signum vel significans, et sic formaliter est dictio; et rationem *consignificandi*, quae vocatur *modus significandi* {307/249} *activus*, per quam vox significans fit *consignum* vel consignificans et sic *formaliter* est *pars orationis*.[4]

Thus, the word initially receives meaning through the act of consciousness. Something objective confronts consciousness, which it intends. This does not mean that a real object that exists independent of consciousness is created. The word thus becomes an *expression*; it *signifies* something. Neither does Duns Scotus think of the meaning of the word in the sense of a sensualistic psychology, as if the meaning were nothing more than a fantasy image of the intended objects that is associatively bound with the sensory word as sounded. In his view, meanings are not psychic realities; they do not belong in a real context, within which they are *caused*. Rather, they must be understood as *intentional contents*, as achievements of intentional acts (intentiones inductae per animam). A meaningful expression that is understood is *more* than the sound of a word that is merely sensorily perceived; this "more" lies in the acts of meaning.[5]

> But the objectification of the content so first constituted is not the whole of this
> first act of thought; consciousness cannot simply present the content to itself,

---

4. Notandum, quod cum intellectus vocem ad significandum et consignificandum imponit, *duplicem rationem ei tribuit*, scil. rationem *significandi* quae vocatur *significatio*, per quam efficitur signum vel significans, et sic formaliter est *dictio*; et rationem *consignificandi*, quae vocatur *modus significandi activus*, per quam vox significans *fit consignum* vel consignificans et sic formaliter est *pars orationis*. De mod. sig. cap. I, 1b sq.

5. Rationes significandi non inducuntur per motum, sed sunt *intentiones inductae per animam*. Quaest. sup. elench. qu. VIII, 11a.

it can only do so by giving it a definite position; it cannot simply distinguish it from an emotional mood of its own, without accrediting it with some other sort of existence instead of that which belonged to it as such a mood. The meaning of this requirement ... is most easily shown by the way in which language actually satisfies it.... The rest of its stock of words {308/250} [with the exception of interjections—Heidegger] is in the definite forms of substantives, adjectives, verbs, and the familiar *parts of speech* in general.... I prefer to comprise the primary activity of thought in a single operation, which may be indifferently represented as that of giving the content of ideas one of these logical forms by making it objective for consciousness, or as that of making it objective by giving it one of these forms.[6]

I have cited this extensive quotation from H. Lotze's *Logic* intentionally. One could call it an expository translation of Duns Scotus's brief statements.

Meanings are already prefigured in that they become objective through the act. A certain relational context pertaining to meaning is present in the *modus significandi*. We must now clarify the essence of this meaning form as such.

We can understand the expression "modus significandi" in a twofold sense: the modus significandi *activus* and *passivus*. The modus activus is the act of meaning as an activity of consciousness. It is called this because the endowing of meaning through the grasping consciousness is "practically an action." The modus passivus signifies the result of the activity, the objective correlate of the act, which Lotze characterizes as an "impression"—immediate givenness *insofar* as it has been meaningfully grasped, that is, formed.[7] The modus activus is {309/251} nothing other than the subjective side; the modus passivus is nothing other than the objective side of meaning. We can express the same state of affairs in the terminology of phenomenology as follows: "In a noetic respect, the heading 'expressing' is supposed to designate a particular layer of acts to which all other acts are to

---

6. H. Lotze, *Logic*, English Translation, ed. Bernard Bosanquet (Oxford: Clarendon, 1884), 12–13 (translation modified); Heidegger cites H. Lotze, *Logik: drei Bücher vom Denken, vom Untersuchen und vom Erkennen*, Philosophische Bibliothek 141, ed. G. Misch (Leipzig: Meiner, 1912), 17.

7. Est sciendum, quod modus significandi duo importat aequivoce. Dicitur enim de modo significandi activo et passivo. *Modus significandi activus* est modus sive proprietas vocis *ab intellectu sibi concessa*, mediante qua vox proprietatem rei significat. *Modus significandi passivus* est modus sive proprietas *rei* prout est per vocem significata. Et quia significare et consignificare est *quoddam modo* agere et significari et consignificari est quoddam modo pati; inde est quod modus vel proprietas vocis mediante qua vox proprietatem rei active significat, modus significandi activus nominatur. Modus vero vel proprietas rei prout per voces passive significatur, modus significandi passivus nuncupatur. De mod. sig. cap. I, 1b.

conform in a sui generis way and with which they remarkably are to fuse, precisely in such a way that every noematic act-sense—and consequently the relation of objectivity [modus essendi] inherent to it—stamps itself 'conceptually' in the noematic [dimension] of the expressing [modus significandi passivus]."[8]

Meaning attains a definite form through the modus significandi: "All logical differences, and differences in categorial form, are constituted in logical acts in the sense of intentions"[9] [modi significandi activi].

If different forms of meaning exist—and the differentiation of the "parts of speech" establishes this—the question arises: What determines the categorial forms of meanings, [that is to say,] where does the *principle of their differentiation* lie? Duns Scotus formulates this problem in the question: *a quo modus significandi radicaliter orietur?*

As a specific class of intentional acts of consciousness, the modi significandi are subject to a law of essence [Wesensgesetz] that is true of *acts in general*: intellectus ad actum determinatum non vadit *nisi aliunde determinetur.*[10] {310/252} The acts are determined by something; they are determined by something that is not form. This expresses the necessary correlation between the quality and the material of the act, between noesis and noema, between form and content. This principle that every form is materially determined, however, does not yet say anything about the nature of the determining material. A meaning is a meaning only in a definite form, through a specific modus significandi. Consequently, qua act the modus significandi must be determined by a specific material, that is, a specific modus *essendi* corresponds to every modus significandi. We thus gain a new concept that is indispensable for the doctrine of the categories of meaning.[11]

---

8. Husserl, *Ideas I*, 246; Heidegger cites Husserl, *Ideen zu einer reinen Phänomenologie und phänomenologischen Philosophie*, in *Jahrbuch für Philosophie und phänomenologische Forschung*, 257.

9. Edmund Husserl, *Logical Investigations*, trans. J. N. Findlay (London: Routledge, 2001), 2:105; Heidegger cites Husserl, *Logische Untersuchungen*, vol. 2, part 1, 2nd ed. (Halle: Max Niemeyer, 1913), 384.

10. Notandum, quod cum huiusmodi rationes sive modi significandi activi non sint figmenta, oportet, omnem modum significandi activum *ab aliqua rei proprietate* radicaliter oriri. Quod sic patet: quia cum intellectus vocem ad significandum sub aliquo modo significandi activo imponit, ad ipsam rei proprietatem aspicit, *a qua* modum significandi originaliter trahit; quia intellectus, cum sit virtus passiva, de se indeterminata, ad actum determinatum non vadit, *nisi aliunde determinetur.* Unde cum imponit vocem ad significandum sub determinato modo significandi activo, a determinata rei proprietate necessario movetur; ergo cuilibet modo significandi activo *correspondet* aliqua proprietas rei seu *modus essendi rei.* De mod. sig. cap. II, 2a.

11. See the previous note.

However, Duns Scotus raises the following objection against what was said: although the word "deitas" is feminine, the genus is considered a modus significandi. There is nothing in the intended object that corresponds to the genus femininum as a form of meaning that includes the thought of passivity in it that could determine the form in question.[12] This is also true of privations and fictions, because no real being is intended in their meanings. And yet expressions for privations and fictions such as "blindness" and "chimeras" also possess definite forms of meaning, that is, they are subject to definite categories of meaning.[13]

To solve these objections, Duns Scotus points out that the modus significandi of a meaning {311/253} need not be taken directly from the receptive material of the reality intended in the meaning, for which [material] it is the determining form. The form can also be determined by something else. It suffices that it does not contradict the material for which it is supposed to be the form, that is to say, it suffices that this form can be determinative for this material or that the material tolerates such formation. This conclusion is especially significant for the modi significandi of abstract, *nonsensory* meanings, for we grasp them in forms of meaning that are originally tailored to sensory meanings. The objection concerning the expression "deitas" is, in essence, no objection, because one may not interpret the "genus" as a form of meaning. However, Duns Scotus takes the ostensible objection seriously and solves it with the aid of a *valid principle*. He also cites this principle to eliminate the difficulty concerning privations and fictions. The privations receive the form of meaning of the "habitus" corresponding to them, just as meanings with a fictive content are determined by the forms of meaning of the *partial meanings* having *real* content that constitute them.[14]

---

12. Sed contra hoc objicitur; quia haec vox significativa scil. *deitas* habet femininum genus, quod est modus significandi passivus; tamen in re significata sibi proprietas non correspondet, quia est proprietas patientis, a qua sumitur femininum genus. De mod. sig. cap. II, 2b.

13. Item privationes et figmenta sub nullis proprietatibus cadunt, cum non sint entia, et tamen voces significativae privationum et figmentorum modos signifcandi activos habent, *ut caecitas, chimaera* et similia. De mod. sig. cap. II, 2b. See above p. 72.

14. Dicendum quod non oportet, quod semper modus significandi activus dictionis trahatur a proprietate rei illius dictionis, cuius est modus significandi; sed potest accipi a proprietate rei alterius dictionis et rei illius dictionis tribui et sufficit quod ipsi non repugnet; et quia substantias separatas non intelligimus nisi ex istis sensibilibus, ideo sub proprietatibus sensibilium eis nomina imponimus et nominibus eorum modos significandi activos attribuimus. Unde licet in Deo secundum veritatem non sit proprietas passiva, tamen imaginamur ipsam *tanquam* patientem a nostris precibus. l. c. 2b.

Similiter privationes intelligimus ex suis habitibus, sub proprietatibus habituum eis nomina imponimus et nominibus eorum modus sig. activos attribuimus. Similiter in

But this does not appear to resolve the difficulty concerning privations satisfactorily. For someone could further object that if the forms of meaning are determined by the "habitus" as their material, {312/254} they determine the meaning content of the privations through the form of the "habitus," and hence with respect to formal determination, they are "false" (*consignificative falsa*).[15] The "falsehood" touched on here is not the opposite of the truth as it applies to judgment and *only* to judgment. Not without reason, Duns Scotus therefore adds "*consignificative*." What is meant is a [form of] falsehood that can only exist in relation to the modi significandi. According to the objection raised, the modus significandi is false formaliter; it lacks precisely *that* as *which* it appears. It presents itself as the form of meaning of a privation, but it is precisely not this but rather a form of the habitus, of a meaning content in which a real object is intended.

In reality, however, the form of meaning of the privative expression determined by the habitus is not consignificatively false because the privation must be grasped as an *ens secundam animam*; its being real is its being cognized. If, on the basis of the principle cited earlier, the modus significandi is determined by the modus *essendi*, but the modus essendi is identical with the modus intelligendi in the case of privations, then the privative meaning rightly has the form of meaning determined by the habitus. Privation cannot be grasped without recourse to the habitus that it negates (privatio non cognoscitur nisi per habitum).[16] {313/255}

We can extract a noteworthy idea from this extremely condensed, albeit equally precise, solution to the problem of the material determinacy of the form of meaning: namely, that by modus *essendi*, we should understand not only *existent natural reality* but also the *nonsensory logical*, what is cognized qua cognized, and thus *everything objective whatsoever*. The modus essendi coincides with the universal

---

ncminibus *figmentorum* sumuntur modi sig. activi ex proprietatibus partium, ex quibus imaginamur chimaeram componi quam imaginamur *ex capite leonis cauda draconis*, et sic de aliis. l. c.

15. Et si instetur: si modi sig. activi in nominibus privationum sumuntur a modis essendi habituum, tunc nomina essendi habitus et non privationis designabunt; et hoc posito, nomina privationum per suos modos sig. activos *erunt consignificative* falsa. l. c. 2b.

16. Dicendum quod non est verum; imo nomina privationum per suos modos sig. activos designant circa privationes modos intelligendi privationum, *qui sunt eorum modi essendi*. Juxta quod sciendum, quod licet privationes non sint entia positiva *extra animam, sunt tamen entia positiva in anima*, ut patet IV, Met. text. 9, et sunt entia secundum animam; *et quia eorum intelligi est eorum esse*, ideo eorum modi intelligendi erunt eorum modi essendi. Unde nomina privationum per suos modos sig. activos non erunt consignificative falsa, quia cum modi intelligendi privationum reducantur ad modos intelligendi habitus (nam privatio non cognoscitur nisi per habitum), ideo modi essendi privationum tandem ad modos essendi habitus reducuntur. l. c. 2 sq.

domain of the "something in general" circumscribed by the primordial category of the "ens." Thus, corresponding to the function of meaning, which applies to everything, the doctrine of meaning has a universal tendency. This suggests that Duns Scotus was quite aware of the domain of application [Herrschaftsbereiches] of the categories of meaning.

When Scotus derives the individual forms of meaning from the modus essendi—a derivation we shall present in the next chapter—he almost exclusively allows only existent, sensory, natural reality to appear in its form differentiating function. This is not only a consequence of his thinking, which, despite his great insight into the logical, remains *empirically* oriented; rather, it arises from the quite correct insight that the forms of meaning are originally gauged to immediately given empirical reality.

Lotze once quite appropriately remarked of these forms that their "logical import is only a shadow of the import of these metaphysical concepts [from which they were originally derived—Heidegger]. It only repeats the formal characteristics which the latter assert of the real; but by not confining their application to the concrete external reality, it loses that part of their meaning which they only possess in that application."[17]

Likewise, nowhere does Duns Scotus say that the modi significandi only *reproduce* or reflect the sense of the categories valid of existent natural reality; rather, he says {314/256} that they have their "origin" there. The forms of meaning are peculiarly *faded* when compared with the categories of existent natural reality, as we shall see when we present the doctrine of the forms of meanings. Here we must note a peculiar fact: when treating *nonsensory logical reality* and, likewise, *psychic reality* too, we use expressions that, in terms of their genuine content, are mostly taken from sensory natural reality. We often lack "language" for these domains. It is hence neither accidental nor arbitrary that discussions pertaining to these domains frequently appear awkward and long-winded given the need for circumlocutions.

An adequate grasp of the objects belonging to the regions mentioned and the problems arising thereby is eminently difficult. But we could practically rule it out were the categorial forms of meanings underlying these expressions not faded and indeterminate, because only thus can they apply to everything objective.

Even though the preceding presentation of the principles responsible for the material determinacy of the forms of meaning is undoubtedly correct, the epistemologist will still not be satisfied with it. If existent natural reality is to be determinative of the categories of meaning, then I must be *aware* of this reality and its structure in advance. Natural reality may be the *ultimate* principle for

---

17. Lotze, *Logic*, 14; Heidegger cites Lotze, *Logik*, 19.

differentiating the forms of meaning, but I cannot relate it directly to the latter. A new problem arises: *A quo modus significandi immediate sumatur?* From what do we *immediately* read off the forms of meaning? What is it from which alone they *can* be read off?

The modus essendi must somehow be given to consciousness: it must have it objectively before itself. But I am aware of an object only in cognition: It is truly an object only as the object of cognition. {315/257} The modus *intelligendi* is the *"ratio concipiendi,"* that is, the way I objectively grasp something and am aware of it. Consequently, the modus essendi can only take on its function of differentiating meaning insofar as it is given as an object of cognition (*prout ab intellectu apprehenditur*).[18] Elsewhere, Duns Scotus discusses the issue of whether the meaning of an expression relates to the object as such or to the object given in the species intelligibilis. He affirms the latter. The expression relates immediately to the *conscious* object. Here we must pay attention to a fundamental distinction pertaining to the concept of "consciousness." Whereas we can understand the species intelligibilis, that through which the object is present to consciousness, as a psychic *reality*, that is, as a specific occurrence in the soul, meaning does not relate to the species intelligibilis understood thus but rather to the species insofar as it possesses *objective value*, that is, insofar as it *represents* the object to consciousness. Thus, the meaning of an expression does not relate to an object insofar as it exists in and for itself, independent of consciousness. Rather, it relates to it only insofar as it is cognized. Everything that we mean intentionally must be grasped in meanings, and only something that is somehow objectively present, something that can be intentional for consciousness, can be "expressed" in meanings.[19] {316/258}

---

18. Notandum, quod modi significandi activi *immediate* a modis intelligendi passivis sumuntur. Juxta quod sciendum est, quod sicut est duplex modus significandi, scil. activus et passivus, ita duplex est modus intelligendi, scil. *activus* et *passivus.* Modus intelligendi activus est ratio concipiendi, qua mediante, intellectus rei proprietates significat, concipit vel apprehendit. Modus autem intelligendi passivus est proprietas rei *prout ab intellectu apprehensa.*

Dicatur ergo, quod modi *significandi* activi sumuntur immediate a modis *intelligendi* passivis; quia modi significandi activi non sumuntur a modis essendi, nisi ut hi modi essendi ab intellectu apprehenduntur. l. c. cap. III, 3a.

19. Species intelligibilis immediate significatur per vocem, sed illa dupliciter consideratur, aut inquantum est quid in *se accidens,* scil. *informans animam,* aut *inquantum repraesentat rem.* Primo modo non significatur per vocem ... sed secundo modo. Quaest. sup. lib. perih. qu. II, 541b.

Res non significatur ut existit sed *ut intelligitur.* l. c. qu. III, 545a.

Like the modus significandi, the modus *intelligendi* can be distinguished into an active modus and a passive modus. The active modus enables objectification for consciousness; the passive modus is nothing other than the modus *essendi* insofar as it is objectified for consciousness. Hence, if the determinacy of the forms of meaning has its *ultimate foundation* in the modus essendi, then it is the modus *intelligendi* passivus qua objectively given modus *essendi* that first genuinely *enables* the determination of form.[20]

A peculiar entwinement—a mutual interdependence of the modi essendi, intelligendi, and significandi—has emerged so far. "Noetically [speaking]," this implies a special interpenetration and foundation of different act layers. A further task arises here: namely, clarifying the mutual relationships of the noematic spheres that have been indicated. Simultaneously, once we decide the question *Quomodo modus significandi a modo intelligendi et a modo essendi distinguatur?* the characterization of the modi significandi, on whose clear apprehension everything here depends, will be advanced significantly.

Regarded purely in terms of *what* they contain, their noematic core, the modi essendi, intelligendi passivi, and significandi passivi are identically (materialiter et realiter) the same: namely, the material determined in each case by the form, or more precisely, the *material* that is correlatively assigned to the form insofar as we imagine it freed of the determinacy of form. The material can first be differentiated, and the modes can first be conceived of as distinct *by means of the form*. However, we said of the form that it is determined by the material. Hence, with regard {317/259} to the same material, there can only be *one* form, and consequently we could only speak of *one* modus. But in reality, a differentiation of form exists. This cannot be possible in any other way unless the material takes on a meaning differentiating function for the form in *different respects*.[21]

The modus essendi is the experienceable in general. It is what confronts consciousness in an absolute sense, the "tangible" reality that unavoidably forces itself on consciousness and can never be gotten rid of. It must therefore be called absolute, centered in itself. This given as such exists not only for realism but also for absolute idealism, which aims to dissolve all content into form, be it that it recognizes only the historical fact of science as something *given* for it, [something] that is "*presupposed*." If it does not grant even this, then minimally, at least the "infinite" process is given, in which and through which the X of the object is to

---

20. Modi autem essendi prout ab intellectu apprehensi, dicuntur modi intelligendi passivi; ergo modi sig. activi sumuntur a modis essendi mediantibus modis intelligendi passivis; et ideo immediate modi sig. activi a modis intelligendi passivis sumuntur. De mod. sig. cap. III, 3a.

21. Notandum, quod modi essendi et modi intelligendi passivi et modi significandi passivi sunt idem materialiter et realiter, sed *differunt formaliter*. l. c. cap. IV, 3b.

be radically dissolved into form and formal systems. The modus essendi is immediately given empirical reality [regarded] *sub ratione existentiae*. It should be noted as significant that Duns Scotus characterizes even this empirical reality as subject to a "*ratio*," that is, a perspective, a form, a relational context. This is nothing else than what is nowadays expressed in the formulation: "givenness" already exhibits a categorial determination. This is an instance of the "most elementary logical problems," problems that, as Rickert once remarked, "reveal themselves only to the logician who also draws 'prescientific' cognition into the domain of his investigation."[22] {318/260}

The modus intelligendi passivus is the reality that has entered into cognition, [it is] the modus essendi in the formal determinacy of cognition. One must understand the modus significandi passivus as the modus essendi insofar as it relates to expressions, that is, insofar as it has entered into meanings. One modus is the aspect (ratio) of *givenness*, another modus is the aspect of *cognition*, and the third modus is the aspect of *meaning*. This is how the modi, which have the same identical material at their basis, are distinguished with regard to the *formal determinacy* (*secundum formales rationes*).[23]

The forms are nothing other than the *objective* expression of the different *modes* in which consciousness is *intentionally* related to the objective.

We must now likewise distinguish and provide a description of the act qualities in which these different modes of intentional relationship are actually carried out.

The modi essendi, intelligendi activi, and significandi activi distinguish themselves from each other materialiter and formaliter insofar as they belong to different essential regions. Peculiarly, Duns Scotus once again refers to the modus *essendi*—which he had previously placed {319/261} in a continuum with the modi intelligendi and significandi *passivi*—when characterizing the *active*

---

22. See the essay "Geschichtsphilosophie," 333. See also *Die Grenzen der naturwissenschaftlichen Begriffsbildung*, 31, 36n1. The problem is dealt with in greater detail in the book *Der Gegenstand der Erkenntnis*, 3rd ed. (Tübingen: Mohr, 1915), 376ff.

23. Modus essendi est rei proprietas *absolute*; modus intelligendi passivus est ipsa proprietas rei prout *ab intellectu apprehensa*; modus sig. passivus est eiusdem rei proprietas *prout per vocem significatur*. Et sunt eadem materialiter et realiter (quia quod dicit modus essendi absolute, dicit modus intelligendi passivus, prout refertur ad intellectum) et quod dicit modus intelligendi passivus, dicit modus sig. passivus, prout refertur ad vocem, ergo sunt eadem materialiter. Sed differunt formaliter, quod sic patet: quia qui dicit modum essendi dicit proprietatem rei absolute sive sub ratione existentiae; sed qui dicit modum intelligendi passivum, dicit eandem rei proprietatem ut materiale, et rationem intelligendi sive concipiendi ut formale; sed qui dicit modum sig. passivum, dicit eandem proprietatem rei ut materiale et dicit rationem consignificandi ut formale, et cum *alia* sit ratio *essendi*, alia *intelligendi*, alia *significandi*, differunt secundum *formales rationes*. l. c. cap. IV, 3b.

modi, however without explicitly distinguishing a modus essendi activus and passivus. One could interpret this as a sign that Scotus was not definitively clear about the modus essendi, because he once declares it the absolute objective reality, albeit he does not fail to note that it too stands under a specific ratio—namely, that of existence—and hence approaches the character of formal determinacy to which an act character must correspond.

The modus intelligendi activus belongs in the region of consciousness, specifically in the region of one that is [presently] *cognizing*, whereas the modus significandi activus must be assigned to the region of "expressions." But insofar as the acts of cognition, meaning, and those in which we become conscious of what is immediately given at present are distinguished according to their *ratio* or *the sense of their activity* (to what extent will reveal itself when we separate the doctrine of meaning and logic), they must also be held apart from each other formaliter.[24]

In his description of these acts, Scotus recurs once again to the fundamental distinction concerning *acts as such*, which we already touched on at the outset. The act quality (of both cognitive acts and acts of meaning) and the act material corresponding to it belong to structural regions that are materialiter distinct. Intentional content (modus passivus) and the real [reellen] components (modus activus) must be distinguished in every intentional experience. {320/262} By contrast, the modi activi and passivi are formaliter identical insofar as the functional sense of the acts represents, as it were, the intentional content that has been transposed into the sphere of the act.[25]

Meaning can be understood in a certain sense as belonging to the objectivity of the world of objects; it receives its "content" thence. But as an achievement of the meaning endowing act, it belongs to the expression animated by meaning, as

---

24. Item sciendum, quod modus *essendi* et modus *intelligendi activus* et modus *significandi activus* differunt *formaliter et materialiter*; quia modus essendi dicit proprietatem rei absolute sive *sub ratione existentiae*, ut dictum est supra; sed modus intelligendi activus dicit proprietatem *intellectus*, quae est ratio *intelligendi* sive *concipiendi*; modus significandi activus dicit proprietatem vocis, quae est ratio consignificandi. Sed alia est proprietas rei extra animam et alia intellectus et alia vocis; ita alia est ratio essendi, alia intelligendi alia consignificandi; ergo modus essendi et modus intelligendi et modus significandi activus differunt in utroque. l. c. 3b sq.

25. Sciendum, quod modus intelligendi activus et modus intelligendi passivus differunt *materialiter* et conveniunt *formaliter*. Nam modus intelligendi passivus dicit rei proprietatem sub ratione intelligendi passiva; sed modus intelligendi activus dicit proprietatem intellectus, quae est ratio intelligendi activa; sed eadem est ratio intelligendi, per quam intellectus proprietatem rei intelligit active et per quam rei proprietas intelligitur passive, ergo proprietates sunt diversae et ratio est eadem, ergo materialiter differunt et formaliter sunt idem. Item sciendum, quod modus significandi activus et passivus differunt materialiter et sunt idem formaliter. l. c. cap. IV, 4a.

formaliter identical with it. Insofar as the meaning endowing act is in turn determined by the material, that is, by objectivity, we can say that the act is founded in objectivity. Considered as a psychic reality, the act possesses its efficient cause in the activity of understanding. The act is, as it were, preserved [aufgehoben] in the "constructio," that is, the context of meaning, as its effect (the way an activity is preserved in its achievement).[26]

The forms of meaning (modi significandi) are thus read off from the guiding thread of givenness (modus essendi), which for its part is only given insofar as it is cognized (in the modus intelligendi). {321/263}

Earlier, we could only distinguish preliminarily between the word and its meaning: the inherence of the two phenomena in distinct domains could only be presented quite generally.

But the investigation has now been carried out sufficiently far that the structure of the *expression as such* (*dictio*) can be surveyed in its layers.

As a sensorily perceptible object [Objekt], the word in itself does not have any relationship to objects of cognition. Rather, it first attains this through *meaning*: vox non proportionatur ipsi rei *nisi per rationem significandi.*[27] "The expressivity of an utterance does not consist in mere words, but in expressive acts; the former formulate the correlated acts, which are to be expressed by them, in a new medium; they generate the intellectual expression, whose universal nature constitutes the meaning of the relevant utterance."[28]

The ratio significandi, the "semantic essence [bedeutungsmäßige Wesen]" (Husserl) of the word, however, is founded on the modus intelligendi, through which the relationship to the object is first produced. "The statements 'the cognition of objects' and 'the fulfillment of the meaning-intention' express the same situation, albeit from different standpoints."[29]

---

26. Notandum, quod modus sig. passivus materialiter est in re, ut in subjecto, quia materialiter est proprietas rei; rei autem proprietas est in eo, cuius est ut in subjecto. Formaliter autem est in eo subjecto, in quo est modus significandi activus, quia formaliter a modo significandi non discrepat.

Modus autem significandi activus, cum sit proprietas vocis significativae, materialiter est in voce significativa ut in subjecto, in proprietate autem rei sicut causatum in causa efficienti radicali et remota; et in intellectu sicut causatum in causa efficiente proxima; et in constructione ut causa efficiens in suo effectu proprio. l. c. cap. V, 4.

27. Quaest. sup. elench. qu. XI, 15a.

Quamlibet essentiam contingit intelligere sub ratione propria et etiam significare, *et tali modo intelligendi correspondet modus significandi abstractus.* Quaest. in praed. qu. VIII, 457b.

28. Edmund Husserl, *Logische Untersuchungen* (Halle: Max Niemeyer, 1901), 2:481, 489.

29. Husserl, *Logische Untersuchungen,* 505. "The red object is cognized as red and called red on the basis of this cognition" (500).

Depending on the nature of the intentional attitude, the meaning undergoes a specific formation through this relationship of the meaning to the objective. Scotus explicitly remarks that it is quite possible that *different* meaning-intentions arise from *one* and *the same* objective givenness, {322/264} that is, that [different] forms of meaning can be founded on it: *non est inconveniens ab eadem rei proprietate modos significandi diversos non oppositos oriri.*[30] "Where an expression's meaning-intention is fulfilled by divergent, conceptually disparate intuitions, the sharp difference in the direction of fulfilment shows up the cleavage of meaning-intentions."[31]

The subject that lives in meaningful speech and surrenders itself to objects through it is not immediately conscious of the form of meaning. The formal content of meanings can be highlighted only in reflection. This formal content presents itself in the modi significandi. These categories of meaning constitute the individual "parts of speech" (partes orationis).* However, with the characterization "pars orationis," we must not think of the *aural form* of speech—the word forms, but rather, of the *nonsensory* logical categories of meaning, for Duns Scotus explicitly characterizes them as such: *omnis pars orationes est ens secundum animam.*[32]

The categories of meaning are the formative ideas [Gestaltideen] of the possible concrete meanings. These formative ideas determine their reciprocal relationships because of the content proper to them. There is an immanent lawfulness in the forms of meaning that a priori regulates the possible contexts of meaning. Duns Scotus formulates this as follows: [modi significandi] sunt *principium efficiens intrinsecum constructionis.*[33]

The potential form in which concrete meaning complexes can be arranged lies in the modi significandi. Herewith we have characterized the essential function of the modi significandi within the domain of meaning. In his uniquely nuanced manner, Lotze illustrates this function with a fitting image on the first page of his

---

30. De mod. sig. cap. XXXVI, 32a.

31. Edmund Husserl, *Logical Investigations*, trans. J. N. Findlay (London: Routledge, 2001), 1:212; Heidegger cites Husserl, *Logische Untersuchungen*, 71f.

* Heidegger translates *partes orationis* as *Redeteile*, although he recognizes its limitations. Bursill-Hall notes in his translation of *Grammatica speculativa*, "The traditional 'part of speech' is not satisfactory, since the medieval grammarian excluded phonetics from his province and the actual expression of the concepts as formulated by the mind was accidental to grammatical theory.... 'Word-class' is almost sufficient... 'minimal sentence bit' ... is more exact but clumsy" (23). We maintain the literal "parts of speech" for Heidegger's *Redeteile*.

32. De mod. sig. cap. XXI, 18a.

33. l. c. cap. XLV, 38a; see below, p. 102, n. 35.

Logic. {323/265} If I were to reproduce his thoughts in paraphrase, I would at most do them injustice. They therefore follow in Lotze's own formulation:

> It is in relations within a manifold that the operations of thought usually show themselves to us, and we might therefore expect to have to look for the most original of its acts in some simplest form of connection between two ideas. A slight reflection, however, suggests to us to go a step further back. It is easy to make a heap out of nothing but round stones, if it is indifferent how they lie; but if a structure of regular shape is to be built, the building-stones must be already so formed that their surfaces will fit firmly together. We must expect the same in the case before us. As mere internal movements, the states which follow external irritants may exist side by side in us without further preparation, and act upon each other as the general laws of our psychical life allow or enjoin. But if they are to admit of combination in the definite form of a *thought, they each require some previous shaping* [Heidegger's emphasis] to make them into logical building-stones and to convert them from *impressions* into *ideas.* Nothing is really more familiar to us than this first operation of thought; the only reason why we usually overlook it is that *in the language which we inherit it is already carried out* [Heidegger's emphasis], and it seems therefore to belong to the self-evident presuppositions of thought, not to its own specific work.[34]

The modi significandi must be understood *teleologically,* that is, their operation must be understood proceeding from the concept of the *constructio* at which they aim as its principles.

It is not clear without further ado *what* kind of principles {324/266} the modi significandi are with regard to the constructio. For we can distinguish *four* kinds of principles in this respect: principium materiale, formale, efficiens, and finale.

The *constructibilia,* that is, the individual meanings as *elements* ("building-stones" [Lotze]) of a *context of meaning* are the *material principle.* They represent the *material* out of which the meaning complex is built up. Because it results from the dependence of one element on another, a construction always has two and only two elements: the dependent and the determining element. In the sentence "Homo albus currit bene," several relationships of dependence can be identified: the relationship of the adjectivum to the substantivum, that of the verbum to the

---

34. Lotze, *Logic,* 11 (trans. modified); Heidegger cites *Logik,* 14. See also Hermann Lotze, *Microcosmus: An Essay concerning Man and His Relation to the World,* trans. Elizabeth Hamilton and E. E. Constance Jones, 3rd ed. (Edinburg: T. & T. Clarke, 1888), 613ff.; Heidegger cites *Mikrokosmos: Ideen zur Naturgeschichte und Geschichte der Menschheit,* 5th ed. (Leipzig: Felix Meiner, 1905), 2:240ff.

subject, and that of the adverbium to the verbum. Correspondingly, the sentence also contains several "constructions."[35]

The *union* of the components is the *formal principle* of the meaning complex. The form's function is to give an object its being. This function of forming is accomplished in the contructio by the "unio" of the elements.[36] {325/267}

Regarding the *principium efficiens constructionis*, we must discern the *immanent* principle, which determines the nature of the dependence and, correspondingly, the *potential connections* of the meanings. The categories of meaning, the modi significandi, are responsible for this function. They, as it were, prepare the constructio in that they prestructure the *direction* of the respective complex a priori; they bring the "building stones" into forms. Duns Scotus assigns the function of the principium intrinsecum to them because they remain, as it were, within—or better, between—the meanings as their forms (quasi inter constructibilia manentes).

The activity of understanding is the *principium extrinsecum* of the constructio. It achieves the union of the components in thought and speech *in the present*, for in themselves the meanings are not presently connected; they only possess specific possibilities of connection because of the categories of meaning.[37]

---

35. Primo earum principia in generali videamus. Sunt autem quattuor principia essentialia *construendi* sermonem congrue et perfecte scilicet: *materiale, formale, efficiens et finale*. Principium materiale construendi sunt constructibilia; quia sicut se habet subjectum ad accidens, sic se habent constructibilia ad constructionem; sed subjectum est materia accidentis, nam accidens non habet materia *ex qua* sed *in qua*; ergo constructibilia sunt *materia* constructionis. Et unius constructionis non sunt plura vel pauciora duobus, quia, ut patebit, constructio causatur *ex dependentia unius constructibilis ad alterum*; sed una dependentia non est nisi duorum, scil. dependentis et determinantis; ergo unius constructionis non sunt nisi duo constructibilia principalia, scil. *dependens* et *terminans*. Et ex hoc patet error dicentium hanc constructionem esse *unam*: "homo albus currit bene." Nam hic sunt diversa dependentia: una, qua Adjectivum dependet ad Substantivum, alia, qua Verbum dependet ad suppositum, tertia, qua determinans dependet ad determinabile; ergo non erit hic una constructio. De mod. sig. cap. XLV, 38a.

36. Principium *formale* constructionis est *unio* constructibilium; hoc enim est forma rei, per quod res habet esse. Sed constructio habet esse per constructibilium unionem; ergo constructibilium unio est forma constructionis. l. c. 38b.

37. Principum *efficiens* constructionis duplex, scil.: *extrinsecum* et *intrinsecum*. Intrinsecum sunt modi significandi respectivi, ratione quorum vel unum constructibile est ad alterum dependens vel alterius dependentiam determinans; a quibus modis sig. respectivis abstrahuntur duo modi sig. generales: modus dependendi in uno constructibili et modus dependentiam terminans in altero constructibili. Et hi modi sig. dicuntur *efficere* constructionem pro tanto quia praeparant et disponunt constructibilia ad actualem unionem, quae fit per intellectum ...

The *expression* of what is given in consciousness, which qua object of cognition is categorially determined, that is, represents a totality of relationships, is the *final principle* of the constructio.[38]

We can now define the constructio in sum as: *Constructio est constructibilium unio ex modis significandi et ab* {326/268} *intellectu causata ad exprimendum mentis conceptum compositum finaliter adinventa.*[39]

Herewith, we have brought the important function of the modi significandi, which is all that matters here, to clarity by contrasting it with the remaining principles of construction. The modi significandi are, as it were, the *nerve center* of the meaning complex: they prescribe the arrangement of this complex and constitute a domain with its own lawfulness.

The *combination of meanings as elements* is a part of construction. The *constructio debita* or the *congruitas* results from the lawful context of the categories of meaning to which individual meanings are subject. It is not based on the special factual [sachlichen] content of the individual meanings that are to be combined just now. Rather, it is grounded in the factually "earlier" *forms* of meaning. We must therefore understand congruitas as a constructio that is a priori prescribed by the modi significandi. In normative terms, it is the rule for special concrete connections of meaning.[40]

In the present, Husserl has restored the "idea of a pure grammar" to its dignity and shown that there exist a priori laws of meaning independent of the objective validity of meanings. The laws of complex meanings "set forth the requirements of a merely *significant unity*, i.e. the *a priori* patterns in which meanings belonging to different semantic categories can be united to form one meaning, instead of producing chaotic nonsense. Modern grammar thinks it should build exclusively on psychology and other empirical {327/269} sciences. As against this, we see that

---

Sed principium efficiens *extrinsecum* est intellectus qui constructibilia per modos sig. disposita et praeparata *actu unit* in constructione et sermone. Constructibilia enim, qualitercumque summe disponantur ad unionem per suos modos sig.; numquam tamen unum constructibile actu se altero unit, sed hoc *fit per intellectum*, ut dictum est. Et dicitur intellectus principium extrinsecum, quasi *extra* constructibilia manens. l. c. 38b.

38. Principium *finale* est expressio mentis conceptus compositi. l. c. 38b.

39. l. c. cap. XLVI, 39a.

40. Sicut constructio requirit constructibilium unionem absolute, sic *congruitas* reequirit constructibilium unionem, non quamcumque sed *debitam*. Et haec debita unio potest contingere dupliciter: uno modo *ex convenientia* significatorum specialium, et per oppositum unio *indebita* ex repugnantia ipsorum. Alio modo potest contingere *ex conformitate modorum sig.* et per oppositum indebita ex indebita modorum sig. discrepantia. l. c. cap. LIII, 47a.

the *old idea* [Heidegger's emphasis] of a *universal*, or even of an *a priori grammar*, has unquestionably acquired a foundation and a definite sphere of validity, from our pointing out that there are *a priori* laws which determine the possible forms of meaning."[41]

Thereafter, in his *Ideas for a Pure Phenomenology and Phenomenological Philosophy*, Husserl assigned the domain of meaning its place within the totality of phenomenological tasks, thereby simultaneously casting a new light on the theoretical significance of "a priori grammar."[42]

Before we definitively establish the concept of a doctrine of meaning and delimit it vis-à-vis logic, we must discuss yet another potential approach to the domain of meaning.

Any deeper consideration of meanings, of their relationship to words as well as to the objects intentionally signified in them, encounters the phenomena of *univocation, equivocation*, and *analogy*. Does their treatment belong, strictly speaking, in the doctrine of meaning, that is, do these functional modes stand in an *essential* relationship to the modi significandi?

Duns Scotus notes that univocation, equivocation, and analogy are distinguished from each other *less* in terms of their meaning content (significatio), that is, according to content and form, than in terms of the "word" (vox). {328/270}

Duns Scotus makes a distinction regarding univocation that clarifies where its full essence becomes visible: univocationem *completam* dico, quando est similitudo in forma et in modo essendi formae, *diminutam*, quando est similitudo in forma, licet habeat alium modum essendi, quomodo domus extra est a domo *in mente*.[43] We encounter absolute univocation when meanings coincide with respect to their content and their act quality. If I intend "house" as a real existent object [Objekt] and "house" as a meaning (representation)—that is, if in one case the act of meaning is a *positing* act that intends the meaning content as really existing but in the other case the act is *without positing* and merely encompasses the meaning content as such without having it further at its disposal, then the expression "house" was not used strictly univocally in the two cases.

---

41. Husserl, *Logical Investigations* II, 49. See Husserl, *Logical Investigations*, IV Investigation: The distinction between independent and nonindependent meanings and the idea of pure grammar, 50–76; Heidegger cites Husserl, *Logische Untersuchungen*, 2nd ed., vol. 2, part I, 295, 294–342.

42. See esp. Husserl, *Ideas I*, §118ff., 235ff. [*Husserliana* III, 291ff.]—Already on 25n10 [*Husserliana* III, 30n4] Husserl announces further special contributions to a pure grammar; Heidegger cites *Ideen*, §118ff., 245ff., and the note on 25.

43. Op. Ox. Prol. qu. IV, 291a, n. 45.

Thus, in expressions that are univocal in the strict sense, *the word as the linguistic form*, the *meaning* in terms of form and content, and the *mode of intending* the meaning content (the character of positing) remain in an *identity*. Consequently, to clarify the essence, we must refer not only to the meaning content but also to the linguistic expression and to the object that fulfills the meaning. Only where these moments are given does it make sense to speak of univocation or of one of the other functional modes. These moments, however, are given only in the vital use of words. Scotus expresses this by saying: Really, univocation is not something that *primarily* affects the meaning but the meaning, the concept, *insofar* as it stands in *predicative* application; for it is only in the *assertion* through which the meaning is applied to the object that the *direction of fulfillment* genuinely *attains its validity*.[44] Ultimately, univocatio is nothing other than *the identical positing {329/271} of the identical meaning that applies to the one identical word (linguistic form)*. The direction of fulfillment is identical insofar as the objects that fulfill it present themselves as identical in terms of their *What*.

Thus, the characteristic feature of univocation is *identity* (una ratio), specifically identity as it endures in the individual moments that essentially belong to the use of univocal expressions.[45]

A conceptual clarification of *equivocation* will further elucidate what we just said.

In aequivoco nullus est idem sed *sola vox*.[46] Thus, *in the case of equivocation, only the first* of the moments we listed—linguistic form, meaning, and direction of fulfillment—*endures*. Insofar as by "expression" we do not mean the linguistic form independent of the meaning content but rather the *unity* of word and meaning, we cannot, strictly speaking, say of an equivocal expression that it is *an* expression; but just as little do we mean multiple expressions. By contrast, it can quite correctly be called a *manifold* expression, [in that it is] manifold with respect to the different acts of meaning—and the different directions of fulfillment that are given thereby—applying to the identical verbal form. Consequently, *identity* is also found in *one* respect in the equivocally used expression, namely, identity of the *word*. However, what distinguishes the equivocal expression radically from univocal expressions is the manifold of acts of meaning and

---

44. Univocum et denominativum primo sunt differentiae *praedicati*, quod secundum se inest conceptui, non *primo voci significanti*. See sup. praed. qu. VI, 452b sqq.

45. Univocum apud logicum dicitur omne illud, quod per *unam rationem* devenit apud intellectum secundum quam dicitur de multis. Sup. praed. qu. VII. 455a, b.

46. l. c. qu. IV, 443a.

directions of fulfillment:[47] *aequivocum cum diversis actibus significandi significat multa.*[48] {330/272}

Equivocal expressions refer to many and varied objects. They can hence also be predicated of them. We might therefore be tempted to place them in a continuum with the *universalia.* Only, we must keep in mind an *essential* difference: the objective material that fulfills the different acts of meaning that are essentially proper to every equivocal expression as such does not manifest a *common aspect,* a substantial commonality that we could hold on to in a "universal concept"—inter significata termini aequivoci *nulla est habitudo.*[49] By contrast, every universal is characterized by the *identity of the aspect* in respect of which it is predicated of individual objects.[50] Because equivocal expressions lack this universal aspect common to many individual objects, it is also impossible to specify it by adding moments of meaning; for every species is essentially species, [in that it is] the determination of a "universal" meaning content.[51] {331/273}

---

47. Nomen aequivocum nec debet dici simpliciter unum nomen nec plura nomina sed nomen *multiplex* quasi ab uno multiplicans. Hoc est manifestum: nam nomen dicitur tale eo quod sic per intellectum imponitur, unde intellectus est principium nominum, cum sit imponens ad placitum: nomen ergo est quoddam artificiale, sed in artificialibus tota substantia est ipsa materia . . . ipsa vox est substantia et materia nominis; manente ergo unitate vocis non dicetur illud nomen plura nomina, sed in termino aequivoco vox est una. . . . Nec simpliciter debet dici unum nomen, *nam ibi sunt plures rationes significandi.* Relinquitur ergo dicendum, quod sit nomen multiplex. . . . Si autem pluribus rebus imponatur una vox, illa dicetur nomen multiplex. Sup. elench. qu. VIII, 10b.

48. Op. I, perih. qu. II, 443a.

49. Sup. elench. qu. X, 13b.

50. Licet vox aequivoca in eo quod secundum aliud et aliud respicit aliud et aliud significatum *conveniat cum universali,* quod secundum aliud et aliud respicit sua supposita—in alio tamen est differentia, nam in termino aequivoco non contingit considerare *aliquam rationem communem,* in qua significata conveniant praeter *solam vocem;* sed in toto universale contingit considerare aliquam rationem in qua supposita univocantur et ideo non est simile. In alio etiam est differentia, nam omnis ratio significandi *actu* importatur per terminum aequivocum; sed nullum suppositum importatur actu per terminum communem, ideo non est simile. Sup. elench. qu. X, 12b.

51. Intelligendum est, quod terminus aequivocus proprie loquendo *non* potest contrahi per immediate sibi adjunctum nec per mediate. *Nam contractio est determinatio alicuius communis,* ita quod aggregatum ex contrahente et contracto necesse est repraesentare intellectum determinatiorem, quam sit intellectus ipsius contracti de se. Sed in termino aequivoco non est intellectus communis omnibus significatis, quia cum aequivocata per terminum aequivocum significentur *sub propriis rationibus, nihil est eis commune praeter solam vocem,* quae contrahi non potest, cum sit singularis. Sup. elench. qu. XIII, 17 a sq.

We can make the essence of equivocal expressions clearer still by settling the question of whether the combination of such an expression with a "signum universale," for example, "omnis" (every one), specifies and distinguishes all individual objects to which the expression can apply. One could say every distinction and specification must be undertaken according to a uniform aspect to which all the objects to be specified are subject. However, in an equivocal expression, we cannot discover a semantic [bedeutungsmäßig] "universal." What is common to the individual meanings is solely the word form, and this is a singular reality. Consequently, a "distributio" appears impossible among the expressions under discussion. A more precise reflection, however, convinces us of the possibility [of such a distributio], as Duns Scotus demonstrates through an astute argument.

We can use an equivocal expression with a determinate meaning "as though" no other meaning pertained to it that did not actually apply to it. Likewise, the signum universale can make a meaning distributively relatable with *one* distributive act of meaning and another meaning with *another* distributive act of meaning.

By "distribution" I mean the apprehension of a universal and its comprehension and positing as an object affecting the individual objects subsumed under it, each of which this object itself is. But as we already emphasized several times, no such common element exists in equivocal expressions that would permit such distribution. Hence, in the expressions listed, distribution inheres in the meaning intended *at the time,* as though it would not touch on any other, but it also *simultaneously* inheres in every other indifferent meaning that accrues to the expression {332/274} as such, *albeit it does so only through a different act of distribution in each case.* The reason for this is as follows: the signum universale posited in one instance relates to one meaning alone; hence, distributive positing constitutes an act. However, we must note that the extent of the function of dependent forms of meaning such as the signum universale is limited by the independent meanings associated with them. If, as is the case with equivocal expressions, multiple acts of meaning apply to them and these acts are without relation among themselves, the result is an equal number of unrelated acts of distribution.

Consequently, distribution is also possible in equivocal expressions, albeit only in *multiple* acts. This once again illuminates the essence of these expressions: the manifold nature of meanings or acts of meaning, which have no relationship among themselves, that are attached to an identical verbal form.[52]

---

52. Dicendum quod signum universale [omnis] adveniens termino aequivoco potest distribuere ipsum pro omnibus suppositis cuiuslibet significati. Sed intelligendum est, quod sicut terminus aequivocus significat unum significatum *ac si aliud non significaret,* et unum repraesentat respectu praedicati *ac si aliud non repraesentaret,* hoc est sub nulla habitudine, sic etiam signum universale distribuit unum significatum ac si aliud

We already dealt more thoroughly with *analogy*, the third mode {333/275} of using expressions belonging here, in another context.[53] We shall only touch on it again here to the extent that the distinction between univocation and equivocation thereby becomes clearer.

In univocation, the identity of the linguistic expression, the meaning, and the direction of fulfillment reigns. By contrast, the identity of the meaning and of the direction of fulfillment decreases in equivocal expressions, such that only the identity of the word remains. Thus, with regard to the meaning content of these expressions, what reigns is the absolute *difference* of the potential acts.

Analogy stands, as it were, "between" univocation and equivocation. It is not entirely the one, nor does it coincide with the other. What reigns is *neither thoroughgoing identity nor complete difference*, but rather a peculiar intertwining of both: identity in difference and difference in identity. This can also be said of equivocal expressions when one focuses on the identity of the word. But in the case of analogy, it is not just this *external* identity of the word form; rather, it simultaneously applies to the content of meaning. Analogy thereby approaches univocation. Insofar as analogous expressions have several *different* meanings, they overlap with equivocal [expressions]. However, the difference [in meanings] is not radical, [for] the meanings are not unrelated but rather are subject to a common identical universal meaning. What differs in analogous expressions is the *direction of fulfillment*, insofar as it aims at different domains of reality and differentiates the universal meaning content of the expression out of these domains. Earlier, we cited the word "principle" as an example of an analogous expression: applied to logical relationships, it means "reason," whereas in the domain of natural reality, it means "cause." Similarly, as a medical term, "cut" {334/276} means

---

non distribueret, hoc est, unum distribuit sub uno actu distribuendi et aliud sub alio. Et huius ratio est: nam distributio est acceptio alicuius communis pro quodlibet eius supposito, quorum quodlibet est ipsum; nunc autem in termino aequivoco non est aliquod commune, super quod possit cadere distributio, quia nihil est ibi commune nisi sola vox. Et ideo distributio cadit super uno significato *ac si super aliud non caderet*, et super quodlibet, sed hoc est alio actu distribuendi et alio ...

Signum universale possit distribuere terminum aequivocum pro omnibus suis significatis, ... sed non *unico actu*. Contra hoc potest argui sic: Signi semel positi est unum significatum et unus modus signifcandi ergo et unus actus distribuendi. Dicendum quod syncategoremata finitatem suae significationis trahunt ex adjunctis, cum ergo hic sint actu plura significata, quorum nullum ad aliud habet habitudinem, ut dictum est, *diversi hic erunt actus* distribuendi, quorum nullus ad alium habet habitudinem ... patet quod causa apparentiae in aequivocatione est *unitas actualis vocis incomplexae* secundum materiam et formam. Sup. elench. qu. XIV, 19.

53. See part I, chapter 1, p. 47ff.

something other than "cut" in the Dedekindian theory of irrational numbers. And yet both meanings have something in common: an identical universal meaning as a point of reference.

We can mathematically symbolize the different functional modes of expressions and say: The identity of univocation can be represented as *a line*, the complete difference of the acts of meaning in equivocal expressions can be represented as divergent lines crossing each other in space, and the identity in difference in analogous expressions can be represented as a bundle of rays converging on a point.

The *reflexive* categories' dominant role in the functional modes of the expressions suggests that we should understand them in general in terms of the universal essence of the relevant categories.

Lotze's and Windelband's investigations have, to be sure, significantly advanced the clear conceptual definition of their essence, the precise demarcation of reflexive categories vis-à-vis the constitutive categories, and the secure measurement of their domain of validity, but it is Lask who first decisively completed these tasks.[54]

Lask defines the reflexive categories in contrast to the constitutive categories as "created by subjectivity." This ought not be taken to mean that their application and validity is perfectly arbitrary. Rather, like the constitutive categories, they are determined in this respect by the material, albeit not by specific material but by content [Gehalt] that has faded to the mere fact of being content [Inhaltlichkeit]. Corresponding to this "constructivity" of the reflexive categories, on the side of the functional modes is the modes' *origin from the use* of expressions in living thought and cognition. The modes are likewise products of subjectivity in a certain sense, but they are nonetheless objectively secured by the objective constancy of the linguistic expression, the meanings, {335/277} and the directions of fulfillment. Further, they also possess the *general* character that Lask reserves for the reflexive categories insofar as their application is not determined by peculiar contents and forms of meaning.

We can now also clarify the relationship of these functional modes to the modi significandi. The latter are held to be objective forms of meaning that are determined by the material. However, the forms of meaning are not affected at all in the functional modes we mentioned; they remain identically the same in the manifold modifications that reveal themselves in the functional modes

---

54. Lotze, *Logic*, Book III, chapter 4; Heidegger cites *Logik*, Book III, chapter 4. See also Windelband, "Vom System der Kategorien," 41ff.; Emil Lask, *Die Logik der Philosophie und die Kategorienlehre: eine Studie über den Herrschaftsbereich der logischen Form* (Tübingen: Mohr Siebeck, 1911), 148ff.

of expressions. For, regardless of how far apart the individual meanings of an equivocal expression lie, the nominal form of meaning remains the nominal form of meaning. The same thing applies to analogy. Thus, univocation, equivocation, and analogy do not affect the meaning as meaning in the mode of the forms of meaning. Rather, they are potential relationships established by subjectivity within the totality of relations—linguistic form, linguistic content, and the object that fulfills them—that constitutes the constancy of expressions that are used predicatively. What is revealed in them is a peculiar *lability* of meaning and of its fulfillment in contrast to the singular reality of the word—a lability that is given with living speech and assertion. Duns Scotus saw the difference of the functional modes we discussed vis-à-vis the modi significandi insofar as he understood them relative to the expression as such rather than to a pure and isolated meaning.[55]

Within the domain of meaning, the modi significandi constitute a specific *order*.[56] But this a priori structured combination of meanings into complexes of meaning does not yet constitute what we call valid *sense*. {336/278} The truth value proper to the *sense of judgment* is not yet realized in the complexes of meaning as such as structured by the modi significandi. But insofar as they, as it were, establish the valid sense of judgment, which can be expressed in propositions, in its basic scaffolding, they also realize a value within the domain of meaning—one that, along with Lotze, we can call "syntactic value."[57]

Thus, the functional sense of the modi significandi must be understood from out of the syntactic value, whereas that of the modus intelligendi must be understood from out of the truth value. The modi significandi first constitute the object [Objekt] that is then evaluated with respect to the truth value. The order that the modi significandi prescribe is the precondition for the complex of meaning to enter into the context of valid sense. The order of the complex of meaning also remains in the domain of valid sense, albeit not as an independent formation but only as a component of a higher sense. The categories of meaning attain greater importance, an epistemological dignity, through this relation to the sense of the judgment. The doctrine of meaning thereby enters into the closest relationship to logic. Indeed, it is nothing other than a *subfield* of the latter provided we understand logic as the *theory of theoretical sense*, which contains within itself the doctrine of the components of sense (*doctrine of meaning*), the doctrine of the structure of sense (*doctrine of judgment*), and the doctrine of structural differentiations and their systematic forms (*doctrine of science*).

---

55. See part I, chapter 3, "Linguistic Form and Linguistic Content," p. 74 ff.

56. Modi significandi respectivi sunt principia *ordinandi* dictionem cum alia ... significata et modi significandi sunt *essentialia* dictioni. See sup. elench. qu. XVII, 27a, 30b.

57. Lotze, *Microcosmus*, 614; Heidegger cites Lotze, *Mikrokosmos* II, 239.

By belonging together with logic, the doctrine of meaning participates in the specific nature of logical inquiry. That is to say, the doctrine of meaning from the beginning excludes every preoccupation with *psychological* problems. The concept we have established here is accordingly much narrower than the one that has been used of late to summarize the tasks of the doctrine of meaning.[58] {337/279}

A doctrine of meaning in the sense in which it occurs in the treatise *De modis significandi** must therefore exclude problems that are concerned with *facts* and *processes* (although they are not insignificant in themselves), or that explicate questions about the *practicality* of signs, or those that answer questions about the difficulty or ease of understanding meanings. It is as little concerned with psychic dispositions that enable the apprehension or understanding of meanings, however important they may be as factual conditions of actual understanding. Neither is the logical doctrine of meaning interested in how meanings *emerge* or in the physiological and psychological chain of causes that runs from a sign to its meaning. Likewise, investigations into the historical development of meanings and into the transformation in meaning [over time] are excluded from its domain of problems. The doctrine of meaning considers only *meaning in itself* and its structure. Unless we recognize this fundamental truth, the treatment of psychological problems of meaning will forever remain uncertain.

The demand for a logical doctrine of meaning that, following Duns Scotus's treatise, we have raised here appears to dignify yet again all those errors of which "the logical grammars have been accused and continue to be accused. The simple truth that linguistic thought is a thing unto itself, something independent and, above all, essentially other than logical thought—this simple truth is constantly misunderstood. Correspondingly, the amorphous creation that is logical grammar has failed its calling, it has squandered its right to existence."[59] {338/280}

---

58. See Eduard Martinak, *Psychologische Untersuchungen zur Bedeutungslehre* (Leipzig: J. A. Barth, 1901).

   * That is, the alternate title of *Grammatica speculativa*. See the translators' preface for clarification.

59. Karl Voßler, "Grammatik und Sprachgeschichte oder das Verhältnis von 'richtig' und 'wahr' in der Sprachwissenschaft," *Logos: Internationale Zeitschrift für Philosophie der Kultur* 1 (1910): 86.

   "But, in and for itself, all speaking is *alogical.*" "Logic first begins either *within* language or by its means, but not before it or without it." Karl Voßler, *Positivismus und Idealismus in der Sprachwissenschaft: eine sprach-philosophische Untersuchung* (Heidelberg: C. Winter, 1904), 25 and 26.

   At the end of his treatise "Das System der Grammatik," *Logos: Internationale Zeitschrift für Philosophie der Kultur* 4 (1913): 203ff., in which he establishes "a language that is free of all more intellectual activity and all spiritual life" as the "essential object of grammar," this author writes, "Perhaps today once again philosophers of language

If the concept "logical grammar" is supposed to mean that grammar must be derived from logic, the concept contains something impossible. Then again, if someone were to point out that logically untrue judgments can be expressed grammatically quite correctly and conclude from this that grammar is consequently not logical, he understands something completely different by the logical or alogical character of language than what the expression "logical" means in the logical doctrine of meaning. "Logical" and "logical" are not the same in both cases.

The demand for a logic of grammar need not presuppose the theoretical opinion that the grammatical use of language must be derivable from logical laws. The question of how language came to be and to which creative factors it owes its existence is not a problem of logic. Regardless of how one regards the essence, task, and structure of linguistics, one must grant that linguistic constructs have meanings. Philosophical reflection begins here, in order to reductively return to the categorial moments and to evaluate them from the perspective of the system of the doctrine of categories. However, we may not reinterpret these logical conditions of language—more precisely, of meanings—as *factual* [*sachlichen*] *causes* of the verbal development of language, and least of all as the *sole* causes. Qua *spirit*, the spirit of language, the creative factor of linguistic development, possesses a definite *logical* structure in the sense we discussed. The logic of language seeks to highlight this and only *this*.

Consequently, the doctrine of meaning does not *explain* language in terms of {339/281} its real existence. Rather, it merely *understands* it from its rational side, that is, the side of its content.

Werner calls Scotus's treatise the "central achievement of the Scholastic Middle Ages in the area of the logic of language, that is, of the attempt to unify grammar and logic."[60] [But] Scotus does not seek to "integrate grammar into logic"; rather, he seeks to understand the logical structure of meanings. Werner overlooks the peculiarity of the domain of meaning as the genuinely "expressive layer."

Werner does not wish to commit himself to a "judgment about the theoretical [sachlichen] value" of the treatise, but he nonetheless remarks that "a logic of language composed from the standpoint of medieval thought cannot claim to be a philosophy of language in the contemporary sense of the term." In his

exist, who demand an independent, general, pure, speculative, and universal grammar, a grammar of grammars[!]. These Neo-Platonists and Neo-Scholastics will learn as much from my observations as I have from theirs" ("Das System der Grammatik," 223).

What we said in the text should have reinforced the possibility and necessity of *both* "standpoints."

60. Werner, "Die Sprachlogik des Duns Scotus," 549.

opinion, a philosophy of language must pay attention to the "genetic development of language."[61]

Psychological and historical investigations into language, however, do *not* belong in a philosophy of language. The latter must seek its problems in a completely new dimension. It must develop the ultimate *theoretical* foundations that underlie language. Unless we have a clear conceptual grasp of "meaning as such," of "the object intended in the meaning," of "the category of meaning," and of "the relationship of the forms of meaning," it is impossible for the inquiry into language to proceed securely, apart from the fact that by solving these problems, the doctrine of meaning treats of a fundamental area of logic.

Incidentally, Werner's judgment about Scotus's "logic of language" shows just how dependent value judgments in the history of philosophy are on one's own systematic standpoint. {340/282} If the latter cannot be theoretically defended, then the historical value judgment must likewise undergo revision.

We shall see how correct Duns Scotus was with the individual statements of his treatise in the following chapter on his doctrine of the forms of meanings.

---

61. Werner, "Die Sprachlogik des Duns Scotus," 550.

THE DOCTRINE OF THE FORMS OF MEANINGS

THE TASK OF INVESTIGATING THE presentation and characteristics of the individual meaning functions necessarily follows on the general clarification of the sense of meaning and meaning function in general. The basic concepts and leading perspectives necessary to achieve this *special* task should have received a sufficient clarification and determination in the previous chapter that we can now choose a manner of presentation that, though not ideal, is without the danger of misleading equivocations: We mean the *simultaneous* consideration of the objective and subjective perspectives in the explication of the doctrine of meaning. Along with the forms of meaning, we shall also present the functional sense, the function of the meaning endowing acts, so that the correlation that exists between the two can be kept constantly in mind. Such a *mixed* method, as it were, best corresponds to the way Duns Scotus conducts the special portion of his doctrine of meaning. The foregoing discussion should put to rest the danger of a psychologistic confusion of the sphere of objective meaning content with the sphere of empirically recordable psychic facts.

Investigations such as the following can easily give {341/283} the impression of a haphazard concatenation of randomly chosen phenomena. Logical and aesthetic conscience demands *order*. The *system* should fulfill this wish, but frequently we are dissatisfied with a rudimentary classification and strive further to derive individual phenomena from an ur-phenomenon. This quite often and easily results in the objects to be treated "suffering violence" while the content of the corresponding concepts is obscured.

The following presentation should clarify the extent to which Duns Scotus avoids shipwreck on an a priori system that endangers sense and seeks an order of the forms of meaning that is grounded in and suggested by the "things."

Objects are expressed by meanings and, in turn, determine the meanings. The distinction between independent and dependent objects is basic in the domain of the objective as such, to which meanings belong as well. Accordingly, meaning endowing acts can be divided into two main groups: those whose activity manifests as the constitution of an *independent* meaning, and those whose content presents itself as a *dependent* form in need of support. Duns Scotus places this fundamental division of the modi significandi at the head of his more specialized investigation. Regarding their genus and species, the modus significandi *essentialis* constitutes the basic forms of meanings, namely, the parts of speech qua essences that exist in an unqualified sense. All content of meaning shaped by the form of the modus essentialis needs no further formal determination to exist. Applied to the act, this means that to be what it is, an act does not require a supporting, more fundamental act of meaning. By contrast, *by its very nature* the modus significandi *accidentalis supervenes* on the modus essentialis (advenit); it is built on the latter. The formal determination that it confers [the object] {342/284} cannot exist unless it exists with an independent "essential" determination. Inherently, it cannot exist purely and simply for itself. This is an objective impossibility that we must accept and not one that, say, might be due to our psychic constitution.[1]

In empirical reality, we encounter this distinction between independent and dependent objects, which is mirrored in the modus significandi, as the distinction between a thing and a property. The distinction between an *ens simpliciter* and an *ens secundum quid* corresponds to that between the ens primum and the ens secundum. The distinction between substance and accident that holds in existent reality is subject to this universal division. The expressions ens simpliciter and ens secundum quid best render the difference that Scotus grasps in its essential universality as given with objects in general and which he foregrounds in the doctrine of the forms of meanings.[2]

The two fundamental categories we encountered earlier[3] as valid in the domain of existent reality reveal themselves in light of this renewed distinction as modifications conditioned by the unique nature of the field of application (of reality) proper to them. Thus, when it is said that the modus significandi essentialis

---

1. De modis significandi cap. VII, 5a, n.1.

2. Accipiendo *esse simpliciter* prout dividitur contra secundum quid, dico, quod sicut ens dividitur in prius et posterius vel primum et secundum, et prius continet sub se substantiam et posterius accidens, ita simpliciter in isto intellectu aequivalet ei quod est primum naturaliter et secundum quid aequivalet ei quod est posterius naturaliter. Op. Ox., dist. IV, qu. III, n. 43.

3. See above part I, chapter 1, p. 51.

confers an *esse*, this cannot mean real existence, but rather, the esse proper to the meaning and that one can grasp as "perdurance."

In the present, Husserl in particular has paid attention to the difference between independent and dependent objects, presented it in the greatest possible theoretical clarity, and developed the essential lawfulness resulting from it. {343/285} The essence of independent objects "by itself, i.e., considered in an a priori fashion, requires no other essence to be interwoven with it"; "the content is by its nature bound to other contents."[4] These definitions can be easily applied to the fundamental division of the modi significandi that Duns Scotus carries out.

We can now further specify the modus significandi essentialis. As modus *generalissimus*, it has the function of constituting the essence of a "part of speech," for example, of generating the essential form for the *noun*. The meaning function of the noun in general becomes manifest in it. It circumscribes the region of the nouns, each of which bears the universal essence in itself. Starting with the modus generalissimus, the series progresses to the lowest specific differences (the "eidetic singularities"), the modus specialissimus. It is something ultimate insofar as it has no subordinate cases, whereas it has necessarily sublated the modus generalissimus within itself.

Fittingly, the modus essentialis that is neither the lowest difference nor the highest genus is called the modus *subalternus*. The essence "noun in general," which has no other, higher genus that would contain its substantial essence, is necessarily the highest genus. As such, it delimits a "region."

We must now strictly distinguish between the actual *material* essence of a region and the *formal* essence—the "empty forms," as it were—that in a certain sense lie above all regions. The modus *essentialis* found in all "parts of speech" is of the latter kind.

With these universal determinations concerning the modus essentialis and accidentalis, Duns Scotus has extracted the formal structure of each region, "part of speech," and presented their arrangement. {344/286} He places this formal arrangement of the "empty form" parallel to the "linea predicamentalis," the gradated sequence of genus in general to species in general down to the lowest difference of all. Further, the word "linea" clearly shows that we are in a purely formal region distinct from every substantiality [Sachhaltigkeit].[5] It belongs to the essence of the genus generalissimum that it has neither multiple

---

4. Husserl, *Logical Investigations* II, Investigation III: On the Theory of Parts and Wholes, particularly 9–10; Heidegger cites *Logische Untersuchungen*, 2nd ed., particularly 236.

5. De mod. sig. cap. VII, 5a, n. 1.

species *under* it nor a *higher* genus *above it.*[6] However, it is proper to the genus to have species under it, albeit not in the sense that they really exist but that they can be conceptually grasped. They are grasped inasmuch as the singularities, which sometimes really exist, are brought to givenness and the essence of the corresponding species is intuited in them.[7]

Regarding the *dependent* forms of meaning, Duns Scotus distinguishes two kinds: the modus accidentalis *absolutus* and the modus accidentalis *respectivus.*[8]

Forms of meaning of the first kind merely determine the independent forms of meaning, whereas those of the second kind additionally confer on them a relationship to other meanings.[9]

Duns Scotus has thus, as it were, exposed the formal scaffolding into which the individual "parts of speech" are built.

The task of "etymology" is fulfilled when the individual parts of speech are considered purely in themselves, with a view to the modi significandi constitutive of them.[10] {345/287}

Duns Scotus adopts the sequence in which he investigates the individual parts of speech in relation to their modi significandi from the grammarian Donatus, who lists them in the following order: noun, pronoun, verb, adverb, participle, conjunction, preposition, and interjection.[11]

THE NOUN

In order to present the essence of the category of meaning "noun," we must inquire into the modus essentialis generalissimus nominis. The latter must express what makes every noun a noun, the meaning function proper to it. This general meaning function of the noun is given in the *"modus entis et determinatae*

---

6. De ratione generis generalissimi non est in se habere plures sub se species sed *non habere aliud supraveniens genus.* Op. Ox. I, dist. VIII, qu. III, n. 19.

7. Ad rationem generis requiritur, quot multas habet actu species non quae *existant* actu vel potentia, sed quod tantum ab actu *concipiantur* per speciem intelligibilem ab individuis acceptam quandoque existentibus, et quod actu habeant *aptitudinem participandi genus,* quia talis actualitas est illorum, inquantum dicuntur species generis. Sup. univers. porph. qu. XVIII, 250a.

Quanto genus communius tanto eius minor in re est unitas et ita nomen generis de suo primo intellectu importat aliquid, quod est materiale in speciebus. Quaest. in lib. praed. qu. VII, 455a.

8. De modis significandi cap. VII, 5a sq., n. 2.

9. l. c. 5b, n. 2.

10. l. c. 5b, n. 3.

11. l. c.

apprehensionis," but the sense of this general manner of functioning of the noun is not immediately clear.

However, by now we know at least one thing about every form: it is determined in its meaning by the material. Hence, we must look around in the domain of the real to discover the factors that determine the most universal sense of the category of meaning "noun."[12]

Duns Scotus points out that certain most universal determinations or most universal modes of being can be discovered in the domain of the real. The modus entis is one such mode. Regardless of which of the different domains it belongs to, every real thing is a *What,* an object. Scotus defines this being something [Etwas-sein] that is expressed in the modus entis more precisely as a "habitus," specifically, as an "enduring [habitus]" that is predicable of every object insofar as it *exists.* It is the primary relational context of everything that is or can become an object. This primary relational context also determines the sense of the category of meaning "noun." The {346/288} meaning function of this part of speech thus has the function of *expressing an object as an object.*[13]

However, we have thereby not exhaustively determined the most universal sense of the meaning function. The modus *determinatae apprehensionis* is, as it were, entwined with the modus entis. The form of meaning "noun" first distinguishes itself as a specific category from the other forms through it [the modus determinatae apprehensionis]. This mode is, as it were, the form of the form of meaning. It is responsible for determining and hence distinguishing. One object becomes one thing and another becomes another through the form. Hence, we can say with justification: the form is something qualitative; the qualitative [moment] in general lies in it. Consequently, the most universal qualitative moment can be found in every object. Insofar as the noun in its meaning function means the object as object, the modus determinatae apprehensionis, the *determinate* or *determining* mode of *meaning the object* [die Weise des *bestimmten* bzw. *bestimmenden Gegenstandbedeutens*], must also be contained in this function.[14]

Once the two modes fuse into a unitary act, the noun's general essential mode of meaning results.

In order to illuminate his definition more precisely, Duns Scotus introduces the definition of the ancient grammarians who said: *Nomen significare substantiam cum qualitate.* In Scotus's view, the modus essentialis nominis can also signify this, but in *one* respect it means *more* and in *another* respect *less.* It signifies more insofar as Scotus interprets its definition as widely as possible, indeed, in

---

12. l. c. cap. VIII, 5b, n. 4.

13. l. c. 5b sq., n. 5; see earlier part I, chapter 1, p. 17ff.

14. l. c. 6a, n. 7.

such a way that the meaning function of the noun does *not* remain *restricted* to the substances and qualities of natural reality but rather extends across the world of objects *in general*. For we indisputably use nouns also to express nonexistent logical and mathematical objects; likewise, {347/289} qualitative determinations need not be just those of sensory empirical reality.

It follows that in another respect, the definition of the noun's essential mode of meaning also says less than the definition of the ancient grammarians. The concepts of substance in natural reality and that of the quality belonging to the same domain of reality possess a much richer content that is conditioned precisely by their belonging to natural reality. These differentiations in meaning are extinguished in the modus entis et determinatae apprehensionis. The mode is so general and faded as to suit the limitless range of its domain of application.[15]

Certainly, we must grant that, *genetically*, the occasion for forming the meaning category "noun" lies in empirical natural reality. But we are not interested in the question of its genesis and occasion here, where the only thing that is decisive is to present the *objective ideal* content and *sense* of the meaning functions.

Duns Scotus also holds on to this broad range of the meaning content of the noun and its detachment from specific domains of reality in his other logical writings. Where he establishes the meaning of the ens nomen, he explicitly says that, unlike the ens participium, it does not mean *actual* natural reality [*reale* Naturwirklichkeit] or existence [Existenz]. Rather, it means habens essentiam, possessing an essence, a What, being-an-object [ein Gegenstand-sein]. The noun means its object whether or not it exists. Thus, the name "Socrates" signifies the meaning "Socrates" insofar as this meaning is the content of a meaning endowing act and not the real Socrates insofar as he exists. Hence, the noun does not mean an object as an object measured by time, that is, as something enduring and real; rather, it is applicable to the What of every object (de essentia cuiuslibet).[16] {348/290}

Given this extremely wide interpretation of the noun's mode of meaning, Duns Scotus also has no difficulty in dismissing an objection that was raised earlier.

---

15. l. c. 6a, n. 8.

16. Solet antiquitus dici, quod *ens* potest esse participium vel nomen. Ens participium significat idem, quod *existens*; quia *tenet significatum verbi a quo descendit*. . . . Ens nomen significat *habens essentiam*. Sup. perih. qu. VIII, 554b sq., n. 10.

Nomen significat univoce rem remanente vel existente vel non existente. Ad quod sciendum, quod hoc nomen "Socrates" significat "Socratem" secundum quod est in actu, *non tamen significat "Socratem existere."* II sup. perih. qu. II, 586a.

Ens nomen non significat rem ut *tempore* mensuratam. Anal. post. II, qu. IV, n. 3.

Ens nomen est de essentia cuiuslibet. l. c. n. 2.

Someone could of course say that nouns such as "nothingness" and "blindness" do not mean a real object and that, therefore, for these words there cannot be a meaning function like that of the noun, which, after all, gains its determinacy from the material that is meant: hence these intended objects cannot be expressed nominally. Duns Scotus grants without hesitation that the objects in question are indeed not *realities*. But in his view, they must nonetheless be considered *objects* [*Gegenstände*] that can be objects [Objekte] for the acts directed at them. They are therefore also subject to the most universal determinations that hold of objects as such. Because the noun's mode of meaning gains its sense only from these [determinations], they too can be expressed nominally.[17]

We can now specify the noun's general mode of meaning. At first, there are two modes: the modus *communis* and the modus *appropriati*. They are species with respect to the essential mode of meaning; on the other hand, they are themselves general in relation to other modes that are "beneath" them on the scale.

The modus communis must receive the meaning function proper to it from a peculiarity of the objects that does not apply to every object qua object. There, in fact, exist objects from which a common moment {349/291} can be detached and made, in and of itself, into an object of thought and hence of meaning. This detachability simultaneously proves, in another respect, to be a *capacity for distribution* across *individual* objects. By its very nature, the detached objective moment possesses the ability to function as a determination applicable to each of the individual objects from which it has been detached. Objects of this kind are known to logicians by the name "universalia."[18]

The expression "universal representation," which is occasionally used of late, is unclear and confusing. If one understands "representation" as a psychic act, then it cannot be said that a universal *representation* is ever universal, because as realities, acts are always individual. But if the expression in question signifies "representation of a universal," if one thereby keeps the *content* of the representation in view, then this content is also not universal in the strict sense. It can only be called universal with respect to its function, that is, with respect to the potential for *being predicated* of many individual objects that is grounded in it. Indeed, Duns Scotus expressly shows that a universal can be cognized for itself and its essence made the object of a cognition. In demonstrating this, he also lets the essence of the universal appear in all its clarity.

If I seek clarity about the essence "tree," for example, I contemplate what makes every tree a tree. Initially, I do not investigate the essence in its What so much as the moments *that hold for every tree*. In a certain respect, I make the

---

17. De mod. sig. cap. VIII, 6a sq., n. 9; see earlier part II, chapter 1, p. 87ff.
18. De mod. sig. cap. IX, 6b, n. 1–3.

essence the object of my investigation. This *respect*, however, is accidental to the essence "tree" as such. I can thus unequivocally recognize the distinctness of my intellectual *orientation*, which is directed, first at the essence *in itself* and thereafter at its *validity for several individual objects*. On further reflection, this {350/292} "validity for" [itself] can be made into an object, and the essence of the universal is thus grasped. As such, the latter can be potentially determined as an individual object. *The universal is not a psychic reality, but an essence (meaning content) that is grasped "in ideation."* Occasionally, we also use the name *universal* to characterize the essence of an existent individual thing, even though, qua reality, the essence is indifferent to determinations such as "universalis" and "singularis."[19]

The mode of "validity for" constitutes the meaning function of the *"nomen commune."*[20]

We traced the mode of meaning of the modus communis back to a peculiarity of the empirically given material of reality, namely, that universal essential concepts can be extracted from it and, in turn, predicated of individual objects. But however significant the role of these universal essences in cognition, they do not contain the whole of reality within themselves; in particular, they do not contain that which makes empirical reality into an unsurveyable manifold of individual objects: *tota entitas singularis non continetur sub universali.*[21] {351/293}

Earlier,[22] we provided a brief characterization of the unique aspect that empirical reality presents. Vital, immediate reality is lost in universal essences. If it is to be grasped in its meaning, then new moments of meaning necessarily must

---

19. Dicendum, quod universale est per se intelligibile, quod patet sic: primum objectum intellectus scil. quod quid est, intelligitur sub ratione universalis; illa vero ratio non est idem *essentialiter* cum illo quod quid est, sed *modus eius accidentalis*, ergo intellectus potest cognoscere differentiam inter suum objectum primum et illam modum, quia potest distinguere inter omnia quae non sunt essentialiter eadem ... *igitur intellectus potest cognoscere modum sive rationem universalis; hoc enim modo reflectendo cognoscit intellectus se et sui operationem et modum operandi et caetera, quae sibi insunt.* Sup. univ. Porph. qu. V, 106a, n. 2.

Universale ex hoc quod universale natum est determinari ad suppositum. Reportata I, dist XIX, qu. V, 248a sq., n. 11.

Universale *est ab intellectu.* Sup. univ. Porph. qu. IV, 97a, n. 4.

Aliquando autem universale accipitur pro re subjecta intentioni secundae, id est pro quidditate rei absoluta, quae, quantum est de se, nec est universalis nec singularis, sed *de se est indifferens.* De anima. qu. XVII, n. 14.

20. De mod. sig. cap. IV, 6b, n. 2.

21. Op. Ox. II, dist. III, qu. XI, 276b, n. 9.

22. See above part I, chapter 1, p. 44–45.

join the essential concepts (as universalia).[23] In this case, the singular individual object or the meaning that expresses it in the mode of singularity can *no longer* be intentionally related to *several* objects. This would directly contradict its content, because its form of meaning says precisely that it is not that: *singulare enim non est communicabile ut quod.*[24]

Admittedly, the singular and the universal can be combined in a certain respect. On the one hand, singularity can be considered an object—a singular object [Gegenstand] is an intentional object [Objekt des Meinens]. On the other hand, singularity can be grasped as the *essence*. In the latter case, it becomes a *mode of apprehension, a universal.*[25]

Regarding the question of the extent to which the individual can be cognized, Duns Scotus rightly decides that it *cannot be cognized by means of the lowest species concept, the one most directly applicable to it.*

This is so because qua individual it always contains something more, about which the species concept does not predicate anything. Hence one must say that an individual qua individual cannot be fully grasped. An *ineffable* remainder persists, {352/294} one that we can at best approximate, albeit without ever exhausting it. However, this does not mean that generalization is the sole method for presenting the heterogenous manifold, as though we could attain the individual in thought merely by combining universal concepts. Modern logic first laid the groundwork for the unique legitimacy of the individualizing sciences and discovered the problems belonging to them.[26]

---

23. Singulare addit aliquam entitatem supra entitatem universalis. Op. Ox. II, dist. IX, qu. II, 437b, n. 10.

24. l. c. III, dist. I, qu. I, 26b sq., n. 10.

25. Aliud est singularitatem esse conceptam *ut objectum* vel ut partem objecti, aliud est singularitatem esse praecise *modum concipiendi*, sive *sub quo* concipitur objectum … Ita in intentionibus logicis, cum dico: singulare est universale, *quod* concipitur est singularitas, sed *modus concipiendi*, sub quo concipitur, est *universalitas*, quia quod concipitur ut concipitur habet indifferentiam ad plura. Op. Ox. I, dist. II, qu. III, n. 7.

26. Cum dicitur, singulare non est intelligibile nisis in universali, dico, quod sicut in communiori non continetur perfecte quidquid est entitatis in inferiori, sic nec in cognosci vel intelligi. Ideo dico quod in nulla specie, inquantum talis perfecte potest cognosci objectum suum per se singulare, quia *aliquid includit, quod non species et quantum ad hoc non ducit species in eius cognitionem; et ideo* dico, quod *singulare non est per se intelligibile sub propria ratione perfecte.* Reportata II, dist. III, qu. III, n. 15.

De singularibus non est facta scientia isto modo, quo scientia accipitur I. Metaphysicae, prout distinguitur contra experimentum, sed accipiendo scientiam pro *certa notitia bene est scientia singularium.* Miscell. qu. III, n. 13.

For the individualizing sciences' unique legitimacy, see the work of Dilthey, Rickert, and Simmel.

The meaning function "modus significandi *per modum appropriati*" corresponds to the nature of cognition in the mode of singularity. In the domain of meaning functions, this mode and the previously discussed modus communis represent the *two fundamental directions* in which empirical reality can be contemplated and correspondingly meant. Duns Scotus hence rightly lists them *in conjunction [beiordnend]* and classifies them as the most proximate specifications of the modus essentialis generalissimus nominis.[27]

For their part, the two species immediately subordinate to the noun's essential universal mode of meaning—the modus communis and the modus appropriati—represent *genera* with respect to the species subsumed under them. We already noted the function of the universal mode of meaning as follows: to mean an object in general as an object. {353/295} Here there is no question of individual objects delimited in some determinate way, albeit the very first step of differentiating the meaning functions into the universal and the individual must return to individual objects. However, this occurs in a very specific respect: in the modus communis it takes place in such a way that the individual objects are regarded as the *fundament*, as the respective fulfillment of their common abstract essence. This universal essence as such is also not intended [gemeint] in the modus communis; rather, what is intended is the *function* founded in it of referring to—and thereby meaning—many individual objects. Likewise, strictly speaking, nothing is determined in the modus appropriati about the individual and the singular as such, its substantive constitution [inhaltliche Konstitution]. Rather, only the essence of the individual, the mode of *intention [Meinens]* directed to the individual object, is to be brought to light.

The next step in differentiating the meaning function occurs as follows: Initially, from the modus communis we advance to the substantive structure of objects. Every object is not only an object as such. Rather, qua object, it also possesses *substantive determinacy*: every *being* is a *being-thus*, although not every being-thus necessarily exists. Whereas in the modus communis, we were only concerned with the genus in general, through its subaltern case, the modus *per se stantis*, we arrive at a meaning function with the goal of *meaning conceptually determined genera*. This mode constitutes the nomen substantivum in the strict sense.[28] {354/296}

---

27. De modis significandi cap. IX, 6b sq. n. 3.

28. Deinde sub his modis descendamus ad alios modos significandi subalternos minus generales istis, et primo sub modo significandi per modum communis; secundo sub modo significandi per modum appropriati.

Circa primum notandum, quod modus significandi per modum communis, habet duos modos sub se, qui sunt minus generales eo, scilicet modum per se

In a substantively determined essence, one can distinguish the following: the essence as such, its "core," and the determinations that accidentally apply to it. As soon as we focus on the materially determined essence, that is, with the modus per se stantis, the modus *adjacentis*, which represents the form of meaning of the determinations that accidentally apply to the essence, is simultaneously given. Here we encounter the constitutive form of the nomen *adjectivum*: this is clear from other remarks found in Scotus regarding the adjective. Its meaning function is: *to determine*. The description modus *adjacentis* is thus justified, inasmuch as determinacy is always determinacy *for* something that either must be determined or is [already] determinate. Determinacy needs *some thing*, to which it can apply.[29]

Someone could now object that while adjectives like "*animatum*" and "*rationale*" are, as adjectives, combined with a nomen substantivum as in the expression "corpus animatum" or "animal rationale," they nonetheless stand for substantives. How can this be reconciled [with the foregoing account]? The mode of meaning of the nomen substantivum, after all, is an independent mode; it needs no foundation, unlike the {355/297} modus adjacentis, which is "in need of support." Expressions such as "*animatum*" and "*rationale*" surely cannot be simultaneously independent and dependent with regard to their form of meaning. To this we must reply that, applied to the mere words, the figures of speech "independent" and "dependent" yield no sense. What is intended can, naturally, only be the meaning of the words. We cannot see from the word "animatum" as such which meaning function enlivens it. This happens only when we live in the meaning of

---

stantis et modum adjacentis. Modus significandi per modum per se stantis sumitur a proprietate rei, quae est proprietas essentiae determinatae. Sicut enim modus significandi generalissimus sumitur a proprietate essentiae absolutae: sic modus significandi per modum per se stantis sumitur a proprietate ipsius essentiae determinatae: et hic modus constituit nomen substantivum. Nomen ergo substantivum significat per modum determinati secundum essentiam. l. c. cap. X, 7a, n. 4, 5.

Essentia variis modis dicitur de creatura: uno modo secundum rationem determinatam alicuius generis secundum quem modum dicimus *hic* est homo vel corpus vel albedo vel quantitas; *et hoc convenit cuilibet enti* sive existat actu sive in potentia sive per suam essentiam; nam quaelibet res reponitur in determinato genere per suam essentiam *non per suum actum existentiae.* De rer. princ. qu. VIII, 346b, n. 1.

29. Adjectivum formaliter significat *formam ut* forma est eius de quo dicitur; propter istam proprietatem adjectivum non potest praedicari nisi *praedicatione formali.* Quodlibet. qu. V, 203b, n. 6.

Adjectiva si praedicantur, de necessitate *formaliter* praedicantur et hoc quia sunt adjectiva. Nam ex hoc quod sunt adjectiva *significant formam per modum informantis,* de quo videlicet formaliter dicuntur. Op. Ox. I, dist. V, qu. I, 448b, n. 7.

the word or, more precisely, in actualizing the context of meaning from which the meaning function first becomes comprehensible. Here the peculiar fact reveals itself that the form of meaning of the modus per se stantis can indeed be combined with the word "animatum," which in ordinary speech is used as an adjective in the modus adjacentis, and that, consequently, animatum functions as a substantive. When *nominalized*, the predicate "blue" yields "the blue," and so in all other cases. In this objection, the eminent importance of clearly apprehending the mode of meaning of the words used in each case comes to light.[30]

When we descend from the modi per se stantis and adjacentis to further differentiations and seek the modi specialissimi, that is, the lowest differentiations of the modus essentialis nominis, this implies, for the material that determines the forms of meaning in their function, that it itself provides an occasion for further specifications vis-à-vis the substantive [inhaltlichen] genera. Thus, the more we distance ourselves from the noun's universal, practically empty mode of meaning, the more we come into close contact with the peculiar features of the heterogenous, unsurveyably manifold content of reality. We should therefore not be surprised that the number of the most special modes of meaning of the nomen substantivum increases with the concrete fullness of the former [that is, of the manifold content of reality]. {356/298}

Simultaneously, we must bear in mind that the noun's lowest modes of meaning contain in themselves all the generic essences [Gattungswesen] above them and the essence noun as such, and if they do not do so *explicite*, then they at least do so in such a way that a theoretical analysis of the total sense of the meaning function of one of the lowest modes must discover the essences belonging to it and their reciprocal arrangement.

According to Duns Scotus, there are five most special modes of meaning that occur below the modus per se stantis: modus generalis, modus specificabilis, modus descendentis ab altero, modus diminuti ab alio, and modus collectionis.

In order to understand the respective sense of each of these modes, we must return to the material.[31]

In contemplating empirical reality, we encounter certain determinacies, each of which is distinct from the other and which nonetheless have something in common. Blue is distinct from red, but both are colors. We tend to say a specific difference separates them. The substantive "color" is accordingly predicated of individual colors in a quite specific sense. It is characteristic of it qua noun that it does not mean just an object in general or an essence that can be attributed to all possible individual objects. Further, it has not only a clearly demarcated,

---

30. De modis significandi cap. X, 7a, b, n. 7.
31. l. c. cap. XI, 7b, n. 9.

specific essential content, but it additionally signifies in the sense of a *genus, whose individual cases are specifically different.*

This modus generalis constitutes the *substantivum generale.* It is the meaning function that receives its sense immediately from the logical concept of the genus.

The universal, to which we earlier traced back the modus communis, represents the universal essence of the genus. It is characteristic of the universal that it can be predicated of several objects. However, in the case of the genus as a {357/299} *species* of the universal, this essential moment of the universal must have become specific in some way.

Porphyry defines the genus as follows: genus est, quod de pluribus differentibus specie in eo quod quid est, praedicatur.

Duns Scotus accepts this definition and demonstrates its correctness. De pluribus specie differentibus and praedicari in quid, predicating the genus of objects that differ in species and indeed in essence, these two definitions constitute the specific differences through which the species genus "genus" [die Art Gattung "genus"] emerges from the genus "universale." For a universal can also be predicated of objects that differ only in number, and furthermore, it cannot be predicated of them essentially but [only] as a qualitative determination.[32]

But genus is not predicated *only* of objects that differ *in number* and [it is predicated of them] not [just] in quale; it is predicated of objects that *differ in species and* [it is predicated of them also] *in quid.* Therewith, we have sufficiently determined the concept of genus and, simultaneously, the sense of the nomen

---

32. Dicendum, quod est vera definitio [generis], quod sic ostenditur: ratio universalis est praedicari de pluribus, cum ergo in definitione generis ponatur praedicari de pluribus, ponitur genus eius postea ponitur "differentibus specie" et "in quid" quae sunt per se differentiae generis. Probatio: quia per se dividunt superius, scil. praedicari de pluribus: ergo sunt per se constitutivae inferioris, ad quod superius per illa appropriatur. Dividitur enim per se "praedicari de pluribus" in "differentibus specie" et "differentibus numero." ... Dividitur etiam in "praedicari in quid" et "in quale." Sup. univ. Porph. qu. XV, 191a sq., n. 4.

Convenienter ponitur "differentibus specie" ut differentia, quia per illam particulam universale descendit in ipsum definitum, tamquam genus per differentiam. l. c. XVII, n. 2.

Convenienter ponitur "in quid," quia praedicari dividitur in "praedicari in quid" et "in quale," tamquam per primos praedicandi modos; igitur per illa descendit universale in species: genus autem non praedicatur "in quale," igitur "in quid." l. c. qu. XIX, 259b, n. 2.

Nihil praedicatur in quid de illo respectu cuius est accidens, sed respectu cuius est genus: ut "color" non praedicatur de substantia in quid sed de albedine respectu cuius est genus. l. c. 260b, n. 4.

generale's meaning function. The function of the meaning of such a substantive {358/300} is to express objects that differ essentially in species.[33]

The distinction of the "praedicari in pluribus" into predictability that applies to objects differing in species and predictability that applies to objects differing only in number suggests that a definite meaning function also corresponds to the latter possibility of predication. Duns Scotus calls this meaning function the modus *specificabilis*. The objects at which this meaning function aims thus need only differ in number and not in species.[34] The third species of the meaning function "per modum per se stantis" is the modus *descendentis ab altero*, which circumscribes the sense of patronyms.

Certainly, there is a major difference in meaning function, [depending on] whether we express different color species by "color" or different members of the lineage in question with "primogenitor." Every member of the lineage differs from the other, and yet in one respect, they are identical. This also applies to color species. But the members of a lineage are distinct in *another* respect, namely, their position in the genealogical tree, and identical in *another* respect, namely, their membership in the same genealogical tree.

This indisputable inner structural difference in the material understood or meant is sufficient reason {359/301} for a new differentiation of the modus per se stantis via the modus descendentis ab altero.[35]

Duns Scotus places *diminutives* alongside patronymics and defines their form of meaning as intending the object that they express in "*diminutive form*": "floret" instead of "flower" and "pebblestone" instead of "stone." It is certainly correct

---

33. Sicut enim a proprietate rei, quae est communicabilis pluribus, absolute sumitur modus significandi per modum communis absolute, sic ab eadem proprietate strictius sumpta, scilicet a proprietate communicabili pluribus specie differentibus, sumitur modus generalis. Ab hac autem proprietate, apud Logicum sumitur secunda intentio generis, et sic iste modus constituit Nomen substantivum generale, ut *animal, color,* et sic de aliis generibus. Nomen ergo *substantivum generale est, quod significat per modum communicabilis pluribus, non solum numero, sed specie differentibus.* De modis significandi cap. XI, 7b, n. 9.

34. Secundus modus per se stantis, est modus significandi per modum specificabilis, sumptus a proprietate rei, quae est proprietas communicabilis pluribus non absolute sed solum numero differentibus. l. c. cap. XI, 7b sq., n. 10.

35. Tertius modus per se stantis, est modus significandi per modum descendentis ab altero; ut ab avo, vel a patre: et hic modus constituit nomen substantivum patronymicum, ut *Priamides.* Et quia nomen patronymicum a propriis nominibus patrum vel avorum derivatur, ideo merito *patronymicum* nomen nuncupatur. Nomen ergo *patronymicum est quod a propriis nominibus patrum vel avorum derivatur, significans per modum descendentis ab altero, ut a patre vel ab avo.* l. c. 8a, n. 11.

that diminutives possess this sense, but this quantitative characteristic does not, as it were, exhaust their sense. We [also] use diminutives to express joy, humor, tenderness, affection, et cetera. But this is, after all, no objection against Scotus's formulation of the meaning function involved, for it does not assert anything about the variously changing content of meaning that can stand, as factual [sachlicher], in one and the same form. Further, we might question whether psychic moods and emotive acts—which are already not simple in themselves—really belong to diminutive expressions or whether these acts are not united in some peculiar and as yet unclarified manner with the relevant diminutive's act of meaning and, as component acts, form a "phenomenological unit" with it.

The assumption of such a unitary act is all the more plausible, as the diminutive is not used in these cases as a purely theoretical expression. Whatever the solution to these complex phenomenological problems may be, {360/302} it does not affect Duns Scotus's characterization of the meaning function,[36] which appears almost trivial if we do not heed the simplicity of the relationship that reigns in the domain of the forms of meaning.

The final modus specialissimus of the modus per se stantis that Duns Scotus lists is the modus *collectivus*, the form of meaning of collectives. In every collective noun, we intend an aggregate or indeed a commonality of individual objects that are separate among themselves. But contrary to Duns Scotus, the aspect under which they form a unity need not be a common *local* determination. The latter may be true of meanings such as "sand dune" or "housing block." By contrast, for meanings such as "people" or "tribe," we must invoke a "higher" aspect of unity. It is indisputable that we intend an aggregate of individual members in these meanings. [But] if we bear in mind that *different* unifying aspects are present in different collectives and that spatial commonality constitutes only *one* class among them, then Duns Scotus's characterization reveals itself to be excessively narrow and partial.

In this regard, then, it also does not seem justified to place patronymics *alongside* collectives as a special form of meaning. Rather, they are more correctly subsumed *under* collectives, because they share their universal function of combining individual objects to a unity under a specific aspect. Although patronymics combine objects under a highly specific aspect, they do not do so such that they would constitute a unique meaning function. However, we maintain that collectives are distinguished from the unity of the genus in respect of their unifying activity and hence are rightly distinguished from the modus generalis.[37]

---

36. l. c. 8a, n. 12.
37. l. c. 8a, n. 13.

We divided the modus communis of the noun into the modus per se stantis and the modus adjacentis. {361/303} We traced the former down to its most specific differentiations. We shall now also do this for the modus adjacentis.

We can see its universal meaning function from the fact that it intends an accidental determination of the object, or, more precisely, from the fact that it intends the *accidental attribution* [des *Zufallens*] of a determination.

Duns Scotus makes a distinction before listing twenty-four special ways in which adjectives signify. We shall mention only the *most significant* of these. A meaning function can have the sense that *it intends the applicability of a determination as a determination* without differentiation, that is, without further moments of meaning that state *in what respect* and *how* a determination applies to the object to be determined. This mode of meaning is therefore more universal than the following ones, in which the modus adjacentis results under specific aspects.[38]

An analogous differentiation of meaning functions exists in the close relationship of substantives and adjectives. An adjective can be a general adjective such as "colored." It then means individual determinations that, though differing among themselves in species, {362/304} are subject to an identical formal determination that is intended in the mode of the adjectivum generale.

The adjectivum speciale lacks this specific difference of the potential individual determinations applicable to the object. Duns Scotus explicitly notes that the adjectives in question here can certainly alter their mode of meaning without the identity of their external word form, which is preserved [in these adjectives], being affected.[39]

---

38. Deinde sub modo adjacentis alteri ad modos specialissimos descendamus: qui continet sub se viginti quatuor modos; quorum:

Primus est modus significandi per modum adjacentis alteri, seu denominantis ipsum simpliciter et absolute, speciali ratione non superaddita, et hic modus constituit nomen adjectivum denominativum, ut *albus, niger, croceus.* Nomen ergo *Adjectivum denominativum significat per modum adjacentis alteri, sive denominantis alterum simpliciter et absolute.* Et iste modus est generalior omnibus modis sequentibus, qui dicuntur modi adjacentis alteri, sive denominantis alterum, superaddita ratione speciali, ut postea patebit.

Secundus modus adjacentis est modus significandi per modum denominantis alterum, sub ratione communicabilis pluribus specie differentibus, et iste modus constituit nomen adjectivum generale significans sub ratione communicabilis pluribus specie differentibus, ut *coloratus.* Nomen ergo *Adjectivum generale est, quod significat per modum denominantis sub ratione communicabilis pluribus specie differentibus.* l. c. cap. XII, 8a, b, n. 1, 2.

39. l. c. 8b, n. 2, 3.

The adjectivum *possessivum* represents a unique mode of meaning in that it attributes a determination to the object that does not merely attach to it—as "colored" does, for example—but rather, means the substance, the material, *of which* it is composed.

The sense of the adjectivum diminutivum results automatically from what we said about the substantivum diminutivum. The same holds of the adjectivum collectivum, for which Scotus lists the examples "urban" and "tribal." Analogous to the way patronymics belong to collective concepts, the adjectivum gentile must be counted among the ones we just considered.[40]

Scotus also includes the adjective's comparative and superlative forms in its special modes of meaning. He calls these forms an excessus citra terminum, that is, something that goes beyond the adjective's positive meaning content.[41]

Adjectives such as "similar" and "identical," which express the mode of meaning "*ad liquid,*" that is, in its *relatedness [Bezüglichkeit]*, are noteworthy.[42]

I merely note [the existence of] the adjectivum temporale (diurnus, nocturnus, and annuus), the adjectivum *locale* (vicinus and propinquus), and the adjectivum *ordinale* (primus, secundus, et cetera).[43] {363/305}

Already from this list of the adjective's different modes of meaning it is evident that the more specific the content of the relevant meanings turns out to be the more forms of meaning we can list. But note that it is less the meaning *function* than the content that it affects that varies. These modes of meaning are therefore less relevant for the doctrine of meaning.

In our initial differentiation of the noun's meaning function, which in itself aims at the object as such, we identified two basic forms of the modes of meaning—the modus communis and the modus appropriati—corresponding to the two basic directions the intellectual apprehension of reality follows. We presented the generalizing meaning functions of the noun earlier.

A consideration of individualizing meaning functions in the modus *appropriati* concludes our characterization of the noun's forms of meaning.

The special individualizing modes of meaning are, above all, proper to proper names. They always intend an individuality and this one par excellence. The meaning function does not determine which aspect of the meant or named object is currently the content of the consciousness of meaning. It tells us only that the meaning content of the proper name is "represented" *sub ratione propria*, that is, in the consciousness that it belongs to this intended individual and *only* to him.

---

40. l. c. 9a, n. 5, 6, 8.

41. l. c. 9b sq., n. 16, 17, 18.

42. l. c. 10a, n. 19.

43. l. c. 10b, n. 21, 22, 24.

This individualizing meaning function is the form, which can be separated from the variously changing material of meaning.[44]

The task of the first name is to {364/306} distinguish individuals bearing the same [last] name. Its universal function can be understood thence. Living in this meaning function of the first name, the individual who is named thus appears to us *as* a different individual. The praenomen's [that is, first name's] meaning function is thus founded on that of the nomen proprium.

The form of meaning of the last name makes a further contribution to characterizing the individual personality it designates and intends, namely, regarding this personality's origins; it bears a *historical* moment within itself.

The nickname manifestly achieves this too, but in a different direction. Its form of meaning is defined *a proprietate eventus*, that is, from a unique and particularly significant event, to which the person named thus stands in a specific relationship—one that naturally varies in individual cases.

It is no accident that Duns Scotus lists the *historical* personality Scipio Africanus as an example. For as an individualizing cultural science, history in particular uses proper, family, and first names. This section of the doctrine of meaning, which concerns the noun's individualizing meaning function, thus provides valuable confirmation that our characterization of *historical* concept formation and concept fixation as individualizing was accurate.[45] {365/307}

---

44. Nomen quodcumque aliquid significans quod *huic soli* potest inesse, potest dici proprium nomen huic, sed simpliciter nomen proprius huius non est nisi quod primo significat hoc sub ratione *propria*, quia solum illud est proprium signum vocale huius. Op. Ox. I, dist. XXII, qu. II, 238a, n. 7.

45. Consequenter sub modo appropriati, qui ex opposito dividebatur contra modum significandi communis, ad modos specialissimos, quorum:

Primus est modus propriae denominationis, sumptus a proprietate individuationis absolute; et hic modus constituit Nomen proprium individui, et absolute impositum ut *Socrates, Plato*. Nomen ergo *proprie proprium est, quod significat rem sub proprietatibus individuationis absolute.*

Secundus modus appropriati est modus significandi per modum praenominationis, sumptus a proprietate differentiae, quae est facere differre: et hic modus constituit Nomen proprium praenomen, ut *Marcus Tullius*. Nomen ergo *proprium praenomen est, quod impositum est rei individuae sub ratione differentiae.*

Tertius modus appropriati est modus significandi per modum cognominis vel cognationis, sumptus a proprietate parentali, quae est unum nomen pluribus commune; et hic modus constituit Nomen proprium cognomen, ut omnes de parentela Romuli dicuntur *Romuli*: et dicitur cognomen, quia pluribus cognatis est nomen commune. Nomen ergo *proprium cognomen est, quod impositum est rei individuae sub proprietate parentali.*

So far, we have considered only the noun's independent modes of meaning. In order to conclude the all-around consideration of the noun's form of meaning, we must also characterize the *dependent* modes of meaning.

In contrast to the modus essentialis generalissimus of the noun, which announces the noun's proper and universal essence, the remaining forms of meaning that we specified—modus communis, appropriati, et cetera—can be grasped as *accidental* modes, as is in fact the case in Donatus. But although they contain the universal essence of the noun, these specific modes are nonetheless independent. Their meaning function does not require foundation. What they contain in addition to the noun's universal essence derives from specific content, which modifies the forms of meaning in such a way that the form of meaning is preserved. By contrast, the *purely accidental* modes do not contain the essence of the noun. Regarded in themselves, they are not nomina, specifications of the essence "noun," but rather, forms that first gain a hold on the basis of a noun. They require support from nomina, but do not possess an independent meaning in themselves. For this reason, Duns Scotus rejects Donatus's view and regards "species, genus, numerus, figura, casus, and persona [type, gender, number, form, case, and person]" as purely accidental modes of the noun.[46] {366/308}

As forms of meaning, albeit accidental ones, they are determined, like all forms, by the material.

Regarding the *genus* of the nouns that Duns Scotus traces back to the two categories of acting and suffering, we can justifiably doubt whether it should be included among the forms of meaning. It is a mere modification of the *word*. Considered from the perspective of historical linguistics, the modification is certainly rooted in factual-cognitive motives, but it nonetheless is not based in a comprehensive category of reality and hence cannot enter consideration for constituting the logical sense of a proposition.[47]

Duns Scotus lists "mountain" and "mountain dweller" (mons and montanus) as examples of the dependent mode "species." He argues against the opinion that sees mere differences in the *words* here and seeks to prove the material determinacy of this mode, which falls apart into a primary and a secondary mode.

Quartus modus appropriati est modus significandi per modum agnominis, sumptus a proprietate eventus et hic modus constituit Nomen proprium agnomen, ut Scipio *Africanus* nominatus est, quia ex eventu devicit Africam. Nomen ergo *proprium agnomen est, quod impositum est rei individuae, sub proprietate eventus.* Patet ergo, qui et quot sunt modi significandi Nominis essentiales generalissimi, specialissimi et subalterni, et quae et quot sunt species Nominis per eosdem modos constitutae. De modis significandi cap. XIII, 11a, n. 1–4.

46. l. c. cap. XIV, 11b sq., n. 1, 2.

47. l. c. cap. XVI, 12b, 13a, n. 1–5.

The primary mode, which lies in the expression "mountain," refers to the object's absolute existence, whereas the secondary mode refers to a conditioned reality [Wirklichsein]. For we can only speak of a mountain dweller to the extent that mountains exist. Mountains, by contrast, can certainly exist without mountain dwellers. To be sure, the expression "mountain dweller" is certainly independent as a noun. However, its meaning function contains a moment that can only be understood on the basis of the meaning "mountain." According to Scotus, this dependency of such nouns on primary meanings founds the mode of meaning "species."[48]

Duns Scotus likewise considers it improper to interpret the mode "*figura*" only as an *external* distinction between simple and composite words. Nouns such as "scholarly" and "unscholarly" refer to determinations of the material, insofar as it can be simple, composite, or multiply {367/309} composite. This characterization is admittedly quite rough and hardly precise, but its indeterminacy makes it suitable to approximately point out peculiarities in matters that indisputably modify meanings like those we mentioned. What Scotus presents here is rather general and imprecise classifications, whose univocal and definite circumscription would require detailed investigations. We can decide only what are pure, absolute forms of meaning, determined by the objective material as such, and what, in contrast, must be attributed to linguistic development, which never takes place purely theoretically, on the basis of a doctrine of categories that has been developed in detail.

The dependent and ancillary character of the form of meaning appears more clearly from the *mode of number* than it did from the noun's accidental modes. Plurality and singularity are modifications of meaning that only possess sense when a meaning—in this case, a nominal meaning—founds them. *Something* must be one or many. This mode thus determines a meaning to the effect that it intends either *one* object or *several* objects. Interestingly, Duns Scotus does not expeditiously recur to mathematical or real numbers when deriving the form of meaning under consideration, the numerus. Rather, he takes the unum and multum *transcendens* together with the genuine number and lets the form of meaning be determined *by both* of them. The form of meaning is indeed not determined by mathematical number alone. Plural nouns apply not only to objects that have actually been counted but also to *manifolds*, to sets. That means the form of meaning of the numerus is tailored to the one [das Eine] and the other as much as it is tailored to the number one [die Eins] and to counted objects. Thereby, it reveals the *extent of its validity*, which *transcends* individual domains and therewith the colorlessness {368/310} of its sense proper to the forms of meaning. Whereas

---

48. l. c. cap. XV, 12a, b, 3–5.

there can be a justified doubt about the former accidental modes whether they really possess this function or whether they should not [rather] be traced back to historical linguistic factors outside the domain of meaning, the mode of number exists on account of being determined by a category that reigns over everything objective.[49]

We have interpreted the general essence of the noun's form of meaning to the effect that it [the form] means an object as an object. The accidental modes of *casus* (case) reflect *the* peculiarity of the apprehended objects, that they stand in specific relationships to each other. The objects themselves function within the network of relationships running back and forth between them as originating "starting points" [Ausgangs-"Ansatzpunkte"] (principium) from which relationships proceed or, in another respect, as reference points [Bezugspunkte] (terminus) toward which a relationship tends. The accidental forms of meaning of the case are reflexes of the most universal determinations of thought native to the domain of meaning. In subjective terms, they [that is, the forms of meaning of the case] derive their sense from thought's primordial activity of distinguishing and comparing. This does not exhaust the characterization of these forms, but it already suffices to distinguish the six cases—nominative, genitive, dative, accusative, vocative, and ablative. The nominative determines the meaning content of the underlying noun as the point of departure of the relationship; the vocative makes the meaning take on the relational context of a referent; whereas the remaining four cases can form the contents of meaning belonging to them in either respect [that is, as either point of departure or referent].

We must consider a further peculiarity of objects if we wish to determine the formal content of individual cases more unambiguously: namely, that, in its essence, {369/311} an object is what it is but it can also simultaneously be something else.[50]

Accordingly, the nominative's form of meaning implies: the meaning content of the noun standing in the nominative case is intended as the starting point of a determination in the sense that the intended object, while remaining identical, is also another thing. This is how Duns Scotus interprets the sentence Socrates amat: Socrates is the principle of the determination "love." In his identity as Socrates, he is simultaneously another thing, [he is] something that applies accidentally to him. He loves, he is a loving Socrates. Because a sentence's sense refers to natural reality, we can make a further substantive determination of the principle. The starting point of the determination is simultaneously an *active* principle, the originating ground of an occurrence. By contrast, in mathematical

---

49. l. c. cap. XVII, 13a, b, n. 6, 8.
50. l. c. cap. XIX, 14b, n. 1–16b, n. 12.

propositions, the nominative's meaning function cannot undergo such a definite differentiation from out of natural reality, because their sense refers to a nonsensory domain, and it is not proper to speak of an occurrence given the peculiarity of this domain of objects.

Scotus rejects as erroneous the view that the nominative displaces the meaning content of the noun to which this meaning content is attached into the function of an object "of which" something is predicated or "in which" something else exists. [If it were correct,] this characterization would not distinguish the nominative sufficiently from the other cases, for we can also predicate something of the meaning contents that stand in other cases.[51]

As a form of meaning, the *genitive* endows the meaning the property of being the principle or terminus, that is, the starting point or reference point of a relation, albeit with the further determination that something else is *its* (ut cuius est alterum). {370/312} However, with this latter determination, which is supposed to distinguish the genitive as such from the dative, we seem to have advanced a mere tautology: the genitive means in the form of the genitive. In the sentence, Socratis interest, "Socrates" functions as the principle, whereas in the sentence, Socratis misereor, "Socrates" functions as the terminus, as it also does in the sentence, Filius Socratis est.

The *dative* likewise posits the meaning as the starting point or endpoint of a relationship, though with the further determination that something else is "given" to or conferred on the thing that is posited as either the starting point or the endpoint.[52]

The *accusative* endows the meaning with sense as the endpoint in which an act attains, as it were, rest and completion. The accusative is thus the fulfillment of the act. Occasionally, the accusative intends the content of meaning that founds it as a principle tout court, without the determination proper to the nominative. This is the case in the so-called accusativus cum infinitivo. Further, we should note that in sentences, the accusativus sometimes appears on its own and sometimes in conjunction with prepositions: Lego librum, curro ad campum.[53]

The *vocative* brings the meaning that founds it in the form of a terminus that is dependent on the immediate performance of an act. We cannot discover a further determination here as we did in the three cases we mentioned previously. With regard to the acts, we must note the distinction between *actus signatus* and *actus exercitus*.

---

51. l. c. 15a, n. 3.
52. l. c. 15b, n. 6.
53. l. c. 16a, n. 8–9.

The first is expressed in the verb and the participle. For example, with "nego" I announce *that* I enact an act of negation; the act itself is enacted with and by "non." In the address "O Henrice," the enactment of the act lies in [saying] "O." The act is not simply announced but enacted. The vocative constitutes the terminus of such an immediate enactment.[54] {371/313}

Like the genitive and the dative, the *ablative* gives the meaning the form of a principium or terminus with the determination *quo*. For this determination of the essence of the cases, it is valuable that Duns Scotus fixes the ablative's function generally as intending a starting point or an endpoint. This function applies generally to every case. The more specific determinations [of the cases] change as the cases' domain of application and the expressions that found them change. Further, it is noteworthy that Duns Scotus does not investigate the meanings that stand in the individual cases in isolation, but rather, [he investigates them] in the context of sentences.

By contrast, the different *declensions* of nouns are not modi significandi; rather, they are based on different *modifications of word forms*. Declension as such only exists on the basis of the different cases and these are assuredly forms of meaning. Insofar [as this is the case], we can also call declension a form of meaning: namely, one that "declines" the content of meaning, that is, forms it qua standing in various relations.[55]

THE PRONOUN

While establishing the noun's essential form of meaning, we emphasized that the noun means the object as object. But we simultaneously noted that this determination was insufficient to delimit the noun from other parts of speech. For the "part of speech" we shall now discuss, the *pronoun*, means per modum entis, that is, [it also] refers to an object as object. However, what distinguishes it from the noun is that in pronouns, the object is not determined in its contents as this object and no other. The pronoun's meaning function therefore can rightfully be called indeterminate, or better, *not determinative* (indeterminata apprehensio). Duns Scotus derives this essential property of the pronoun {372/314} from the materia prima. The latter is namely indeterminate in itself; it lacks all form *such that it neither includes nor excludes form*. Materia prima does not possesses any *specific* tendency to be determined by a *definite* form. It, as it were, "rests" in any indifferent form; it is accessible to every form. This peculiarity is not "imposed" on it but belongs to it as such. It constitutes its essence. Materia prima is characterized by

---

54. l. c. n. 10.
55. l. c. cap. XX, 17a, b, n. 3.

a *capacitas quedam formarum,* a certain neutral availability for indifferent formal determinations.

The pronoun's essential mode of meaning derives from this property of the materia prima of being indeterminate yet determinable.

Admittedly, we should not understand this determination by the materia prima as though pronouns had the materia prima for the object meant and named by them. Rather, the materia prima only renders the pronoun's meaning function comprehensible.

Ancient grammarians expressed the same state of affairs in that they asserted that the pronoun means the substance without [its] qualities. Compared with this explication of the pronoun's meaning function, the one Scotus provides proves far more general because it does not apply exclusively to existent natural reality.[56]

{373/315}

Against Scotus's interpretation, someone could object that the meaning function of a part of speech that itself represents something positive must likewise be positive. But according to what we [just] said, the pronoun functions in a *privative* form: as the modus *indeterminatae* apprehensionis. Consequently, the pronoun's meaning function cannot be correctly characterized by this mode.

Regarding this, Duns Scotus notes that we call privative something that is indeterminate in *such* a way as to exclude all form and permit no formal determination

---

56. Modus significandi essentialis generalissimus Pronominis *est modus significandi per modum entis et indeterminatae apprehensionis*; a qua vero proprietate modus significandi per modum entis sumitur, prius dictum est, nam in hoc modo Pronomen a Nomine non distinguitur, ut dictum est.

Modus vero indeterminatae apprehensionis oritur a proprietate seu modo essendi materiae primae. Materia enim prima in se, extra indeterminata est, respectu cujuslibet formae naturalis, quae inest de se, ita quod nec includit formam, nec determinationem formae. Ab ista ergo proprietate materiae primae, quae est proprietas de se indeterminata, determinabilis tamen per formam, sumitur modus significandi per modum indeterminati, qui est modus significandi essentialis generalissimus Pronominis, non quod Pronomen materiam primam significet tantum, sed ex modo essendi reperto in materia prima, intellectus movetur ad considerandum aliquam essentiam sic indeterminatam et ad imponendum sibi vocem sub modo significandi per modum indeterminati. Et hunc modum generalissimum essentialem Pronominis Grammatici expresserunt dicentes, *Pronomen significare substantium meram, vel substantiam sine qualitate*; dantes intelligi per substantiam modum entis, qui in substantia principaliter reperitur, ut dictum est: per meram, vel sine qualitate, modum indeterminatae apprehensionsis. l. c. cap. XXI, 17b, n. 5, 6.

Materia prima ad nullam formam determinate inclinatur et ideo sub quacumque quiescit, *non violenter sed naturaliter* quiescit propter indeterminatam inclinationem ad quamcumque. Op. Ox. I, dist. I, qu. I, 311b, n. 6.

whatsoever. Something that *neither includes nor excludes* formal determinacy, however, is not privative. The pronoun's meaning function, however, turns out to be *of this nature* [that is, it is not privative]. But even if we did not want to grant that this meaning function is not privative, we could say that, as a privative function, it circumscribes the pronoun's genuine modus significandi, which is such that it refers to absolutely everything.[57] And even if we were to accept that the modus significandi pronominis is, in fact, privative and not merely privatively circumscribed, it would be delimited with sufficient determinacy from other parts of speech. For parts of speech ought not be thought of as [merely] word forms but rather as nonsensory, primordial categories of meaning. As such they are *entia secundum animam*;[*] consequently, they are also positive in nature and hence positively distinguishable as well.[58]

We said that the pronoun means in the modus *communis* and relates, in every object, to objectivity as {374/316} such. But this also occurs with the noun *ens*; consequently, *ens* is actually a pronoun. Duns Scotus seeks to counter this objection by noting that the *extent* of validity of the noun "ens" is restricted in comparison with the pronoun's domain of validity [Herrschaftsbereich] insofar as, in its meaning, it is not applicable to the transcendentals "unum, res, and aliquid." Likewise, it is not applicable to privations and negations (nihil est *non ens*). Hence, it cannot coincide with the pronoun and itself possess the character of the latter.[59]

But this argument might not be conclusive. Duns Scotus surely declares the ens to be *convertible* with the transcendentals; they thus belong in the domain of its validity. Furthermore, he understands the concept of ens so generally that it really is applicable to any random cognizable thing (quodlibet intelligibile). The ens thus has the same breadth of application as the pronoun. The two are not distinct in this respect and the objection holds, but only as long as we overlook the fact that for all its indeterminacy, the meaning function of the noun "ens" *differs* from that of the pronoun. With the noun, I intend an object *as* an object. With the pronoun I intend a *highly specific* object, albeit the pronoun does not determine it in its content. The pronoun's meaning function is geared toward determinancy (determinabilis), and it results from the pronoun's application in a specific context of meaning (a sentence).

The pronoun's meaning function, which in itself is not restricted to a definite object, receives the univocal [eindeutige] direction of its fulfillment, which comes to light in individual instances of application, from diverse moments that stand

---

57. De modis significandi cap. XXI, 17b sq., n. 7, 8.

*Reading *sie* for Heidegger's *die*.

58. l. c. 18a, n. 10.

59. l. c. 18a, n. 9.

ir relation to the phenomenon of the direction of fulfillment in general. And different pronouns can be identified in each case depending on the nature of these moments that condition fulfillment (substantive determinacy). {375/317}

In immediate *intuition*, objects can be present "in the flesh" such that we cannot doubt their existence and their conceptually graspable What. The meaning function of the demonstrative pronoun is to indicate an object that is given in the flesh. The meaning function, which, though it does not *determine* in itself, is nonetheless determinate in its essence, is fulfilled by the immediately "represented" objects [given] at the time.

Duns Scotus makes an interesting distinction here. The demonstrative *ad sensum* also means and intends the object that it refers to. In the judgment "ille currit," we grasp the full givenness: "the person running over there." The demonstrative *ad intellectum* likewise refers to an immediately given object, but it does not intend it only as such [that is, immediately given]. In the judgment "haec herba crescit in horto meo" [this herb grows in my garden] "haec," to be sure, refers to the herb in my hand, but it does not intend it only as the herb in my hand; rather, it simultaneously refers to it as the herb growing in my garden. The latter state of affairs is not visually given. Hence, "haec" is used *ad intellectum*.[60] {376/318}

In the demonstrative pronoun, fulfillment occurs directly and immediately (*notitia prima*). Not so with the relative pronoun, which intends the object in an *actus secundus*, that is, it does not refer to the immediately given object but to

---

60. Modus ergo significandi, qui vocatur *demonstratio,* sumitur a proprietate rei, quae est proprietas certitudinis et praesentiae seu notitiae primae intellectus, et hunc modum Donatus vocat *qualitatem finitam*: et hic modus constituit Pronomen demonstrativum.

Pronomen ergo demonstrativum significat rem sub ratione vel proprietate praesentiae seu notitiae primae. Semper enim Pronomini sex demonstrationes correspondent praesentiae, sive sit ad sensum, sive ad intellectum, differenter tamen, quia Pronomen demonstrativum ad sensum hoc quod demonstrat, significat, ut *ille currit.* Sed Pronomen demonstrativum ad intellectum hoc quod demonstrat, non significat, sed aliud: ut si dicam de herba demonstrata in manu mea, *haec herba crescit in horto meo,* hic unum demonstratur, et aliud significatur: et hunc modum demonstrandi habent propria nomina: ut si dicam demonstrato Joanne, *iste fuit Joannes,* hic unum demonstratur et aliud in numeros significatur. Et sic contingit dare diversos modos certitudinis et praesentiae: et secundum hoc erunt diversi modi demonstrationum: et ex consequenti diversa Prononima adjectiva. Contingit enim rem esse praesentem et certam et maxime certam vel praesentem, et sic demonstratur per hoc Pronomen *ego,* vel non maxime esse certam et praesentem, et sic demonstratur per hoc Pronomen *tu,* et alia simila. l. c. cap. XXII, 18b, n. 2, 3.

the object as having already attained givenness but *henceforth* no longer given. The object is, as it were, "repeated" by the relative pronoun, and as "repeated," it is said to be not immediately given.[61] In subjective terms, this means that the moment of recall (recordatio) is present in the relative pronoun. This is the awareness of something that the knower knows *as something he has once known*.[62] The relativum therefore intends the intended object as something that was previously intended.

The modus per se stantis, which we already encountered in the noun and which intends an object existing in itself as distinct from others, also characterizes personal pronouns (I, you, it . . .). The [pronoun] "I" intends the most certain and most immediate object, the person currently executing the meaning function of the pronoun. The meaning function is highly determinate; its fulfillment differs every time another I actualizes the meaning. [The pronoun] "you," although it does not mean the person executing the act of meaning himself, also contains a reference to the person currently speaking, insofar as the person "addressed" by him is intended. The "you" is an "I" that is an "it" (Fichte). He, she, and it are indicative pronouns (most often demonstrativa ad intellectum) and mean in the modus per se stantis. Hence their frequent use as placeholders for proper nouns.[63] {377/319}

The modus adjacentis, which we already encountered in the noun, constitutes the meaning function of the possessive pronoun, which intends an object that either belongs to the speaker or belongs to some other object that the speaker intends in thought.[64]

Duns Scotus does not treat the pronoun's accidental modes of meaning further. He merely declares that they are the same as the ones he presented and already discussed when treating the noun.[65]

Duns Scotus is manifestly conscious of the pronoun's preeminent significance in the domain of meaning. Otherwise, he would not return after the discussion of its different modes of meaning to the pronoun's meaning function in detail and secure the sense he has established against potential objections—something he omits to do for the other parts of speech.

It is said that a pronoun in itself, when taken absolutely, is without meaning; it only has a "suitability" (habilitas) to mean something, and this in the sense of

---

61. l. c. 19a, n. 4.

62. Recordatio est cognitio seu cogitatio actus alicuius praeteriti ipsius recordantis *et hoc inquantum praeteriti*. Op. Ox. IV, dist. XLV, qu. III, 326b, n. 5.

63. De modis significandi cap. XXII, 19b, n. 6, 7; ib. 18b, n. 3.

64. l. c. 19b, n. 8.

65. l. c. cap. XXIII, 20a, n. 2.

demonstrative and relative acts. This opinion is based on Priscian, who declares pronouns to be empty and vain without these acts.[66]

Duns Scotus demonstrates the error of this opinion by reverting to the essence of the modus significandi and its relation to meaning. We can only speak of a specifically differentiated meaning function if meaning in general is present. If the pronoun is to have modi significandi at all, a foundational primary meaning must accrue to it. But in fact, something like modi significandi really exist for the pronoun too. Hence a meaning that first makes the modi significandi possible is proper to it also.

Regarding Prician's assertion, we should note that for Aristotle, {378/320} something may be called "empty and vain" only when it is ordered toward a specific goal and *fails to reach it.* By contrast, the pronoun's tendency is such that it intends an object *without determining it in its content.*

We can understand "empty and vain" in a twofold sense. First, the pronoun does not mean anything at all; second, it means something but without *determining it.* The pronoun is "empty and vain" in the latter sense. We can call it "empty" insofar as its meaning function is not "determinative." But although it is not determinative, its meaning function is *nevertheless determinate* and hence not empty insofar as it explicitly has the function of *intending something without determining it.* The objection that Scotus astutely rejects can only rest on a confusion of the determinate meaning *function* as such with the *content* of meaning that changes from case to case and is hence indeterminate (empty).

There exists another view, which grants that the pronoun must necessarily have a determinate meaning function, for otherwise we could neither think anything with the pronoun nor predicate something of it as the subject of a judgment. But this meaning [that we intend with the pronoun] is the *determinate concept* of being, objectivity in general, which like the concepts genus, species, et cetera applies to every individual sensory and supersensory object. But this interpretation of the pronoun's meaning function also cannot be maintained because we cannot relate any real predicate to the pronoun in itself as the subject. The judgment "I am a human" would be impossible—just as impossible as the judgment "the concept 'human' is a living being" is absurd.[67]

Duns Scotus summarizes the essentials of the pronoun's meaning function in the sentence "Illud est significatum pronominis, significant scil. essentiam de se indeterminatam *determinabilem tamen.*"[68] {379/321}

---

66. l. c. cap. XXIV, 20a, n. 3.

67. l. c. 20a, b, n. 4–8.

68. l. c. 21a, n. 9.

Werner considers it "striking that for Duns Scotus's thought, which strives to grasp the concrete and the individual, the concretizing character of pronouns did not become apparent. Consequently, medieval logic of language was as far from a philosophy of language as Scholastic-medieval philosophy was from a conception of the philosophy of language that penetrated into the concrete essence of things."[69]

In the main, it is indisputable that Scholasticism was still far from the proximity to reality and from the intensive, analyzing treatment of existent reality that we encounter in the modern empirical sciences. But philosophy is not an empirical science, and what is in question in a doctrine of meaning is not the individual details and particularities of objects but what is fundamental, the categorial, the *formal content*. Where forms of meaning appear that are designed to grasp the individual—but are, *as forms*, nonetheless general in themselves—Duns Scotus recognizes them as such, as we showed of the most special modes of meaning of the noun. As surely as pronouns are applied to individual objects, just as surely is their meaning function a universal one. It really belongs to the tasks of a *philosophy* of language to work out this universal function, provided it keeps itself free of psychologistic confusions.

An interesting passage from Hegel (whose *Logic*, so rich in productive distinctions and conceptual determinations, has even now not been sufficiently explored) illuminates how justified Duns Scotus is in his interpretation of the pronoun's meaning function: "When I say '*the singular*,' '*this* singular,' 'here,' 'now,' all of these expressions are universalities; *each* and *every* thing is a singular, a this, even when it is sensible—here, now. Similarly when I say 'I,' I *mean* {380/322} me *as this one* excluding all others; but what I say ('I') is precisely everyone, an 'I' that excludes all others from itself . . . 'I' is the universal in and for itself . . . taken abstractly as such, 'I' is pure relation to itself."[70]

THE VERB

Next to the noun, the verb is considered one of the *most important* parts of speech. This privileged position of the verb within a meaningful whole (propositional sense) is immediately evident from the material determinacy of its form

---

69. Werner, *Die Sprachlogik des Duns Scotus*, 560.

70. G. W. F. Hegel, *The Encyclopaedia Logic (with the Zusätze): Part I of the Encyclopaedia of Philosophical Sciences with the Zusätze*, trans. T. F. Geraets, W. A. Suchting, and H. S. Harris (Indianapolis: Hackett, 1991), 51; Heidegger cites Hegel, *Enzyklopädie der Philosophischen Wissenschaften*, ed. Georg Lasson, Philosophische Bibliotheke (Hamburg: Felix Meiner, 1911), 33:55ff.

of meaning. The essence of the noun leads back to objectivity as such. Every object is *one* object and [as such] distinct from another. The object's state of affairs [Gegenstands-Sachverhalt] exists just as originally as the object itself. A relational context exists with regard to every object, be it only the one *that it is identical with itself and different from another.*

Duns Scotus rightly calls the object [Gegenstand] and the object's way of comporting itself [Gegenstandsverhalt]—the modus *entis* and the modus *esse*—the most universal determinations in the domain of the objective as such.[71]

The modus *esse*, the object's way of comporting itself [Gegenstandsverhalt], determines the {381/323} meaning function of the verb. But this mode does not suffice to equivocally determine the part of speech in question because the modus *esse* is also proper to the participle, and hence a further determination is required in order to establish the full essence of the verb.

The *genuine* essential form of the verb, which distinguishes it from all other parts of speech, is the modus *distantis*.

The verb expresses an object's way of comporting itself [Gegenstandsverhalt]. In this meaning function, it isolates, as it were, the comportment [Verhalt] from the object [Gegenstand], but it does so in such a way that, in and through this isolation, it again relates the content [Gehalt] to the object: the verb predicates the comportment [Verhalt] *as valid of the object.* The distinction between the verb and the participle should also be apparent now. The latter, although it intends the same state of affairs as the verb, does not mean it in the modus distantis; it does not predicate it as valid of the object; rather, it intends the state of affairs as somehow identified with the object, as *linked* with it.

However, it does not seem possible to trace the essential form of the meaning of the verb—the modus distantis—consistently back to the "content [Gehalt]" distinguished from the object. This would imply that the mode, because it does not apply to all verbs, cannot be the essential form [of the verb]. In the sentence "ens est" (being is), the state of affairs that the verb "is" intends, that is, "being,"

---

71. Et ut sciamus a qua rei proprietate iste modus significandi sumatur, notandum est, quod in rebus invenimus quasdam proprietates communissimas, sive modos essendi communissimos, scilicet modum entis et modum esse. Modus entis est modus habitus et permanentis, rei inhaerens, ex hoc quod habet essentiam. Modus esse est modus fluxus et successionis, rei inhaerens ex hoc quod habet fieri.

Tunc dico, quod modus significandi activus per modum entis, qui est modus generalissimus Nominis, trahitur a modo essendi entis, qui est modus habitus et permanentis. Sed modus significandi activus per modum esse, qui est modus essentialis generalissimus Verbi, trahitur a modo essendi ipsius esse, qui est modus fluxus et successionis, ut postea patebit. De modis significandi cap. VIII, 5b sq., n. 5, 6.

does not appear to be distinguished from the object—from "being" in the way that the object and the object's way of comporting itself [Gegenstandsverhalt] are otherwise distinct. Distinguished from being, it would be nonbeing.[72]

How does Duns Scotus solve this difficulty? He concedes that "est" here does not mean something essentially distinct from the object "ens," but he then notes that in the judgment in question we should regard the subject as matter and the predicate as form. Insofar [as we do this], "ens" and "est" are *essentially* distinct (*at tamen in ista propositione subjectum* {382/324} *accipitur ut materia et praedicatum ut forma, quae essentialiter differunt*).[73]

This short sentence is less significant as a refutation of the objection than for Duns Scotus's deep insight into the essence of judgment, which is a worthy addition to—indeed, possibly even surpasses—his earlier statements about this basic phenomenon of logic.[74]

Here, Duns Scotus anticipates, in principle, one of the most modern and most profound theories of judgment. Lask says, "Cognition is associated solely and exclusively with the addition of logical *form* to [what was formerly] a logically amorphous material mass. Hence, what lies at the basis of cognition is matter, that which is 'given' to it, the support of cognition, that on which it must carry out its activity. By contrast, the category represents a mere logical supplement, that which supervenes on the material substrate. Consequently, the true subject is matter and the true predicate is . . . the 'category'!"[75]

The near verbatim agreement in formulation is interesting in its own right. But above all, we must not overlook the fact that Duns Scotus reaches this interpretation in relation to a judgment that is meaningful for its content. In the proposition "the entity is," he could not do otherwise than to declare the material the subject and the form the predicate. Scotus thus also agrees with Lask in the way he arrives at and solves the problem insofar as the latter [also] arrived at the theory of judgment while trying to establish the domain of validity [Herrschafts-bereiches] of *logical form.* {383/325} As a fundamental inquiry, Lask's inquiry is far more comprehensive, whereas Duns Scotus only achieves insight into the essence of *this* judgment while analyzing the unusual proposition "ens est." But

---

72. l. c. cap. XXV, 21a sq., n. 1, 9, 10, 11.

73. l. c. n. 11.

74. See above, part I, chapter 2, p. 57ff.

75. Lask, *Die Lehre vom Urteil*, 58. In his repeatedly cited essay on *number*, Rickert writes: "By predicate, we should initially understand only the form that the act of judgment adds to the content. The subject is correspondingly only the content that is formed. In this original combination or 'synthesis' of subject and predicate as the combination of form and content, we possess what is, in fact, the simplest judgment" ("Das Eine, die Einheit, und die Eins," 48).

he did not expand this profound and valuable insight into a universal theory of judgment. The reason for this is not only his *metalogical* "standpoint" but also, above all, his lack of intellectual freedom vis-à-vis the fetters of tradition—notwithstanding his critical and independent manner of thinking.

The ens and the est are distinguished "secundum rationem." A different relational context exists with regard to each of them—what these were, we just said. And this difference with respect to relational context already suffices to differentiate between the object and the object's way of comporting itself [Gegenstandsverhalt].

Every object has two determinations: the *What* of its content, and that it is this object and [as such] distinct from every other [Dieser-sein und Unterschieden-sein].[76]

The modus esse, which is common to the verb and the participle, derives from the phenomenon of *change* and succession in existent reality, to which its enduring substantial determinacy stands contrasted. But it is also clear that the verb expresses not only real events but also timeless relationships. Duns Scotus says that not every being has an esse *successivum*. [The nature of] God's being is not change, and *yet* we say "God is." Scotus sidesteps this difficulty with the following explanation: God's being {384/326} is successive in an *eternal* and not a temporal succession. But this formulation too is merely analogical. Inspired by the concept of temporal succession, we imagine God's being to ourselves *as if* it would lie in eternal succession.[77]

Alongside relationships from the domain of supersensory metaphysical reality, nonsensory mathematical and logical relationships are also expressed verbally. It therefore seems fitting to determine the verb's meaning function as generically and colorlessly as possible, as *intending an object's way of comporting itself* [*Gegenstandsverhaltes*].

The verbum *substantivum*, whose meaning function is not yet specified by determinate modes of being that change along with individual domains of reality, expresses the utterly general relationships existing between objects in general.

---

76. Vel dicendum est, quod licet non sit dare ens praeter hoc, vel illud: et cum omne quod est, sit hoc vel illud, quia ens est concretum et significat duo, scilicet rem et esse, et illud esse non est ens; ideo hoc verbum *est* significat aliquid essentialiter distans *ab* ente.

Vel aliter, licet in ista propositione significatum Verbi non differat essentialiter et secundum rem a significato suppositi, differt tamen ab eo secundum rationem: et hoc sufficit ad distantiam et diversitatem Verbi a supposito, quae sunt entia secundum rationem; *Verbum* ergo *est pars orationis significans per modum esse distantis a substantia.* De modis significandi cap. XXV, 22b, n. 12, 13.

77. l. c. 21b, n. 2, 3, 4.

If we descend into the object region of natural reality where it makes sense to speak of events, actions, doing, and suffering, the meaning function of the verbum substantivum undergoes corresponding determinations. This is how the verbum activum, passivum, neutrum, and commune can be distinguished. The latter can be present in the mode of meaning of the verbum activum or passivum. By contrast, the neuter verb signifies neither in the passive nor in the active form, so that we might be tempted to classify it under the concept of the general mode of meaning, the verbum substantivum. However, this mode of meaning is not determined *in itself*, whereas this is true of the mode of the neuter verb [that is, it is determined in itself]. Verbs such as "vivo" [live] and "sto" [stand], which Scotus lists as examples of the neuter, can in a certain respect be reckoned among the verba activa. However, they describe an activity that does not immediately and as such aim at an object [Objekt], as is the case with "doceo" [instruct], for example. But as this {385/327} difference is not categorial [in nature], it does not justify the division of these classes.[78]

What Duns Scotus teaches about the *compositio* is more significant for the further clarification of the essence of the verb's meaning function. Fundamentally, we already referred to this accidental mode of meaning of the verb when we remarked that the verb does not just mean an object's way of comporting itself [Gegenstandsverhalt] distinct from the object; rather, it means this simultaneously *as belonging to the object*. Duns Scotus remarks that whereas ancient grammarians do not explicitly mention compositio, they were in fact familiar with it given Aristotle's statement concerning the "est," which describes a certain connection without which the elements connected cannot be understood.

According to Duns Scotus, this "est" is included in all verbs as their "root," as it were. Compositio therefore *belongs* to the *verb as such* and determines its meaning function such that the state of affairs is understood as "tending" toward the object, as intentionally related to it and *valid for it*.

Duns Scotus, however, does not include compositio in the essential meaning function of the verb because this aims at meaning the state of affairs as such, whereas the compositio builds on it.

The modus per se stantis is to the noun what the modus compositionis is to the verb. Through it, an object is intended as this determinate object. The compositio is the genuine principle that connects verb and noun into a unitary sense.

If we wish to apply this interpretation of the judgment "ens est" to every judgment, we would have to say that the function of *form* is proper to the verb, whereas the compositio—the accidental mode of meaning of the verb—expresses a

---

78. l. c. cap. XXVI, 22b–23b.

specific {386/328} moment of the form; namely, the *character of being valid* (*inclinatio*) of the material (*suppositum*), of the "given." A relational context is always a relational context of or with regard to something; a *state* of affairs [Sachverhalt] is always a state of *affairs* [Sachverhalt].[*]

This is how the modus distantis and the modus compositionis, which at first glance seem to counteract and contradict each other, can be united in the *one* meaning function of the verb.[79]

The verb can just express the state of affairs, name it, that is, predicate it as a state of affairs—and, as such, as either valid or invalid—of the object. But in addition to acts of predication, the subject can adopt other attitudes toward a state of affairs. The state of affairs can be *wished*, *asked*, *commanded*, or *doubted*. Corresponding to these different act qualities, different accidental modes of the verb's meaning function arise. These modes are different attitudes the subject adopts, and as such they modify the compositio. Even today, imperative, optative, interrogative, and subjunctive sentences have not been sufficiently clarified and distinguished from each other. Their relation to the judgment is particularly unclear. The circumstance that Duns Scotus reckons them among the *accidental* modes, that is, to the *founded* meaning functions, hints that he too understands them *not as utterly simple* acts but rather as acts laden with manifold complications. Quite correctly, Duns Scotus emphasizes that the distinction of the act qualities—above all, the distinction of the compositio—affects the way a state of affairs relates to an object.

The infinitive, which Scotus includes in a series with the previous modes, is the form of the verb that names the contents of {387/329} the state of affairs it intends as such. A state of affairs is simply re-presented in the infinitive. This also explains why the previous modes can all be dissolved in the infinitive: they all contain a state of affairs but as somehow colored by act qualities.[80]

Duns Scotus bases another species of the special modes of meaning on *forma*. He distinguishes the forma perfecta, meditativa, frequentativa, inchoativa, and diminutiva. However, the modifications that are expressed in these forms relate less to the verb's genuine meaning functions than to its respective contents, the What of the state of affairs that is intended.[81]

---

*This phrase makes more sense with a nonstandard translation: "the way things *relate* [Sachverhalt] is always the way *things* relate [Sachverhalt]."

79. l. c. cap. XXVII, 24a, b.

Compositio est modus significandi mediante quo verbum primo et principaliter *dependet ad quemlibet suppositum ante se.* l. c. cap. XXIX, 26a, n. 3.

80. l. c. cap. XXVIII, 24b sq., n. 2, 3, 4.

81. l. c. 25b, n. 6.

As a moment of the meaning function, the compositio signifies that the relational context denoted in the verb exists in regards to an object. A relational context is only conceivable as a relational context *in regards to something*. The modus esse of the verb, that is, its essential feature that it intends a relational context, analytically demands an object on which this relational context, as it were, can be founded. Qua signifying the state of affairs, the modus esse also simultaneously demands supports for the state of affairs. A state of affairs can, in turn, only be imagined as a *relationship [Verhältnis]* between "things [Sachen]," as a relation between relata. Thus, objects are given at the same time along with the modus esse, and the state of affairs intended in the mode is based on them.[82] {388/330}

There is yet another accidental moment of the verb's meaning function alongside the compositio that intends the state of affairs as belonging to the object and connects it, as it were, "forward" to the sentence subject: the *significatio*. It implies that the state of affairs is connected to objects that are not thought of as the contents of the sentence subject and hence stand in the oblique case. The explanation for the term *"significatio"* is that it expresses a property of the verb founded on the verb's conceptual meaning. The changing content of the verb also conditions the multiplicity of the nouns in the different cases that depend on this content. The conceptual determinacy of the relational context expressed in the verb results in a greater or lesser variation of the states of affairs.[83]

The relational context intended in the verb can be variously determined depending on the respective difference in relation to the objects that are not the sentence subject. The genus accidentale verbi thus further specifies the significatio, which was already grasped, in itself, as an accidental determination of the verb's universal meaning function. It is, as it were, a quality of the significatio.[84]

------

82. Item sicut Verbum per modum *distantis* exigit modum *per se stantis* pro supposito, ita per eundem modum *esse* exigit modum *entis* esse in obliquo. Et sicut Verbum per modum *compositionis* exigit modum *entis per se stantis* in ratione principii in supposito; sic per modum *generis* exigit modum *entis per se stantis* in ratione termini in obliquo. Item sicut Verbum per modos proportionales casibus modo Verbi superadditos exigit in supposito rationem principii, aliter et aliter conjunctam, et ex consequenti aliud et aliud suppositum; sic etiam Verbum per modos proportionales casibus generi Verbi superadditos Verbum exigit in obliquo rationem termini, aliter et aliter conjunctam: et ex consequenti alium et alium obliquum. l. c. cap. XXX, 27b sq., n. 11.

83. l. c. cap. XXIX, 26a, n. 3.

84. Consequenter de *Genere* videamus. *Genus* in verbo sumitur a proprietate rei Verbi, quae est proprietas dependentiae rei Verbi post se ad obliquum sub ratione termini non contracti sed contractibilis. *Genus ergo in Verbo est modus significandi accidentalis Verbi, mediante quo proprietatem dependentia rei Verbi post se ad obliquum*

Duns Scotus remarks of the genus verbi, {389/331} which is subdivided into the genus activum, passivum, neutrum, and commune, that it is based *"primarily"* on the difference in the *word form* of verbs. He thus indicates that the genus verbi cannot be understood in purely semantic terms, and we must rely more on identifying the bare grammatical relationships.[85]

Finally, we must clarify how Duns Scotus determines the relationship of the category of "time" to the verb. The German term for the verb, "Zeitwort [timeword]," might be taken to mean that the category of time should be assigned to the essence of the part of speech in question. It should already be clear from what has been said that Scotus is not of this opinion. For him, time is only an accidental mode, albeit not in the sense that it is a respective mode based on the verb's relation to the subject of the proposition or its objects (nouns in the oblique cases). Rather, time is a mode based on the state of affairs as such, *but for this reason* it *need not* be given along with the state of affairs. Logical and mathematical states of affairs have no temporal determinations.[86]

THE PARTICIPLE

The meaning function of the verb can be summarily characterized as intending a *state of affairs*; specifically, *as valid* of an object (per modum distantis).

The general function of the participle is also to intend a state of affairs, albeit *not* in the modus distantis *but* in the modus *indistantis*. This means that the emphasis of meaning in the participle is not so much on the *inherence* of the state of affairs in the object as on the state of affairs conceived of as *united* with the object. This moment of meaning, in which {390/332} the tension between the object and the state of affairs is, as it were, sublated and erased, distinguishes the participle from the verb.[87]

---

sub ratione termini significat. Et hoc patet per Petrum Heliam, qui diffinit Genus per significationem accidentalem, sic dicens: *Genus est significatio accidentalis cum determinatione in o vel in or:* dans intelligere per *significationem accidentalem* modum significativum transeuntis, ut dictum est, id est, dependentiae ad quemlibet obliquum post se. Per terminationem in *o* vel in *or* dat intelligere species generis, quarum diversitas maxime attenditur penes vocis terminationem secundum Grammaticos, ut patebit. l. c. cap. XXX, 26b, n. 1.

85. l. c. 27a, n. 4.

86. l. c. cap. XXXII, 28b, sq., n. 3, 4, 6.

87. Modus significandi essentialis generalissimus Participii est modus significandi per modum *esse indistantis* a substantia, circa quod notandum quod modus *esse* in Participio et in Verbo ab eadem rei proprietate oritur, quae est proprietas fluxus et successionis; et in hoc modo Participium a Verbo non discrepat.

Duns Scotus clarifies the characterization of the part of speech under discussion to the effect that it *participates*, as it were, in the meaning function of the noun and that of the verb, but not in relation to their essential moments, *as though* the participle could simultaneously mean an object as an object and a state of affairs as a state of affairs. This interpretation must be rejected as incorrect, for if it were correct, it would not be understandable why the participle constitutes an *independent* form of meaning—one *specifically* distinct from the others. The "participation" mentioned can *only* refer to the *accidental* modes, insofar as "numerus" and "casus" are proper to the participle as they are to the noun, but "tempus" and "significatio" are also simultaneously proper to it as they are to the verb.[88] {391/333}

The division of the participle's special modes of meaning is carried out analogously to those of the verb.[89]

The nominal accidents do not appertain to the participle as such, except on the basis of the *association* with the object that is entailed in its essence.[90]

THE ADVERB

The adverb means per modum *esse*, that is, the thought of the state of affairs is included in its meaning. On closer examination, its function aims to *determine* the *compositio*, that is, the moment of the inherence of a state of affairs in an object, in some way. Because the moment of compositio is excluded from the

---

Modus autem *indistantis* a substantia seu modus uniti substantiae, sumitur ab eadem rei proprietate in Participio, a qua sumitur modus *adjacentis* in Nomine: et *compositio* in Verbo: et haec est proprietas inhaerentis alteri secundum esse. Et non est inconveniens ab eadem rei proprietate modos significandi diversos, non oppositos, oriri: cum modi significandi oppositi in eadem voce possint fundari. Et per hunc modum significandi Participium a Verbo distinguitur, et per ipsum Participium in suum suppositum in constructione et in situ collocatur.

Participum ergo est pars orationis significans per modum esse indistantis a *substantia, sive* uniti *cum substantia quod idem est.* Et dicitur *Participium* quasi partem Nominis et partem Verbi *capiens* non partem essentialem id est modum essentialem utriusque. Et quidam dicunt, quod Participium significat per modum *entis* et per modum *esse*, quod falsum est: quia tunc Participium non esset ab utroque distinctum specifice, quod est inconveniens. Sed pro tanto dicitur Participium capere partem Nominis et Verbi: quia habet quosdam modos significandi accidentales modis accidentalibus Nominis et Verbi consimiles, ut statim apparebit. l. c. cap. XXXVI, 32, a, b.

88. l. c. cap. XXXVIII, 33a, n. 1–3.
89. l. c. cap. XXXVII, 32b, n. 4–6.
90. l. c. cap. XXXVIII, 33b, n. 3.

participle (this circumstance distinguishes it precisely from the verb), properly speaking, we cannot call adverbs determinations of the participle. But insofar as a state of affairs is intended in the participle, this state of affairs must also— qua state of affairs—be susceptible to the determining form of the adverbial meaning function. But the general, essential meaning function of adverbs only affects verbs.[91] {392/334}

If, however, this general meaning function receives particular specifications (for example, the moment of meaning of limitation or exclusion), the adverb can be applied to all meanings that have been preformed for this particular meaning function. It follows that nouns and pronouns can also be connected with adverbs.

This seems to contradict the functional meaning of the adverb that we noted at the outset when we said that the thought of the state of affairs is included in the adverb's function, whereas nouns and pronouns intend objects as objects. Someone could object that states of affairs can also be *named* in nominal and pronominal forms of meaning, and hence it is not inconsistent that *they* are also *adverbially* determined.

However, the difficulty cannot be resolved this way. For when a state of affairs is found in the meaning function of the noun or the pronoun, I *no longer* intend it *as a state of affairs* but *as an object*. In my view, the contradiction can be resolved if we recognize that the full content of the meaning of the adverbial determinations of nouns and pronouns is such that these determinations only allow themselves to be "thought of" in a complete sentence in which *states of affairs* are intended. For example, Duns Scotus cites the sentence: homo tantummodo legit, "Only man

---

91. Modus significandi essentialis generalissimus Adverbii est modus significandi per modum *adjacentis* alteri per modum esse, significans ipsum simpliciter, id est: absolute determinans. Et quia Participium significat per modum *esse* sicut Verbum, ideo Adverbium determinat Participium sicut Verbum: licet Adverbium dicatur Adjectivum Verbi secundum Priscianum. Hoc est ideo, quia Adverbium secundum omnes species eius determinat Verbum sed non Participium: quia Adverbia determinantia Verba genera compositionis et genera sui modi, qui est qualitas compositionis, Participia determinare non possunt, cum Participium compositionem et modum Verbi non habeat. Et sumitur iste modus determinantis a proprietate terminantis in re.

Adverbium ergo est *pars orationis significans per modum adjacentis alteri, quod per modum* esse *significat, ipsum* esse *absolute determinans.*

Et notandum, quod Adverbium de suo modo significandi essentiali generalissimo tantum determinat ea, quae per modum esse significat: licet de aliquo modo essentiali speciali et accidentali possit alia determinare, ut patet de Adverbiis exclusivis, quae sunt *tantummodo, solummodo* et huiusmodi; quae propter modum significandi per modum excludentis possunt determinare omne illud, quod habet se per modum exclusibilis, l. c. cap. XXXIII, 29a sq., n. 1, 2.

reads." Hence the adverb always has some relation to states of affairs, that is, to the verbs that express them.[92] If it does not stand in relation to {393/335} verbs or participles, that is, it does *not* stand in the function of determining states of affairs, its meaning is "mangled," as Duns Scotus expressly notes.[93]

The nature of the adverbial meaning function permits a specification in which the adverb's *genuine* character of determination is articulated. An adverb can determine verbs and participles in two ways: first, with respect to their meaning *content* in itself, and second, with respect to their *mode* of meaning. Both kinds of adverbial determining function can be further specified; through this specification, we arrive at the different concrete forms of adverbs.

A state of affairs expressed by a verb can undergo stricter adverbial determination with respect to the categories of space, quantity, and quality, as can the act quality of the verbal *act* of meaning.[94]

The meaning *function* of the verb as such and not the substantive What [das inhaltliche Was] of the states of affairs that is expressed in it at any given time can be determined with respect to *compositio*, time, and the quality of the verb.[95]

We shall not pursue in detail the [different] adverbial determinations that are possible on the basis of the differentiation of the states of affairs in accordance with the categories listed [space, quantity, quality, time, et cetera] as they do not further impinge on the meaning *function* of the verb but, instead, represent *material* differentiations.

By contrast, it is interesting to look into how, while discussing the adverbial determinations that aim at the meaning *function* of verbs, Duns Scotus clarifies problems {394/336} that are otherwise familiar from phenomenology or, at the least, assigns them a place within his doctrine of meaning.

In our discussion of the verb's compositio and the act qualities that modify it, we already intimated how Duns Scotus indicates a problem domain that has still not been sufficiently treated in the least. The adverbs, which are under consideration here solely as determinations of the compositio, attain their specific character from the relevant act qualities; these are: questioning, doubt, affirmation,

---

92. l. c. n. 2.

Adverbium licet sit adjectivum verbi non tamen habet modos significandi speciales, *quibus ipsi soli verbo proportionatur.* Unde quia habet modos significandi generales, ideo determinare potest participium, pronomen et ipsum nomen. Sup. elench. qu. XXXIII, 48a.

93. Adverbium enim nisi habeat participium vel verbum, *semper est truncata locutio sive incongrua.* Op. Ox. IV, dist. L, qu. VI, 567a, n. 10.

94. De modis significandi cap. XXXIV, 29a, n. 5; cap. XXXV, 30a, n. 7.

95. l. c. cap. XXXV, 30b, n. 13.

and negation. The adverbs associated with the indicative, optative, and imperative moods—the act qualities of wishing and commanding—as their more proximate determinations also belong here. By contrast, temporal adverbs should be classified in the previously mentioned group of adverbs, which concern the *substantive* side of the state of affairs.[96]

THE CONJUNCTION

As the name already indicates, the task of the conjunction is *to connect clauses.* With this very general characterization, nothing is determined either about the *kind* of connection or about the nature of the clauses to be connected. We can distinguish two fundamental kinds of connection and two corresponding classes of conjunctions. A connection of clauses is possible *quae inter se dependentiam non habent,* that is, the substantive What [das inhaltliche Was] of the clauses that are connected does not, as such, require this particular connection. The connection is imposed on them "from outside," as it were. Conjunctions of this kind are not unfittingly called *conjunctio per vim.*[97] {395/337}

Copulative conjunctions—for example, "and"—belong to this class. The "and" can link two substantives or adjectives or entire sentences with each other, whose content does not exhibit any immanent articulation and hence *does not require* the copulative connection. It is characteristic of the relation occurring in such conjunctions that it does not remain *limited* to *two* elements but can extend to a third and then to any number in succession. Disjunctions are also conjunctions per vim, but they have *the* peculiarity that they connect

---

96. l. c. cap. XXXV, 30b sqq., n. 14–19.

97. Modus significandi essentialis Conjunctionis generalissimus est modus significandi *per modum conjungentis duo extrema.* Et sumitur iste modus significandi a proprietate conjungentis et unientis in rebus extra. *Conjunctio ergo est pars orationis per modum conjungentis duo extrema significans.*

Sub modo essentiali generalissimo Conjunctionis ad modos subalternos per divisionem descendamus. Dividitur autem iste modus *conjungentis duo extrema* in modum conjungentis duo extrema per *vim* et in modum conjungentis duo extrema *per ordinem.* Et hos duos modos Donatus appellat *potestates.* Et habet se similiter *potestas* in Conjunctione sicut *significatio* in Adverbio. Nam sicut significatio in Adverbio consistit in speciali modo determinandi: sic potestas in Conjunctione consistit in speciali modo conjungendi. Et istius modi modus est modus conjungendi *per vim et per ordinem.* Ex hoc patet quod *potestas* in Conjunctione non est modus significandi accidentalis, nisi pro tanto, quia est extra rationem Conjunctionis simpliciter et absolute sumptae, ut dictum est de significatione in Adverbio. l. c. cap. XXXIX, 33b sq., n. 5, 6.

two clauses *such that* they are distinguished from a *third*. Duns Scotus cites a sentence of Boethius, who remarks of the disjunctive conjunction that it brings two clauses into relation, while simultaneously *prohibiting* both from existing at the same time.[98]

Conjunctions per *ordinem* constitute the second kind. *The meaning content* of the clauses to be connected *requires* specific forms of connection. As examples, Duns Scotus cites conjunctions that mediate, on the one hand, between cause and effect (*real* objects and states of affairs) and, on the other hand, between antecedent and consequent (logical objects and states of affairs).[99]

In addition to these two kinds of genuine conjunctions, whose sense is grounded in the essence of speech, that is, of sentences, there also exist conjunctions for the sake of *embellishment*. As they essentially do not belong {396/338} to the genuine forms of meaning, closer treatment is superfluous.[100]

THE PREPOSITION

The *preposition* can also be understood as a kind of connective. However, it cannot be reduced to one of the other connectives that appear in the context of meaning and hence constitutes a new, independent form of meaning. The connection occurs with nouns found in particular cases. The cases permit us to think of the objects intended in the respective meanings as occurring in specific relationships. In the context of meaning, the prepositions have the function of determining the respective relationships and hence enabling further contexts of meaning.

However, when prepositions combine with other forms of meaning (for example, verbs) so that they constitute a grammatical unit with them, they lose their meaning function. They no longer constitute an independent expression. Rather, they receive the form of meaning of the word with which they are grammatically linked. They can still have a determining effect on the content of meaning, *but not in the specific function of the preposition*.[101]

THE INTERJECTION

Duns Scotus considers the interjection a more proximate determination of the verb or the participle. Accordingly, we might think that it is not an independent meaning function but coincides with the adverb. However, it should be

---

98. l. c. cap. XXXIX, 34a, n. 7.
99. l. c. cap. XXXIX, 34a, b, n. 8, 9.
100. l. c. 34b, n. 11.
101. l. c. cap. XLI, XLII, 35a sqq.

noted that its meaning content always represents moods; it is thus related to *emotional acts*. {397/339} Accordingly, the interjection does not determine the meaning content of verbs as such either, that is, the *state of affairs* intended in them. Its determining function bears on *the relation of the verbal acts of meaning to consciousness*.[102]

Concrete forms of interjection occur according to the various emotions such as pain, sorrow, joy, wonder, fear, and shock.[103] {398/340}

---

102. l. c. cap. XLIII, 36b sq., n. 10.
103. l. c. cap. XLIV, 37a sq.

—ɷ—

CONCLUSION

The Problem of Categories

Motto:

"We seek the Absolute everywhere
and always only find things."

NOVALIS, *FRAGMENTE*, VOL. II (MINOR), 111.

THE GENUINE GOAL OF THIS investigation as an investigation into the history of the *problem* requires with systematic necessity as its conclusion—in addition to a retrospective summary that processes and evaluates the main points of its result—a preview of the *systematic* structure of the problem of the categories. However, we cannot do much more than bring to light the *essential powers of the problem and their context,* for our treatment of the problem thus far did not make them available in a *fundamental manner.* This is also the reason why until now, the systems of categories that have been proposed could not allay the impression of a certain deadly hollowness.

In the preceding inquiry, where our aim at first was to present one *historical* formation of the problem of categories while simultaneously raising it to a systematic level, it was not expedient to posit fundamental theses with determinate content at the outset, because their far-reaching relationship to a special configuration of the problem would undoubtedly have remained controversial without previous knowledge of this configuration. Moreover, our presentation, which aimed at a simple, systematic understanding, would have been greatly hampered by the oft-sprawling problems that inevitably follow from taking a fundamental position; by constantly bringing forth open questions, these problems would have exasperatingly interrupted our presentation. By contrast, this is now the appropriate place to voice {399/341} the intellectual *unrest*, which we have so far suppressed, that the philosopher must constantly experience when studying historical formations of his world of problems.

The essential powers of the problem of the categories, however, can be brought to light only if the categories are isolated and analyzed one by one. It is thus all the more important that we emphasize from the outset that they condition each other reciprocally and that what appears direct and unmediated is always mediated, and furthermore, that what we establish individually in what follows receives its full sense only within the totality.

If we conceive of the categories as elements and means for interpreting the sense of the experienceable—of the objective as such—it follows that a basic requirement of the doctrine of categories is the *characterization and delineation of the different domains of objects into sectors that are categorially irreducible to each other*. The entire *plan* of the previous investigation already emphasized the fulfillment of this task.[1] It simultaneously had to accomplish the destruction of the formerly sterile and unproblematic aspect of the logic of medieval Scholasticism. This was done by bringing to light the determining elements that fundamentally characterize the individual domains of objects. The fact that these elements reach all the way into the ultimate categorial sphere of the objective (the transcendentals) provided the fundamental, unifying aggregation of these regions, which were [otherwise] falling apart. In order to do so, a strictly *conceptual* and in a certain sense one-sided presentation {400/342} was needed, one that consciously excluded the more profound metaphysical implications of the problem.

These metaphysical implications can be understood as being ultimately decisive for the problem of categories only if a second fundamental task for any theory of categories is recognized: *situating the problem of the categories within the problems of judgment and of the subject*. This aspect of the problem of the categories is also at least broached in Scholastic logic. Admittedly, our presentation of Duns Scotus's doctrine of judgment had a different aim: it was intended

---

1. Oswald Külpe also emphasizes "the differentiation of the domain of validity of the categories." See "Zur Kategorienlehre," in *Sitzungsberichte der Königlichen Bayerischen Akademie der Wissenschaften, philosophisch-philologische und historische Klasse*, Jahrgang 1915, Abhandlung 5 (Munich: Königliche Bayerische Akademie der Wissenschaften, 1915), 46ff. This last, most valuable work by Külpe appeared *after* the present investigation was completed. Given the significance of Külpe's treatise and, overall, the philosophical position that this scholar, who died too young, was able to achieve, a comment is needed, but only insofar as the upcoming thoughts call for it. In any case, it should be particularly noted that this is not intended to infract our piety toward the author in the least.

to characterize the domain of the logical, and in this, the essential relationship of the judgment to the category remained fundamentally obscure at first. By contrast, the doctrine of meaning enabled access to subjectivity (meaning not individuality, but the *subject in itself*). Duns Scotus's task, the analysis of a particular stratum of acts—the modi significandi—requires him to attend to the sphere of *acts in general* and to make fundamental determinations about the individual strata of acts (modus significandi, intelligendi, essendi) and their relations to one another.

The existence of a doctrine of meaning in medieval Scholasticism reveals a refined disposition for confidently listening in on the immediate life of subjectivity and its immanent contexts of sense, without having acquired a precise concept of the subject. We might be tempted to "explain" the existence of such "grammars" by way of reference to the operation of medieval schools and their traditions. An "explanation" of this sort is often cherished in the historical sciences, but it is utterly suspect for problems in intellectual history. Admittedly, it is justified *to a certain degree* even in our case. But when a living understanding of an "epoch" and of the effective achievements of its spirit is at stake, what is needed is *an interpretation* of its sense *guided by ultimate telic ideas*. We often use the facile label "construction" to arrogantly reject such an undertaking out of hand as unhistorical and hence worthless. {401/343} Because of a fundamental ignorance of the nature of historical cognition and of historical concept formation, we fail to notice that merely shuffling and amassing as much "factual material" as possible leads away from the vital life of a historical past and, curiously, verges on a leveling construction that puts out of play the sense that confers unity and purpose.

Notwithstanding its immediately schematic character, the doctrine of meaning is particularly significant for a philosophical exposition of medieval Scholasticism in the context of the problem of categories, *because it returns to a fundamental sphere of the problem of subjectivity* (the strata of acts). The investigation of the relation between the modus essendi and the "subjective" modi significandi and intelligendi leads to the principle of the *material determination* of every form, which in turn includes the fundamental correlation of object and subject.[2] This essential relatedness of the object of cognition and the cognition of the object has its clearest expression in the concept of *"verum"* as one of the *transcendentals*, the determinations of the object *as such*. Nevertheless, we still lack—and this has to do with our understanding of the epistemological problem itself—on the

---

2. I hope to be able to show on another occasion how *Eckhart's mysticism* first receives its philosophical explication and evaluation from this vantage point in conjunction with the metaphysics of the problem of truth that we shall touch on later.

one hand, the explicit integration of the problem of judgment into the subject-object relationship and, on the other hand, bringing the category into relation with judgment.

Because fundamental clarity has not yet been attained regarding these problem contexts even today in the places that champion realism, this fundamental task of the doctrine of categories (next to the demarcation of the domains of objects) deserves a closer discussion. In doing so, the opportunity presents itself {402/344} to indicate, at least in very general outline, the necessity of a metaphysical closure to the epistemological problem.

The category is the most universal determination of an object. The object and objectivity have, as such, sense only *for* a subject. Objectivity is constituted in the subject by means of the judgment. Consequently, if we want to comprehend the category decisively as the determinacy of the *object*, we must establish its essential relation with the structure that constitutes objectivity. It is hence no "accident" but rather is grounded in the innermost core of the problem of the categories that the problem manifests both for Aristotle and for Kant in some sort of connection with predication, that is, with judgment. This could mean that the categories are to be reduced to mere *functions of thought*, but this possibility is hardly conceivable for a philosophy that has acknowledged the *problems of sense*. And precisely transcendental idealism—whose contemporary form we may not simply identify with Kantian epistemology and the way it has been formulated—emphasizes from the outset that all thought and cognition is always the thought and cognition *of an object*. The validity of treating the categories as mere "forms of thought" must likewise be evaluated in relation to this.[3] {403/345}

---

3. Külpe's failure to consider the fundamental significance of the problem of judgment for the *grounding of objectivity* is also the reason why he succeeds just as little at refuting transcendental idealism in *Die Realisierung*, vol. 1 (Leipzig: Hirzel, 1912) as he does in his previously mentioned essay "Zur Kategorienlehre"—indeed, why he could not succeed. Particularly in the crucial passage where Külpe rejects the characterization "theory of representation" as unsuitable for critical realism and emphasizes that "the objects of the real world that are to be represented and determined [!] in cognition are not preexisting constituents of perception, are not simply given in consciousness, *but can be grasped only by a cognitive process, in particular by scientific research*" ("Zur Kategorienlehre," 42; Heidegger's emphasis), he leans on an argument that transcendental idealism consciously placed at the center of the problem. If critical realism can be persuaded to take judgment fundamentally into consideration when developing the problem of cognition and, conversely, transcendental idealism succeeds in organically integrating the principle of the material determination of form into its basic position, then we shall necessarily succeed in elevating the two most important and fruitful epistemological "orientations" in the present to a higher unity.

Even the most general and—in terms of their content—faded determinations of objects, the reflexive categories, cannot be fully understood without relation to the *judgment* that constitutes objectivity. This means that a *merely* "objective" universal theory of the object that does not include the "subjective side" necessarily remains incomplete. Thus, every distinction is assuredly a distinction of some objective thing, but it is this once again only *as* a distinction that is *cognized, judged*. The reason for a multiplicity of *domains of validity* within the totality of the categories lies *primarily, though not exclusively*, in the multiplicity of the object regions, each of which conditions a correspondingly structured form of the formation of judgment, from which [form] the categories can first be "read off" in their *full content*.

Likewise, the problem of the "immanent and transeunt (that is, lying 'outside of thought') validity" of the categories can be solved only by setting out from the judgment. Without taking "subjective logic" into consideration, it does not even make sense to speak of *immanent and transeunt* validity. Immanence and transcendence are relational concepts that first acquire a definite meaning once we establish *that in relation to which* something must be thought of as immanent or transcendent. It is indisputable that "all transeunt validity stands and falls with the recognition of objects."[4] But the *problem* is, after all, *just what kind* {404/346} *of objectivity can this be* if we bear in mind that objectivity only has sense for a judging subject and that without this subject, we shall also never succeed in bringing to light the full sense of what is called *validity. We need not decide here* whether validity means a special kind of "being" or an "ought," *or neither of these, but rather can first be comprehended from more fundamental groups of problems that are contained in the concept of the living spirit and are doubtless closely connected with the problem of value.*

The intimate connection between the problem of the categories and the problem of judgment likewise permits us to make the *form-matter relationship* and the meaning differentiating function of matter once again into a problem. The form-matter duality is such a key means of treating epistemological problems

---

4. See Külpe, "Zur Kategorienlehre," 52. Heinrich Rickert, in his *Gegenstand der Erkenntnis*, has in the present particularly called attention to the necessity of including the logical, judging subject. We shall have to abstain from taking a final position on the problem of "judging consciousness as such" and that of the "unquestioned yes" (Rickert, 318ff. and 334ff.; cited above) until the necessary universal foundations have been laid by the doctrine of value that is under development. This also holds for Edmund Husserl's valuable conclusions about "pure consciousness," which provide a crucial look into the riches of "consciousness" and destroy the oft-expressed view that in itself, consciousness is empty. Husserl, *Ideas I*, 136 [*Husserliana* III, 174]; Heidegger cites Husserl, *Ideen*, 141ff.

today that a *fundamental* investigation into the value and limits of this duality
has become unavoidable.

Of course, a final clarification of this question cannot be attained by remaining within the logical sphere of sense and the structure of this sense. At most, we chance on exponentiation (Lask's theory of the levels of forms), which undeniably accomplishes the important task of illuminating the structural manifold of the logical itself yet further complicates the problem of the meaning differentiating function of matter and projects it into a new sphere without adequately accounting for the fundamental difference between sensory and nonsensory matter.

We cannot see logic and its problems in the true light at all if they are not interpreted *from* a translogical perspective. {405/347} In the long run, *philosophy cannot dispense with its proper optic, metaphysics.* For the theory of truth, this poses the task of an ultimate, metaphysical and teleological interpretation of consciousness. Everything that has value already lives within consciousness in a primordial and genuine manner, provided it is a living act that is meaningful and productive of meaning. We have not in the least understood what such an act is when we neutralize it in the concept of a blind, biological fact.

The theoretical attitude is merely *one* among the myriad of formative directions of the living spirit. It must therefore be considered a fundamental and perilous error of the philosophy of "worldview" that it is satisfied with cataloguing reality rather than aiming, beyond the ever-provisional summary of the totality of the knowable, at a *breakthrough* to true reality and real truth, as is its most proper vocation. Epistemological logic will be preserved from being exclusively restricted to the study of structures, and it will make logical sense *even in its ontic meaning into a problem* only if it orients itself in this way toward the concept of the living spirit and its "eternal affirmations" (Friedrich Schlegel). A satisfactory answer as to how "unreal," "transcendent" sense secures true reality and objectivity for us will then become possible for the first time.

The more radically Lask explicated the structural problems in the doctrine of judgment and in the doctrine of categories, the more inexorably he was impelled from his constellation of problems into metaphysical problems, without himself perhaps becoming fully aware of this. And precisely in his concept of an object that is characterized by its transcendence of opposites, there lies a fruitful element capable of unifying epistemological theories that diverge in many respects even at present. But in doing so, we should not underestimate the difficulties {406/348} entailed in the problem of opposition and the problem of values, the problem of the ontic interpretation and logical understanding of the "object."[5]

---

5. The author hopes to be able to present fundamental conclusions regarding this problem at a later date in a more thorough investigation of being, value, and negation.

Where this kind of *transcendental-ontic* understanding of the concept of the object is present, the problem of the "application" of the categories loses all sense. This is all the more certain to be the case the more resolutely we take seriously the fundamental meaning of the *principle of immanence* (this must not be construed "individualistically"). The latter's *ultimate* grounding, which I consider necessary, will have to be accomplished on the basis of the concept of the living spirit that has been indicated—and it can only be carried out metaphysically. If there is any point at which we must recognize that the *merely* objective and logical way of treating the problem of categories is only half the solution, then it is precisely in regards to the problem of the *application* of the categories, provided we even grant that it is a *potential* problem.[6]

The epistemological subject does not explain the metaphysically most meaningful sense of the spirit, to say nothing of its full content. And it is only when the problem of the categories is placed within the latter that it acquires its proper dimension of depth and enrichment. *The living spirit is as such essentially historical spirit in the broadest sense of the term.* The true {407/349} worldview is far removed from the merely discontinuous existence of a theory detached from life. Spirit can be comprehended only if the complete abundance of its achievements, that is, *its history*, is preserved in it; and insofar as this steadily expanding abundance is comprehended philosophically, we are given an ever intensifying means for the living comprehension of the absolute spirit of God. History and its cultural, philosophical, and teleological interpretation *must become a meaning determining element for the problem of categories* provided we want to work out the *cosmos* of categories and go beyond an impoverished schematic table of categories. Along with demarcating the domains of objects and including the problem of judgment, this is the third fundamental requirement for a promising solution

---

6. Unfortunately, Külpe gets into Lask's *Lehre vom Urteil* (1912) as little with regard to *this* problem in particular (which we can understand given his constant preference for "objective logic") as he does in general at any point. I am compelled to attribute *even* greater significance to *Lehre vom Urteil* for the doctrine of categories than I do to Lask's *Logik der Philosophie*. This book on judgment is unusually rich in fruitful perspectives, and it is therefore all the more regrettable that Külpe, in his exemplary, distinguished manner of disputation, could no longer present to expert circles his position on Lask regarding what, in my opinion, is the absolutely crucial problem of judgment. Indeed, the same thing that he wrote of Lask in his final work holds today of Külpe himself: "Surely this highly talented researcher would not have evaded the consequence of his trenchant reflections [on the problem of differentiating forms; Heidegger's insertion] in the latter course of his development, had he not been torn from us all too soon by a harsh fate" ("Zur Kategorienlehre," 26n3).

to the problem of categories. Conversely, only from such a broadly oriented doctrine of categories can we provide the conceptual means and objectives required for a living comprehension of particular epochs of intellectual history. Even today, if it is treated more profoundly at all, the problem of the "medieval worldview" touched on in the introduction, which ought to be particularly interesting in the context of the present investigation, lacks the *proper conceptual foundation in the philosophy of culture* that can first give clarity, certainty, and unity to the whole. The peculiar will to live and the refined spiritual composure of such a time call for a concordant *openness* of empathetic understanding and a broadly (that is, philosophically) oriented evaluation. For example, the concept of *analogy* that we discussed in this investigation[7] with regard to the problem of metaphysical reality seems at first to be a completely wan and no longer meaningful Scholastic concept. But as the dominant principle in the categorial sphere of sensory and supersensory reality, it harbors the conceptual expression {408/350} of the *qualitatively* full, value-laden, transcendence-oriented experiential world of medieval humanity. It is the conceptual expression of the specific form of inner existence, anchored in the transcendent primordial relationship of the soul to God, that was alive with unusual integrity in the Middle Ages. The multitude of quotidian connections between God and the soul, between the afterlife and the here and now, changes as the distance or nearness (understood in a qualitative, intensive sense) in this relationship changes. The metaphysical conjointment resulting from transcendence is simultaneously the source of a multitude of oppositions and hence also of the richest life of the immanent personal life of the individual.

Transcendence does not mean a radical, vanishing removal from the subject: rather, there is a living relation based on correlativity, which as such does not have a *single* rigid orientation but can be compared with the back-and-forth flow of experience among spiritually congenial individuals. Of course, here we have not considered the absolute incommensurability of one of the members of the correlation. The scale of values accordingly does not gravitate exclusively toward the transcendent but is, as it were, reflected back by the abundance and absoluteness of the transcendent and comes to rest in the individual.

For this reason, we also find a whole world of manifold differentiations of value throughout the medieval worldview, and this already because it is so radical in its consciously *teleological* orientation. The possibility and fullness of experience resulting from these differentiations of value for subjectivity is hence conditioned by that dimension of spiritual life that reaches forth *into the*

---

7. See p. 47ff. above.

transcendent and not, as is the case today, by the *breadth of its fleeting content*. The possibilities of rising insecurity and complete disorientation are far greater and almost unlimited for such a superficially unfolding attitude to life. By contrast, the fundamental orientation of the form of life of medieval humanity from the outset does not lose itself in the voluminous content of sensory reality; rather than anchor itself therein, it precisely subjects the latter itself, {409/351} as *in need of anchoring*, to the necessity of a transcendent goal.

In the concept of the living spirit and this spirit's relation to the metaphysical "origin," an insight opens up into the spirit's basic metaphysical structure, in which the uniqueness and individuality of *acts* is conjoined with the universal validity and self-subsistence of *sense* into a living unity. In objective terms, we encounter the problem of the relation of time and eternity, change and absolute validity, world and God—a problem that is reflected in the theory of science in [the distinction between] *history* (the formation of value) and *philosophy* (the validity of value).[8]

If we contemplate the deeper essence of philosophy as worldview, the view of Christian philosophy in the Middle Ages as a Scholasticism standing in opposition to the *mysticism* of its time must be exposed as fundamentally erroneous. Scholasticism and mysticism belong together essentially in the medieval worldview. The two pairs of "opposites," rationalism-irrationalism and Scholasticism-mysticism, *do not coincide with one another*. Any attempt to equate them rests on an extreme rationalization of philosophy. Philosophy as a rationalistic construct detached from life is *impotent*; mysticism as irrational experience is *without a goal*.

---

8. The concept of *"perennial philosophy"* can first be analyzed and established in terms of the theory of science setting out from this point, which has *not* been done to this day in a satisfactory manner even to a remote degree. Just as little has the problem of an examination *of Catholic theology in terms of a theory of science*, which is closely related with what we have said, been recognized as a problem, to say nothing of its solution having been tackled. The reason for this lies partly in the way of treating *logic* so far, which has been overly traditional and blind to the problems. Geyser, whose *Grundlagen der Logik und Erkenntnishlehre* (1909) we already mentioned earlier, undertook the first fundamentally conscious new orientation in this area. (See my review article "Neuere Forschungen zur Logik," *Literarische Rundschau* 38, no. 11 [1912]: 522f. [GA 1, 35f.].)

Tr.: See GA 1, "Neuere Forschungen zur Logik," 17–43; Thomas Sheehan, trans., "Recent Research in Logic," in *Becoming Heidegger: On the Trail of His Early Occasional Writings, 1910–1927*, ed. Theodore Kisiel and Thomas Sheehan (Evanston, IL: Northwestern University Press, 2007), 30–44.

The philosophy of living spirit, active love, and reverent devotion to God, whose most general tenets {410/352} we could only allude to here, and even more so, a doctrine of categories guided by its basic tendencies, faces the major task of a fundamental confrontation with what is in abundance as well as profundity, wealth of experience and concept formation, the most powerful system of a historical worldview, a system that has, as such, subsumed all the fundamental philosophical problem motifs that preceded it within itself—that is, a confrontation with Hegel. {411/353}

AUTHOR'S NOTICE

THIS INVESTIGATION INTO THE HISTORY of a *problem* ultimately has a *systematic* goal: the doctrine of categories, whose fundamental grounding and organic development philosophy today clearly recognizes as one of its basic tasks. As an investigation into the *history* of a problem, it has the philosophy of the Scholastic Duns Scotus for its object. It aims to gain a deeper understanding of one of the intellectually most accomplished and richest paradigms of medieval Scholastic thought with regard to the problem of categories *and logic as such*, and to counter the conventional estimation of medieval Scholasticism and its logic. With this in mind, the major emphasis in part I (the doctrine of categories) was placed on what is the basic requirement for any treatment of the problem of categories: demarcating the different domains within the objective as such. To begin with, the most universal determinations of objects in general and the individual domains (logical, mathematical, physical, psychic, and metaphysical reality) had to be subjected to an interpretive characterization. Part II (the doctrine of meaning) then provided an opportunity to present a particular sphere of objects, that of meanings, in greater detail. In doing so, it could work out basic theses about acts (and about the sense of these acts) of meaning and cognition, and furthermore about the basic forms of meaning in general (the "categories of meaning"). The final chapter attempts to provide preliminary determinations of the structure of the problem of categories and the potential path to its solution.

Freiburg im Breisgau

Martin Heidegger {412/354}

167

BIBLIOGRAPHICAL REFERENCES

Die Kategorien- und Bedeutungslehre des Duns Scotus. Postdoctoral thesis, University of
Freiburg im Breisgau, 1915. First published as *Die Kategorien- und Bedeutungslehre
des Duns Scotus* (Tübingen: J. C. B. Mohr, 1916), 245 pages, including an index of
names and a subject index. The concluding chapter was composed retrospectively
for publication.

The *Selbstanzeige* was first published as "Die Kategorien- und Bedeutungslehre des
Duns Scotus," *Kant Studien* 21, no. 4 (1917): 467–68.

EDITOR'S AFTERWORD

I.

"Ways—not works" is the motto that Martin Heidegger wrote down in his own hand, along with the title page for his complete edition of the last hand [Gesamtausgabe letzter Hand], a few days before his death. In February of the same year, he had composed the dedication to his spouse, Elfride Heidegger (née Petri). "Her fervent support on the long path" began with their engagement in 1915 and lasted for over sixty years. The title page, motto, and dedication are reproduced as facsimiles.[*]

Martin Heidegger had intended to include a foreword in volume 1 of his complete edition explaining the sense and task of this edition, which was personally sketched out and begun by him. The swift death, whose portent the philosopher clearly perceived in the final days of his earthly existence, no longer left him the time to carry out his plan. Instead of the foreword, which never advanced beyond preliminary drafts, he composed the motto.

From the surviving notes for the foreword, two texts clarifying the edition's motto, which were written down on separate sheets, may be shared.

> The complete edition should reveal in different ways a being-underway in
> the itinerant field of the dynamically changing questioning of the equivocal
> question of being. The complete edition should thereby instruct one to take up
> the question, to join in questioning and, above all, thereafter, to question more
> questioningly. To question more questioningly—that is, to enact the step back;

---

[*] See GA 1, iii–v.

171

back to what is withheld; back into the speech that names ("back" as itinerant character of thought, not temporally-historiographically). {437}

What is at stake is awakening the confrontation over the question concerning the matter of thought (thought as the relation to being as presence; Parmenides, Heraclitus: *νοεῖν, λόγος*), and not relaying the author's opinion or characterizing the writer's standpoint or locating [him] in the series of other historiographically determinable philosophical standpoints. Of course, something of this sort is possible at any time, above all in the age of information, but it is entirely without relevance for preparing the questioning access to the matter of thinking.

The second note reads as follows:

The large number of volumes attests only to the lingering question-worthiness of the question of being and provides manifold occasion for self-examination. On its part, the effort collected in the edition remains only a weak echo of the beginning that withdraws itself ever further: the restraint of *Ἀλήθεια*, which cleaves to itself. In a certain way, it is manifest and constantly experienced, but its unique characteristic remains necessarily unthought in the beginning, a state of affairs that saddles all subsequent thought with a peculiar reticence. To seek, now, to transform what was familiar in the beginning into something known would be delusory.

II.

Compared with the separate edition that appeared in 1972, the *Frühe Schriften* have been supplemented in this first volume of the complete edition of the last hand with seven works by the young Heidegger. The volume now fully encompasses all the early writings that were published by Martin Heidegger between 1912 and 1916. The two earliest essays, "The Problem of Reality in Modern Philosophy" (1912) and "Newer Research in Logic" (1912), are as yet from the pen of the student—one year {438} before Heidegger obtained his doctorate (1913). The other five newly included smaller works are critical reviews (1913–1914). The two essays as well as the three larger reviews are thematically related to the treatises that follow them [in *Frühe Schriften*]: Heidegger cites the two essays as well as the longest of the reviews in the dissertation, the postdoctoral thesis, and the trial lecture.

Martin Heidegger's personal library contains his personal copies of the dissertation, the postdoctoral thesis, and the trial lecture. In contrast to the later writings, they contain very few marginal remarks. Judging by the handwriting and their contents, they belong to the years immediately after the publication of these writings. As in all volumes of Division I, the marginal notes are reprinted as footnotes; in order to distinguish them from the textual notes provided with running numbers, they are marked by lowercase letters.

Dr. Hartmut Tietjen is owed thanks for looking up all the quotations, which are particularly numerous in the *Frühe Schriften*, and for revising and expanding the index of names and the subject index. The circumstance that volume 1, contrary to Martin Heidegger's general instruction not to provide the volumes of his complete edition with an index, contains an index of names and a subject index is due to the prehistory of this index. The postdoctoral thesis, *Duns Scotus's Doctrine of Categories and Meaning*, appeared in 1916 with an index of names and a subject index compiled by its author. When Martin Heidegger decided to combine his dissertation, postdoctoral thesis, and trial lecture into the volume *Frühe Schriften* in 1972, he commissioned the editor of the present volume to expand the existing index of his postdoctoral thesis by including the two other writings, such that the separate edition of *Frühe Schriften* appeared with both indexes. {439} The supplementation of the *Frühe Schriften* with the seven works mentioned now poses the same task of expanding the index while preserving its original character as established by Martin Heidegger himself.

The numbers set to the side, sometimes called page marginalia, refer to the page numbers of the separate edition of *Frühe Schriften* that appeared in 1972.

The years set in parentheses in the table of contents indicate the date the writings were completed.

The afterword to volume 5, *Holzwege*, expounds on the character of the complete edition as an edition of the last hand in contrast to a critical edition.

I sincerely thank Dr. Hartmut Tietjen and Klaus Neugebauer for their carefully executed proofreading work.

Freiburg im Breisgau, July, 1978

Friedrich-Wilhelm von Herrmann {440}

ENGLISH–GERMAN GLOSSARY

THE GLOSSARIES PROVIDE THE MOST frequent equivalents for each entry. When more information is needed to follow the nuances of Heidegger's terminology, or when it facilitates the use of the subject index, less frequent equivalents are also included. Every entry in the German–English glossary appears in the English–German glossary's column of equivalents. For some entries, the English–German glossary contains additional German equivalents that do not appear in the German–English glossary. Important but rarely used equivalents, explanatory notes, and examples are given in parentheses.

absolute, the	das Absolute
accrue	zukommen
achievement	Leistung
act	Akt
act of judgment	Urteilsakt
act of meaning	Bedeutungsakt
act of thinking	Denkakt
act quality	Aktqualität
activity	Leistung
activity of willing	Willenstätigkeit
actualization	Vollzug
add	hinzukommen
adjective	Adjektivum
adverb	Adverbium
aggregate	Anzahl
analogy	Analogie
antecedent	Grund

application	Anwendung, Geltung, Verwendung
apply	zufallen
apprehension	Auffassung, Erfassen, Erfassung
area	Bezirk, Gebiet, Gegend
arrangement	Anordnung, Gliederung, Zusammenordnung
array	Anordnung
articulation	Gliederung
aspect	Gesichtspunkt
assert	aussagen
assertion	Aussage
associatively	assoziativ
attitude	Einstellung
attunement	Einstellung
authentic	echt, eigentlich
awareness of methodological issues	Methodenbewusstsein
befall	zufallen
being	Sein, Wesen
see also existent (n.)	
being real	Wirklichsein
bespeak	besagen
cardinality	Mächtigkeit
category	Kategorie
causality	Kausalität
cause (n.)	Ursache
cause (v.)	verursachen
certainty	Gewißheit
circumscribe	abgrenzen
circumscription	Abgrenzung
classification	Artung
cognition	Erkenntnis, Erkennen
complex meaning	Bedeutungskomplexion
comportment	Verhalt
comprehension	Auffassung
concept	Begriff
conceptual	gedanklich, inhaltlich
conceptually determining	inhaltlich bestimmend
conclusion	Schluß, Festsetzung, Folgerung
condition	Bedingung, Sachlage
confer	verleihen
conjunction	Konjunktion
consciousness	Bewußtsein, Bewußtheit

also bring to light	zum Bewußtsein bringen
also become aware	zum Bewußtsein kommen
consider	betrachten
constancy	Bestand
constitution	Verfassung
construct	Gebilde
contemplation	Betrachtung
content	Gehalt, Inhalt (Sachverhalt)
content-related, content-specific, in terms of content	inhaltlich
content of meaning	Bedeutungsgehalt, Bedeutungsinhalt
context	Zusammenhang
context of meaning	Bedeutungszusammenhang
continuum	Kontinuum
convertibility	Konvertibilität
copula	Kopula
copy	Abbild
cultural sciences	Kulturwissenschaften
definite	bestimmt
definition	Bestimmung
delimit	abgrenzen
delimitation	Abgrenzung
demarcate	abgrenzen
demarcation	Abgrenzung
dependent	unselbstständig
designate	bezeichnen
determinability	Bestimmbarkeit
determinacy	Bestimmtheit
determinate	bestimmt
determination	Bestimmung, Bestimmtheit
determinative	bestimmend
determined	bestimmt
determining	bestimmend
dialectic	Dialektik
difference	Differenz, Verschiedenheit
different in kind *or* in species	artverschieden
discreteness	Diskretion
discrete quantum	Diskretum
distinction	Verschiedenheit
distribution	Distribution
district	Bezirk
divisibility	Teilbarkeit

doctrine of categories	Kategorienlehre
doctrine of meaning	Bedeutungslehre
doctrine of the form of meanings	Formenlehre der Bedeutungen
domain	Bereich
domain of application	Anwendungsbereich, Geltungsbereich, Herrschaftsbereich
domain of number	Zahlbereich
domain of objects	Gegenstandsbereich, Objektbereich
domain of reality	Wirklichkeitsbereich
domain of validity	Geltungsbereich, Herrschaftsbereich
dominance	Herrschaft
dominate	herrschen
dualism	Dualismus
emotive act	Gefühlsakt
enact	vollziehen
enactment	Vollzug
endow	verleihen
endowed with meaning	bedeutungsbehaftet
endpoint	Zielpunkt
entwinement	Verschlungenheit
entwining	Verschlingung
epistemology *or* epistemological theory	Erkenntnistheorie
equivocation	Äquivokation
essence	Wesen
also formal essence	formales Wesen
also material essence	materiales Wesen
essential form	Wesensform
essential moment	Wesensmoment
eternity	Ewigkeit
evaluation	Werten, Wertung, Auswertung
also aspect of evaluation	Wertgesichtspunkt
also evaluation of value	Wertbeurteilung
evidence	Evidenz
execute	vollziehen
execution	Vollzug
exhibit	aufweisen
existence	Existenz, Bestand (Realität)
existent (n.)	das Seiende
also domain of beings	Bereich des Seienden
existent (adj.)	real, existierend, seiend
experience (n.)	Erlebnis, Erleben, Erfahrung

experience (v.)	erleben
experienceable, the	das Erlebbare
expression	Ausdruck
fact	Tatsache, Tatsächlichkeit
fact of being content, the	Inhaltlichkeit
factual	tatsächlich, sachlich
falsehood *or* falsity	Falschheit
feeling	Gefühl
fictions	Figmenta
field	Feld (Gebiet, for example, Arbeitsgebiet)
form	Form, Formung, Gestalt
formal content	Formgehalt
formation	Formung, Gebilde
formative	gestaltend
formative function	Formungsfunktion
formative ideas	Gestaltideen
formative principle	Gestaltungsprinzip
form of meaning	Bedeutungsform
function	Funktion, Leistung
functional mode	Funktionsweise
functional sense	Leistungssinn
fundamental (n.)	das Prinzipielle
fundamental (adj.)	prinzipiell
genus	Gattung
genuine	eigentlich
given	gegeben
given, the	das Gegebene, Gegebenheit
givenness	Gegebenheit
God	Gott
grammar	Grammatik
grasping	Auffassung
ground (n.)	Boden, Grund
ground (v.)	fundieren, begründen, gründen
grounding	Begründung, Fundierung
heterogeneity	Heterogeneität
heterothesis	Heterothesis
hint	hinweisen
historical science	Geschichtswissenschaft
history	Geschichte, Historie
hold sway	herrschen

homogeneity	Homogeneität
I	Ich
idea	Gedanke, Gedankengut, Idee, Vorstellung
idealism	Idealismus
identity	Identität
ignorance	Unkenntnis
immanence	Immanenz
imply	besagen
independent	selbständig
indicate	hinweisen
individuality	Individualität
intellect	Geist
intellectual	gedanklich, geistig
intellectual-historical	geistesgeschichtlich
intellectual history	Geistesgeschichte
intelligible	gedanklich
intend	intendieren, meinen
intending	Meinen, Meinung
intention	Intention, Meinen
intentionality	Intentionalität
interjection	Interjektion
interpretation	Auffassung
intertwining	Verflechtung
interweaving	verflechten
interwoven	verflechten
interwovenness	Verflechtung
intuition	Anschauung
judgment	Urteil
also sense of judgment	Urteilssinn
also structure of judgment	Urteilsstruktur
also theory of judgment	Urteilstheorie
also doctrine of judgment	Urteilslehre
kind	Art, Artung
knowing	Wissen
knowledge	Kenntnis, Wissen (Erkenntnis)
language	Sprache
law	Gesetz
law of series	Reihengesetz
linguistic constructs	Sprachgebilde

linguistic content	Sprachgehalt
linguistic form	Sprachgestalt
linguistic formations	Sprachgebilde
living element	Lebenselement
logic	Logik
logical, the	das Logische
manifest	aufweisen
manifold *or* manifoldness	Mannigfaltigkeit
manner	Weise
manner of meaning	Bedeutungsweise
material	Material, Stoff
material of meaning	Bedeutungsmaterial
mathematics	Mathematik
matter	Material, Stoff, Sachverhalt
meaning	Bedeuten, Bedeutung
meaning complex	Bedeutungskomplexion
meaning content	Bedeutungsgehalt, Bedeutungsinhalt
meaning context	Bedeutungszusammenhang
meaning endowing	bedeutungsverleihend
meaning function	Bedeutungsfunktion
measurement	Messung
memory	Erinnerung
mensurability	Meßbarkeit
metaphysics	Metaphysik
methodological consciousness	Methodenbewusstsein
methodology	Methodologie
Middle Ages	Mittelalter
mode	Weise
mode of consideration *or* considering	Betrachtung
mode of meaning	Bedeutungsweise
modes of meaning	Bedeutungsmodi
monism	Monismus
mood	Zustand, Stimmung, Gemütsbewegung
motion	Bewegung
multiplicity	Mannigfaltigkeit, Mehrerleiheit
multitude	Mannigfaltigkeit
mysticism	Mystik
naturalism	Naturalismus
natural reality	Naturwirklichkeit
also existent natural reality	reale Naturwirklichkeit

see also reality	
natural science	Naturwissenschaft
nature	Natur, Art, Wesen
negation	Negation, Verneinung, Verneinen
noema	Noema
noematic	noematisch
noesis	Noesis
noun	Nomen
nonsensory	unsinnlich
nothing, the *or* nothing	das Nichts
nothingness	das Nichts
number	Zahl, Anzahl
also domain of number	Zahlbereich
also principle of number	Zahlprinzip, Prinzip der Zahl
see also One, the number	
numerical, the	das Zahlenmäßige
object	Gegenstand, Objekt
objective	gegenständlich, objektiv
objective entity	Gegenständliche, das
objective, the	Gegenständliche, das
objectivity	Gegenständlichkeit, Objektivität
object region	Gegenstandsgebiet
object's way of comporting itself, an	Gegenstandsverhalt
observation	Beobachtung
one, the	das Eine
one, the number	die Eins
operation	Leistung
opinion	Meinung, Meinen
opposition	Gegensatz
order *or* ordering	Ordnung
over against	gegenüber
participle	Partizipium
particular	besondere, bestimmt
peculiarity	Eigentümlichkeit
perception	Wahrnehmung
perform	vollziehen
performance	Vollzug
perspective	Gesichtspunkt
phenomenology	Phänomenologie
philosophy	Philosophie
also history of philosophy	Geschichte der Philosophie

also medieval philosophy	Philosophie des Mittelalters, mittelalterliche Philosophie
also modern philosophy	moderne Philosophie
physical, the	das Physische
also physical reality	physische Wirklichkeit
see also natural reality	
physics	Physik
place	setzen
plurality	Vielheit
point of departure	Ausgangspunkt
point out	hinweisen
posit	setzen
predicable	zukommen
predicate (n.)	Prädikat, Eigenschaftswort
predicate (v.)	aussagen, aussagbar sein, prädizieren
predication	Aussage, Prädikation, Prädizierung
preposition	Präposition
primary relational context	Urbewandtnis
principle	Prinzip, Principium, Grundsatz (Satz)
principle, in	prinzipiell
privation	Privation
problem of categories	Kategorienproblem
pronoun	Pronomen, Fürwort
proper	eigentlich
property	Eigenschaft, Eigentümlichkeit
proposition	Aussage, Satz
psychic, the	das Psychische
also psychic reality	psychische Realität, psychische Wirklichkeit
see also natural reality	
psychologism	Psychologismus
psychology	Psychologie
also modern psychology	moderne Psychologie
also Scholastic psychology	Psychologie der Scholastik
quality	Qualität
see also act quality	
quantity	Quantität, Anzahl
quotidian connections	Lebensbezüge
real (adj.)	real, reell, wirklich
see also natural reality	
see also reality	
real (n.)	das Reale, das Wirkliche
realism	Realismus

reality	Wirklichkeit, Realität, Wirklichsein
also existent reality	reale Wirklichkeit
reason	Grund
recall	Erinnerung
recognition	Anerkennung
refer	hinweisen
reference	Hinweis
reference point (terminus)	Bezugspunkt
reflection	Reflexion, Überlegung, Besinnung
regard (n.)	Hinsicht
regard (v.)	betrachten
region	Gebiet, Gegend
reign (n.)	Herrschaft
reign (v.)	herrschen
relation	Relation, Beziehung, Verhältnis, Zusammenhang
relational context	Bewandtnis
relationship	Beziehung, Verhältnis, Zusammenhang
representation	Abbildung, Vorstellen, Vorstellung
respect	Hinsicht
reveal	aufweisen
Scholasticism	Scholastik
science	Wissenschaft
also doctrine of science	Wissenschaftslehre
also history of science	Wissenschaftsgeschichte
also system of sciences	System *or* Systematik der Wissenschaften
also theory of science	Wissenschaftstheorie, Theorie der Wissenschaft
sector	Bezirk
self-sufficient	selbständig
semantic	bedeutungsmäßig
sensation	Empfindung
sense	Sinn
sensory	sinnlich
sensorily	sinnlich
sensualistic	sensualistisch
sentence	Satz
set (n.)	Menge
set (v.)	setzen
shaping	Gestaltung
sign	Zeichen
significance	Bedeutsamkeit
signification	Bedeutung

signified	Bezeichnete, das
signify	bedeuten, besagen, bezeichnen
signifying	Bedeutung
situation	Sachlage
something *or* some thing	Etwas, das
space	Raum
species	Spezies, Art
specific	besondere, bestimmt
specific difference	Artunterschied
specifically different	artverschieden
speech	Rede
sphere	Bezirk
spirit	Geist
spiritual	geistig
spiritualism	Spiritualismus
starting point (principium)	Ansatzpunkt
state	Zustand
statement	Aussage
state of affairs	Sachverhalt
structure	Gebilde
subject (n.)	Subjekt
subject (v.)	unterwerfen, unterziehen, unterliegen, unterordnen, stehen, rücken
subjective	subjektiv, subjektbezogen
subjectivity	Subjektivität
substance	Substanz
substantive (n.)	Substantiv
substantive (adj.)	inhaltlich
substantiality	Sachhaltigkeit
suggest	hinweisen
sum	Anzahl
supersensory	übersinnlich
supervene	hinzukommen, hinzutreten
theory of representation	Abbildtheorie
theory of the object	Gegenstandstheorie
thing	Ding
think	denken, meinen
thinking *or* thought	Denken
time	Zeit
transcendence	Transzendenz
transcendental philosophy	Transzendentalphilosophie
transcendentals	Transzendentien

truth	Wahrheit
understanding	Verständnis, Verstehen, Verstand, Auffassung, Fassung
uniqueness	Eigentümlichkeit
unit	Einheit
unity	Einheit
universal (n.)	das Allgemeine, das Universale
universal (adj.)	allgemein, universal, universell
universal validity	Allgemeingültigkeit
universal representation	Allgemeinvorstellung
univocation	Univokation
unpacking	Auswicklung
unsurveyable	unübersehbar
use (n.)	Verwendung
use (v.)	verwenden
utterance	Rede
validity	Geltung
valuation	Wertigkeit
value	Wert
value philosophy	Wertphilosophie
vantage point	Gesichtspunkt
verb	Verbum
view	Auffassung, Anschauung
visual orientation	Blickrichtung
vital element	Lebenselement
way	Weise
what is given	das Gegebene, Gegebenheit
word	Wort
word form	Wortgestalt, Wortform
worldview	Weltanschauung

GERMAN-ENGLISH GLOSSARY

Abbild	copy
Abbildung	representation
Abbildtheorie	theory of representation
abgrenzen	delimit, demarcate, circumscribe
Abgrenzung	delimitation, demarcation, circumscription
Absolute, das	absolute
Adjektivum	adjective
Adverbium	adverb
Äquivokation	equivocation
Akt	act
Aktqualität	act quality
allgemein	universal
Allgemeine, das	universal
Allgemeingültigkeit	universal validity
Allgemeinvorstellung	universal representation
Analogie	analogy
Anerkennung	recognition
Anordnung	arrangement, array
Ansatzpunkt	starting point (principium)
Anschauung	intuition, view
Anwendung	application
Anwendungsbereich	domain of application
Anzahl	aggregate, quantity, sum (number)
Art	species, kind, nature
Artung	classification, kind
Artunterschied	specific difference

artverschieden	different in kind *or* in species, specifically different
assoziativ	associatively
Auffassung	understanding, comprehension, apprehension, interpretation, grasping, view
aufweisen	manifest, reveal, exhibit
Ausdruck	expression
Ausgangspunkt	point of departure
Aussage	assertion, statement, proposition, predication
aussagen	predicate, assert
Auswertung	evaluation
Auswicklung	unpacking
bedeuten	mean, signify
Bedeuten	meaning
Bedeutsamkeit	significance
Bedeutung	meaning, signification, signifying
Bedeutungsakt	act of meaning
bedeutungsbehaftet	endowed with meaning
Bedeutungsform	form of meaning
Bedeutungsfunktion	meaning function
Bedeutungsgehalt	meaning content, content of meaning
Bedeutungsinhalt	meaning content, content of meaning
Bedeutungskomplexion	meaning complex (complex meaning)
Bedeutungslehre	doctrine of meaning
Bedeutungsmaterial	material of meaning
bedeutungsmäßig	semantic
Bedeutungsmodi	modes of meaning
Bedeutungsweise	manner *or* mode of meaning
bedeutungsverleihend	meaning endowing
Bedeutungszusammenhang	context of meaning, meaning context
Bedingung	condition
Begriff	concept
begründen	ground
Begründung	grounding
Bereich	domain
besagen	signify, imply, bespeak, mean
besondere	particular, specific
Bestand	constancy, existence
Bestimmbarkeit	determinability
bestimmend	determinative, determining
bestimmt	determinate, specific, determined, definite, particular

Bestimmung	determination, definition
Bestimmtheit	determinacy, determination
Beobachtung	observation
betrachten	consider, regard
Betrachtung	contemplation, mode of consideration *or* considering
Bewandtnis	relational context (*or* idiomatically)
also Urbewandtnis	primary relational context
Bewegung	motion
Bewußtheit	consciousness, being conscious
Bewußtsein	consciousness
also zum Bewußtsein bringen	bring to light
also zum Bewußtsein kommen	become aware
bezeichnen	designate, signify
Bezeichnete, das	signified
Beziehung	relation, relationship
Bezirk	area, sphere, district, sector
Bezugspunkt	reference point (terminus)
Blickrichtung	visual orientation
Boden	ground
Denkakt	act of thinking
denken	think
Denken	thought, thinking
Dialektik	dialectic
Differenz	difference
Ding	thing
Diskretion	discreteness
Diskretum	discrete quantum
Distribution	distribution
Dualismus	dualism
echt	authentic
Eigenschaft	property
Eigenschaftswort	predicate
eigentlich	genuine, proper, authentic
Eigentümlichkeit	peculiarity, uniqueness, property
das Eine	the one
die Eins	the number one
Einheit	unity, unit
Einstellung	attunement, attitude
Empfindung	sensation
Erfahrung	experience

Erfassen *or* Erfassung	apprehension
Erinnerung	memory, recall
Erkennen	cognition
Erkenntnis	cognition (knowledge)
Erkenntnistheorie	epistemology, epistemological theory
Erlebbare, das	the experienceable
erleben	experience
Erlebnis *or* Erleben	experience
Etwas, das	something, some thing
Evidenz	evidence
Ewigkeit	eternity
Existenz	existence
existierend	existent
Falschheit	falsity, falsehood
Feld	field
Figmenta	fictions
Form	form
Formenlehre der Bedeutungen	doctrine of the form of meanings
Formgehalt	formal content
Formung	form, formation
Formungsfunktion	formative function
fundieren	ground
Fundierung	grounding
Funktion	function
Funktionsweise	functional mode
Fürwort	pronoun
Gattung	genus
Gefühl	feeling
also Gefühlsakt	emotive act
Gebiet	area, region (field, e.g., Arbeitsgebiet)
Gebilde	formation, structure, construct
gedanklich	intellectual, intelligible, conceptual
gegeben	given
Gegebene, das	what is given, the given
Gegebenheit	givenness, what is given, the given
Gegend	region, area
Gegensatz	opposition
Gegenstand	object
gegenständlich	objective
Gegenständliche, das	the objective, objective entity
Gegenständlichkeit	objectivity
Gegenstandsbereich	domain of objects

Gegenstandsgebiet	object region
Gegenstandstheorie	theory of the object
Gegenstandsverhalt	(an) object's way of comporting itself
gegenüber	over against, vis-à-vis
Gehalt	content
Geist	intellect, spirit
Geistesgeschichte	intellectual history
geistesgeschichtlich	intellectual-historical
geistig	intellectual, spiritual
Geltung	validity, application
Geltungsbereich	domain of validity, domain of application
Geschichte	history
Geschichtswissenschaft	historical science
Gesetz	law
Gesichtspunkt	aspect, perspective, vantage point
Gestalt	form
gestaltend	formative
Gestaltideen	formative ideas
Gestaltung	shaping
Gestaltungsprinzip	formative principle
Gewißheit	certainty
Gliederung	articulation, arrangement
Gott	God
Grammatik	grammar
Grund	reason, antecedent, ground
gründen	ground
Grundsatz	principle
Herrschaft	dominance, reign
Herrschaftsbereich	domain of application, domain of validity
herrschen	reign, hold sway, dominate
Heterogeneität	heterogeneity
Heterothesis	heterothesis
Hinsicht	respect, regard
Hinweis	reference
hinweisen	indicate, point out, hint at, suggest, refer
hinzukommen	supervene, add
hinzutreten	supervene
Historie	history
Homogeneität	homogeneity
Ich	I
Idealismus	idealism
Identität	identity

Immanenz	immanence
Individualität	individuality
Inhalt	content
inhaltlich	substantive, conceptual, of *or* in terms of content, content-related, content-specific
inhaltlich bestimmend	conceptually determining
Inhaltlichkeit	the fact of being content
intendieren	intend
Intention	intention
Intentionalität	intentionality
Interjektion	interjection
Kategorie	category
Kategorienlehre	doctrine of categories
Kategorienproblem	problem of categories
Kausalität	causality
Kenntnis	knowledge
Konjunktion	conjunction
Kontinuum	continuum
Konvertibilität	convertibility
Kopula	copula
Kulturwissenschaften	cultural sciences
Lebensbezüge	quotidian connections
Lebenselement	living or vital element
Leistung	activity, achievement, function (operation)
Leistungssinn	functional sense
Logik	logic
Logische, das	the logical
Mächtigkeit	cardinality
Mannigfaltigkeit	manifold, manifoldness, diversity, multiplicity (multitude)
Material	material, matter
Mathematik	mathematics
Mehrerleiheit	multiplicity
meinen	intend, think (in the sense of "opine")
Meinen	intention, intending, opinion
Meinung	opinion, intending
Menge	set
Meßbarkeit	mensurability
Messung	measurement

Metaphysik	metaphysics
Methode	method
Methodenbewusstsein	methodological consciousness, awareness of methodological issues
Methodologie	methodology
Mittelalter	Middle Ages
Monismus	monism
Mystik	mysticism
Natur	nature
Naturalismus	naturalism
Naturwirklichkeit	natural reality
also reale Naturwirklichkeit	existent natural reality
also physische Naturwirklichkeit	physical natural reality
see also Wirklichkeit	
Naturwissenschaft	natural science
Negation	negation
Nichts, das	the nothing, nothingness, nothing
Noema	noema
noematisch	noematic
Noesis	noesis
Nomen	noun
Objekt	object
Objektbereich	domain of objects
objektiv	objective
Objektivität	objectivity
Ordnung	order, ordering
Partizipium	participle
Phänomenologie	phenomenology
Philosophie	philosophy
also Philosophie, Geschichte der	history of philosophy
also Philosophie, des Mittelalters	medieval philosophy
also Philosophie, moderne	modern philosophy
Physik	physics
Physische, das	the physical
also physische Wirklichkeit	physical reality
see also Naturwirklichkeit	
Prädikat	predicate
Prädikation *or* Prädizierung	predication
prädizieren	predicate
Präposition	preposition

Principium	principle
Prinzip	principle
prinzipiell	fundamental, in principle
Prinzipielle, das	the fundamental
Privation	privation
Pronomen	pronoun
Psychische, das	the psychic
also psychische Realität	psychic reality
also psychische Wirklichkeit	psychic reality
Psychologie	psychology
also moderne Psychologie	modern psychology
also Psychologie der Scholastik	Scholastic psychology
Psychologismus	psychologism
Qualität	quality
see also Aktqualität	
Quantität	quantity
Raum	space
real	real, existent
see also Naturwirklichkeit	
see also Wirklichkeit	
Reale, das	the real
Realismus	realism
Realität	reality (existence)
Rede	speech, utterance
reell	real
Reflexion	reflection
Reihengesetz	law of series
Relation	relation
Sachhaltigkeit	substantiality
Sachlage	situation, condition
Sachverhalt	state of affairs, matter (content)
Satz	sentence, proposition (principle)
Schluß	conclusion
Scholastik	Scholasticism
seiend	existent
Seiende, das	existent
also Bereich des Seienden	domain of beings
Sein	being
selbständig	independent, self-sufficient
sensualistisch	sensualistic

setzen	set, place, posit
Sinn	sense
sinnlich	sensory, sensorily
Spezies	species
Spiritualismus	spiritualism
Sprache	language
Sprachgehalt	linguistic content
Sprachgestalt	linguistic form
Sprachgebilde	linguistic formations, linguistic constructs
Stoff	material, matter
Subjekt	subject
subjektiv	subjective
Subjektivität	subjectivity
Substantiv	substantive
Substanz	substance
Tatsache	fact
tatsächlich	factual
Tatsächlichkeit	fact
Teilbarkeit	divisibility
Transzendentalphilosophie	transcendental philosophy
Transzendentien	transcendentals
Transzendenz	transcendence
übersinnlich	supersensory
universal *or* universell	universal
Universale, das	universal
Univokation	univocation
Unkenntnis	ignorance
unselbständig	dependent
unsinnlich	nonsensory
unübersehbar	unsurveyable
Ursache	cause
Urteil	judgment
Urteilsakt	act of judgment
Urteilslehre	doctrine of judgment
Urteilssinn	sense of judgment
Urteilsstruktur	structure of judgment
Urteilstheorie	theory of judgment
Verbum	verb
Verfassung	constitution
verflechten	interwoven, interweaving

Verflechtung	interwovenness, intertwining
Verhalt	comportment
Verhältnis	relation, relationship
verleihen	endow, confer
Verneinen *or* Verneinung	negation
Verschiedenheit	distinction, difference
Verschlingung	entwining
Verschlungenheit	entwinement
Verstand	understanding
Verständnis *or* Verstehen	understanding
verursachen	cause
verwenden	use
Verwendung	use, application
Vielheit	plurality
vollziehen	enact, perform, execute
Vollzug	enactment, actualization, execution (performance)
Vorstellen	representation
Vorstellung	representation, idea
Wahrheit	truth
Wahrnehmung	perception
Weise	manner, mode, way
Weltanschauung	worldview
Wert	value
Wertbeurteilung	evaluation of value
Werten	evaluation
Wertgesichtspunkt	aspect of evaluation
Wertigkeit	valuation
Wertphilosophie	value philosophy
Wertung	evaluation
Wesen	being, essence, nature
also Wesen, formales	formal essence
also Wesen, materiales	material essence
Wesensform	essential form
Wesensmoment	essential moment
Willenstätigkeit	activity of willing
Wissen	knowledge, knowing
wirklich	real
Wirkliche, das	the real
Wirklichkeit	reality
also reale Wirklichkeit	existent reality
see also Naturwirklichkeit	

Wirklichkeitsbereich	domain of reality
Wirklichsein	being real, reality
Wissenschaft	science
also System der Wissenschaften	system of sciences
also Wissenschaftsgeschichte	history of science
also Wissenschaftstheorie	theory of science
also Wissenschaftslehre	doctrine of science
Wort	word
Wortgestalt	word form
Zahl	number
Zahlbereich	domain of number
das Zahlenmäßige	the numerical
Zahlprinzip	principle of number
Zeichen	sign
Zeit	time
Zielpunkt	endpoint
zufallen	befall, apply
zukommen	accrue (predicable)
Zusammenhang	context, relation, relationship
Zusammenordnung	arrangement
Zustand	mood, state

INDEX OF NAMES

SUBJECT INDEX

---

*The GA 1 subject index includes an entry for "Willenshandlung (Willensakt)," though the actual term on GA 1, 286 is "Willenstätigkeit."

JOYDEEP BAGCHEE is author of *The Nay Science: A History of German Indology* and *Philology and Criticism*. He specializes in German and Indian philosophies. He lives and teaches in Berlin.

JEFFREY D. GOWER is Byron K. Trippet Assistant Professor of Philosophy and Philosophy, Politics, and Economics at Wabash College. His research focuses on questions of sovereignty, economy, and ecology in Agamben, Derrida, Heidegger, and Aristotle.